T0237794

Lecture Notes in Computer Sci

Commenced Publication in 1973
Founding and Former Series Editors:
Gerhard Goos, Juris Hartmanis, and Jan van Leeuwen

Lin Padgham   Franco Zambonelli (Eds.)

Agent-Oriented Software Engineering VII

7th International Workshop, AOSE 2006
Hakodate, Japan, May 8, 2006
Revised and Invited Papers

 Springer

Volume Editors

Lin Padgham
RMIT University, Melbourne, Australia
E-mail: linpa@cs.rmit.edu.au

Franco Zambonelli
Università di Modena e Reggio Emilia, DISMI
Via Allegri 13, Reggio Emilia, Italia
E-mail: franco.zambonelli@unimore.it

Library of Congress Control Number: 2007920434

CR Subject Classification (1998): D.2, I.2.11, F.3, D.1, C.2.4, D.3

LNCS Sublibrary: SL 2 – Programming and Software Engineering

ISSN	0302-9743
ISBN-10	3-540-70944-4 Springer Berlin Heidelberg New York
ISBN-13	978-3-540-70944-2 Springer Berlin Heidelberg New York

Springer is a part of Springer Science+Business Media

springer.com

© Springer-Verlag Berlin Heidelberg 2007

Typesetting: Camera-ready by author, data conversion by Scientific Publishing Services, Chennai, India
Printed on acid-free paper   SPIN: 12021468   06/3142   5 4 3 2 1 0

Preface

Since the mid 1980s, software agents and multi-agent systems have grown into a very active area of research with some very successful examples of commercial development. At AAMAS 2006 Steve Benfield from Agentis described research on large scale industry system development, which indicated a savings of four to five times in development time and in cost when using agent technologies. However it is still the case that one of the limiting factors in industry take up of agent technology is the lack of adequate software engineering support, and knowledge in how to systematically develop agent systems.

The concept of an agent as an autonomous system, capable of interacting with other agents in order to satisfy its design objectives, is a natural one for software designers. Just as we can understand many systems as being composed of essentially passive objects, which have state, and upon which we can perform operations, so we can understand many others as being made up of interacting, semi-autonomous agents. This paradigm is especially suited to complex systems. However software architectures that contain many dynamically interacting components, each with their own thread of control, and engaging in complex coordination protocols, are difficult to correctly and efficiently engineer. Agent oriented modelling techniques are important for supporting the design and development of such applications.

The AOSE 2006 workshop was hosted by the 5th International Joint Conference on Autonomous Agents and Multiagent Systems (AAMAS 2006) held in Hakodate, Japan. A selection of extended versions of papers from that workshop, along with some additional papers, are presented in this volume, which follows the successful predecessors of 2000 to 2005, published as *Lecture Notes in Computer Science*, volumes 1957, 2222, 2585, 2935, 3382 and 3950.

This book has been organised into four parts: Modelling and Design of Agent Systems, dealing with some specific aspects of modelling agent systems, Modelling Open Agent Systems, dealing with design issues that arise when dealing with agents in the Internet environment, Formal Reasoning About Designs, which looks at the use of reasoning methods to analyse designs, and finally Testing, Debugging and Evolvability.

Part I: Modelling and Design of Agent Systems

The first part focusses on issues of modelling and design in agent systems. This is an extremely important activity and one which has, over the last few years, received a great deal of attention within a range of AOSE methodologies. The three papers in this part address specific aspects of modelling and design for agent systems.

The first paper "An Agent Environment Interaction Model" by Scott De-Loach and Jorge Valenzuela looks in detail at how to design and specify the interface of an agent system with its environment, using *actions* to represent both sensors and effectors. Agents exist over time, in environments which are dynamic and changing, and they typically affect their environments. Consequently the specification of the environment and the agent's interaction with it is a key part of modelling agent systems. The approach described is integrated into O-MASE, the extended version of the well established MASE methodology developed by the first author.

The second paper on "Allocating Goals to Agent Roles during MAS Requirements Engineering" by Jureta et al. explores how to design roles, and ultimately agents, to ensure that non-functional goals are addressed. They provide a systematic approach for assigning non-functional goals to roles, and heuristics for selecting between different options. Focussing on this assignment of goals to roles at an early stage in the process allows agent organisational structures to emerge from the role definitions.

The third and final paper in this part by Garcia, Choren and von Flach, entitled "An Aspect-Oriented Modeling Framework for Multi-Agent Systems Design" is about modelling concerns that cut across all or many parts of an agent application such as mobility, error handling or security. They build on *Aspect Oriented Programming*, introducing a meta-modelling framework for representing these crosscutting concerns in an agent oriented design. They integrate aspect-oriented abstractions into their agent oriented modelling language called ANote.

Part II: Modelling Open Agent Systems

Part two deals with some of the complexities that arise when dealing with agents in the Internet environment. Two papers deal with design of governance structures for providing some control over autonomous agents, while one deals with modelling agent mobility.

Kusek and Jezic's paper "Extending UML Sequence Diagrams to Model Agent Mobility" looks at a number of different ways to potentially model agent mobility, using extensions of UML sequence diagrams. Their aim is to capture agent creation, migration paths, and current location. They evaluate the strengths and the weaknesses of the different approaches based on clarity, space needed for representing larger systems, and representation of mobility. They conclude that choice of the most preferred approach depends on the application characteristics of how many agents and nodes there are in the system to be modelled.

The papers "Applying the Governance Framework Technique to Promote Maintainability in Open Multi-Agent Systems" by Carvalho et al., and "Designing Institutional Multi-Agent Systems" by Sierra et al., both deal with specifying the institutional structures within which agents may interact, and which provide some guarantees about the behaviours. Both focus on specifying agent interaction patterns or templates, and on the ability to express norms or constraints regarding agent behaviour. Carvalho et al. use XMLaw and template structures. Sierra et al. describe the methodology for developing a design in the Islander tool, which also captures interaction specifications, and norms and constraints. The methodology used by Sierre et al. is integrated into the Prometheus methodology as a social or organisational design layer.

Part III: Formal Reasoning About Designs

One of the trends in software engineering, and certainly in agent oriented software engineering, is to incorporate automated reasoning into design tools to aid the designer in various ways. This part presents three papers with this general focus.

The first paper, "Modeling Mental States in the Analysis of Multiagent Systems Requirements" by Lapouchnian and Lespérance looks at formal analysis by taking an i* specification and mapping it to the Cognitive Agents Specification Language (CASL). CASL relies heavily on ConGolog for specification of procedural aspects, and also on modal logics and possible world semantics. The developer annotates an i* specification and specifies how elements are to be mapped to the procedural component of CASL. Some transformations are automated. Once the formal specification exists it becomes possible to do formal analysis of such things as epistemic feasibility of plans or termination.

The second paper, by Brandão et al., entitled "Observed-MAS: An Ontology-Based Method for Analyzing Multi-Agent Systems Design Models" focusses on translating design models to formal ontologies, which describe the Multi Agent Systems domain. The ontologies are represented in a Description Logic system and enable analysis of the design using defined queries, which are represented by ontology instances. Analysis is done in two phases–the first within individual diagrams while the second looks at relationships between diagrams. The authors argue that while it is difficult to analyze and establish the well-formedness of a set of diagrams of a UML-like object-oriented modeling language, it gets far more complex when the language is extended to add a set of agency related abstractions. Their approach helps to tame this complexity.

The third paper entitled "Using Risk Analysis to Evaluate Design Alternatives" by Asnar, Bryl and Giorgini, looks at using planning to propose design alternatives, based on risk-related metrics, which are particularly important in certain kinds of systems where availability and reliability are crucial. While the developer must be involved in the reasoning process to agree to any loosening of constraints, the system they describe provides automated reasoning to suggest viable alternatives. They illustrate their approach using an Air Traffic Management case study.

Part IV: Testing, Debugging and Evolvability

As is well known, implementation is not the final stage of system development. Systems must always be tested and debugged, and typically they also evolve once they are deployed, sometimes becoming whole product lines of related systems. These last four papers look at these aspects of developing agent systems.

Tiryaki et al. describe "SUNIT: A Unit Testing Framework for Test Driven Development of Multi-Agent Systems", which is based on an extension of the JUnit framework. They propose a test driven multi-agent system development approach that naturally supports iterative and incremental MAS construction. This approach is supported by their SUnit system.

The second paper in this part "Monitoring Group Behavior in Goal-Directed Agents Using Co-efficient Plan Observation" by Sudeikat and Renz describes an approach to validating the multi-agent cooperative behaviour of a system. They argue that goal hierarchies developed during requirements engineering, combined with Belief Desire Intention architectures, are suitable as a basis for development of a modular approach to checking crosscutting concerns in (BDI) agent implementations. They provide a case study to illustrate their approach.

The third paper, by Jayatilleke et al., "Evaluating a Model Driven Development Toolkit for Domain Experts to Modify Agent Based Systems" describes evaluation of a toolkit designed to allow domain experts to themselves modify and evolve an agent application that has been built using this toolkit. The toolkit builds on design documentation, but provides increased granularity at the detailed design level, enabling production of fully functional code. Domain experts then need only change at the design level, in order to obtain an enhanced implementation. Meteorologists were able to modify an example system that was based on a real application and actual evolutionary changes to the system.

Finally, the paper entitled "Building the Core Architecture of a NASA Multiagent System Product Line" by Peña et al. describes techniques adapted from the field of Software Product Lines (SPL) to enable building of the core architecture for a multiagent system where components can be reused to derive related concrete products with greatly reduced time-to-market and costs. They illustrate the approach with examples from a NASA mission.

These papers provide a diverse and interesting overview of the work that is currently being undertaken by a growing number of researchers and research groups in the area of Agent Oriented Software Engineering. They represent leading edge research in this field, which is of critical importance in facilitating industry take-up of powerful agent technologies.

December 2006   Lin Padgham
                                                            Franco Zambonelli

Organization

Organizing Committee

Lin Padgham (Co-chair)
RMIT, Australia
Email: linpa@cs.rmit.edu.au

Franco Zambonelli (Co-chair)
University of Modena e Reggio Emilia, Italy
Email: franco.zambonelli@unimore.it

Steering Committee

Paolo Ciancarini, University of Bologna, Italy
Jörg Müller, Clausthal University of Technology, Germany
Gerhard Weiß, Software Competence Center, Hagenberg
Michael Wooldridge, University of Liverpool, UK

Program Committee

Bernard Bauer (Germany)
Federico Bergenti (Italy)
Carole Bernon (France)
Giacomo Cabri (Italy)
Luca Cernuzzi (Paraguay)
Paolo Ciancarini (Italy)
Massimo Cossentino (Italy)
Keith Decker (USA)
Scott DeLoach (USA)
Klaus Fischer (Germany)
Paolo Giorgini (Italy)
Michael Huhns (USA)

Gaya Jayatilleke (Australia)
Juergen Lind (Germany)
Mike Luck (UK)
Andrea Omicini (Italy)
Van Parunak (USA)
Anna Perini (Italy)
Fariba Sadri (UK)
Onn Shehory (Israel)
Michael Winikoff (Australia)
Mike Wooldridge (UK)
Laura Zavala (USA)

Table of Contents

Testing, Debugging and Evolvability

An Agent-Environment Interaction Model

Scott A. DeLoach and Jorge L. Valenzuela

Department of Computing and Information Sciences, Kansas State University
234 Nichols Hall, Manhattan, KS 66506
{sdeloach, jvalenzu}@cis.ksu.edu

Abstract. This paper develops a model for precisely defining how an agent interacts with objects in its environment through the use of its capabilities. Capabilities are recursively defined in terms of lower-level capabilities and actions, which represent atomic interactions with the environment. Actions are used to represent both sensors and effectors. The paper shows how the model can be used to represent both software and physical agents and their capabilities. The paper also shows how the model can be integrated into the Organization-based Multiagent Systems Engineering methodology.

1 Introduction

There is widespread agreement that the environment in which a multiagent system is situated is of fundamental importance in the analysis, design, and operation of the system. However, even with this agreement, few multiagent methodologies include the modeling of the environment or the agent's interactions with it as first class entities [10]. In situated multiagent systems, the *environment* is the entity in which agents exist and communicate [6]. Communication is a critical factor that enables agents to interact and coordinate. Typically, this interaction and coordination is modeled using direct communication through the social environment; however, it can also be modeling indirectly through the physical environment. A *social environment* is the entity that provides the principles, processes and structures that enable the agents to communicate while the *physical environment* provides principles and processes that affect objects within an environment [6]. In [4], Ferber defines a multiagent system as having six basic entities:

- An environment, E
- A set of objects, O, that exist in E
- A set of agents, A, which are active objects (i.e., a subset of O)
- A set of relations, R, that define relationships between objects in O
- A set of operations, O, that agents can use to sense and affect objects in O
- A set of universal laws that define the reaction of the environment to agent operations

Based on Ferber's definition, we have identified *five requirements* for specifying agent-environment interaction model. Essentially, an AEI should define:

L. Padgham and F. Zambonelli (Eds.): AOSE 2006, LNCS 4405, pp. 1–18, 2007.
© Springer-Verlag Berlin Heidelberg 2007

1. A unique entity called the environment
2. The set of objects in the environment (which includes agents)
3. Specific types of relations that may exist between objects in the environment
4. The set of operations that agents may perform upon objects in the environment
5. The laws that govern the effect of those operations on objects in the environment

While capturing these elements is essential, we believe it is also critical that these concepts be captured using a model that shows direct relations between the objects, agents, and actions as well as specifies the intended effect of each action unambiguously. We believe it is also important to provide a model that allows these concepts to be specified and viewed at the appropriate level of abstraction.

While most current multiagent methodologies provide some notion of the environment or the agent's interactions with it, no major methodologies possess a detailed agent-environment interaction model that explicitly defines how the environment is affected by agents or how the agent perceives the environment. Including such an agent-environment interaction model is important because it allows us to explicitly identify (1) how agents directly interact/coordinate with each other, (2) how agents indirectly interact/coordinate with each other, and (3) the effect of agents on objects in the environment, which in situated multiagent systems often determines whether the system has accomplished its goals. In addition, agents in situated multiagent systems also generally require some representation of the environment in order to effectively communicate with other agents and to achieve their goals. By including a well-defined model of the environment in the agent-environment interaction model, the analysis, and design of these agents should be clearer and thus improved over implicit approaches.

The goal of this paper is to present an Agent-Environment Interaction model (AEI) that can be integrated into appropriate multiagent systems methodologies. Specifically, we will integrate the AEI Model into the Organization-based Multiagent Systems Engineering methodology (O-MaSE) [1]. To make the notation as clear and unambiguous as possible, we use standard UML notation with liberal use of keywords to denote specific concepts in the model. Obviously, if our AEI Model is integrated into other methodologies and modeling approaches, the notation can be adapted as needed.

The paper is organized as follow. In Section 2, we discuss how some current multiagent methodologies address environmental issues and provide an overview of O-MaSE [1]. In Section 3, we present our AEI Model and integrate our AEI Model into O-MaSE. In Section 4, we present a detailed example of the AEI Model using a robotics Weapons of Mass Destruction (WMD) simulation system. Finally, in Section 5, we present our conclusions and areas for future work.

2   Related Work

In this section we review four prominent multiagent systems methodologies and how they model interactions with the environment: Gaia, Message, Prometheus, and O-MaSE. We also analyze how well each of these methodologies meets the agent environment interaction requirements stated above.

2.1   Gaia

The extended version of Gaia [12] adds some basic concepts and organizational abstractions to the original version of GAIA [11]. Among these additions is an Environment Model, which is introduced during the analysis phase. Because the authors believe that "it is difficult to provide a general modeling abstraction and general modeling techniques because the environment for different applications can be very different in nature" [12], they model environmental entities in terms of abstract computational resources. These resources are modeled as tuples that the agents may read, (sense), effect, (change), or consume, (remove). Thus the Gaia Environment Model can be viewed as a list of resources that can be accessed using an associated name and acted upon based on the type of action associated with them. An example of a Gaia Environment Model is shown below [12].

```
reads var1 // readable resource of the environment.
var2 // another readable resource.
change var3 // a variable that can be also changed by the agent.
```

Analyzing the Gaia Environment Model using our five AEI model requirements shows that, while it does include a limited notion of objects, it does not include any notion of agents (requirement 2). In addition, the Gaia Environment Model severely limits the types of relations (requirement 3) and actions (requirement 4) that can be performed on those objects. Finally, the Environment Model has no notion of environmental laws that affect the environment objects independently of the agents (requirement 5). A more general notion of an AEI could be of benefit in the Gaia methodology.

2.2   MESSAGE

In the MESSAGE methodology [5], the MESSAGE modeling language defines some knowledge-level-concepts like *Concrete-Entity*, *Activity*, and *MentalStateEntity*. One of the concrete entities defined is *Agents*, which are autonomous entities that can perform actions that affect resources. The *Actions/Activities* are concrete entities and include *Tasks* and *Interaction Protocols*. Agents can also perceive information entries that describe the state of a resource. Another concrete entity is a *Resource*, which represents a non-autonomous entity that agents can access/use.MESSAGE builds five views of the Analysis Model: Organization, Goal/Task, Agent/Role, Interaction and Domain views. The *Organization view* shows the concrete entities in the system, the environment and the relationship among them.

Based on our requirements, we see that MESSAGE defines elements of its environment as containing objects (both agents and resources) that can interact using actions and messages. However, MESSAGE does not include the notion of environmental laws that affect the objects in the environment (requirement 5).

Even though MESSAGE captures most of the required information, it does not explicitly define an agent-environment interaction model and does not provide a flexible way to represent or define actions at an appropriate level of abstraction.

2.3 Prometheus

The aim of the Prometheus System Identification Phase is to identify the basic functionality of the system along with the inputs, outputs, and important data structures [7]. Prometheus models these inputs as *percepts* and defines them as raw data coming from the environment. Outputs are modeled as *actions*, which are defined as the agent's way to modify the environment. Scenarios are used in Prometheus to describe how the system operates nominally. Each scenario consists of a set of steps that can include goals, actions, percepts, scenarios, or "other" for special types of steps.

The architectural design phase focuses on identifying the agents in the system and their interaction. Once the agents are identified, the next step is to define the percepts each agent reacts to and the actions it may perform. Agent interaction is specified by defining messages and the different repositories to be used. All these items are depicted in the system overview diagram. The Detailed Design Phase focuses on defining the capabilities, which are defined in terms of internal events, plans, and detailed data structures of the agents. Each capability is described by a descriptor, which includes the definition of its percepts, actions, data read or written, interaction with other capabilities, and sub-capabilities.

Our analysis reveals that Prometheus does not explicitly define the environment. It does not define the objects in the environment (requirement 1), the relationships between them (requirement 2), or the laws that govern the effect of agent's actions on the environment (requirement 5). However, Prometheus does capture the operations that it uses to get percepts from the environment and perform actions on the environment. Thus Prometheus too could benefit from an explicit AEI Model.

2.4 Organization-Based Multiagent Systems Engineering

The Organization-Based Multiagent System Engineering (O-MaSE) [1] methodology extends the original MaSE [3] methodology to allow the design of organizational multiagent systems. Some of the weaknesses of MaSE addressed by O-MaSE include the tendency to generate static organizations, the inability to model sub-organizations/systems, and the lack of explicit concepts for modeling interactions with the environment. To model interactions with the environment, O-MaSE represents both the sensing and manipulation of the environment as a type of *Capability*, which is defined as an "atomic entity that defines the agents' abilities; these abilities include *soft* abilities such as access to resources or computational algorithms, as well as *hard* capabilities such as sensors and effectors [1]. We use this notion of capabilities as the foundation for our AEI Model, extending it to allow capability composition as well as to model direct interaction with the environment. The current version of the O-MaSE metamodel is shown in Fig 1. The important elements for this paper center on the Capabilities and the Domain Model. In O-MaSE, Capabilities can be either plans or actions, where plans are algorithmic entities that use actions for low-level operations. The domain model is relatively simple, consisting of a set of Environment Objects. Actions interact directly with the Environment Objects.

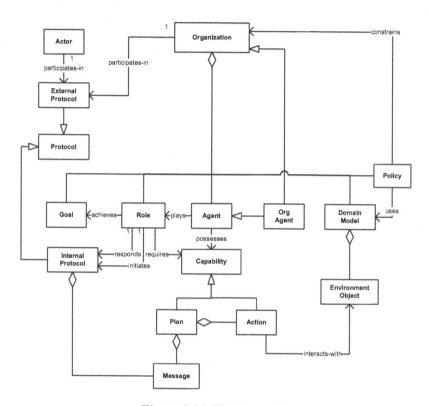

Fig. 1. O-MaSE Metamodel

However, even though O-MaSE does provide the notion of capabilities and a domain model, it does not meet all our requirements for an AEI Model. Specifically, the domain model does not include agents as objects in the environment (requirement 2) or the definition of the laws that govern the effect of those operations on objects in the environment (requirement 5). In the next section, we present our AEI Model that ties together the O-MaSE elements to provide a complete environment interaction model that can be used with O-MaSE and easily adapted to other main stream multiagent systems methodologies.

3 Agent-Environment Interaction Model

Our proposed AEI Model is composed of three main elements: the Capability Model, the Environment Model, and a set of Interactions between capabilities and environment objects. Essentially, agents possess capabilities that sense and act upon objects in the environment via interactions. Fig 2 depicts the integration of these three parts into our AEI Model. The top part of the figure represents the *Capability Model*, which defines capabilities as consisting of a set of actions, each of which has a single operation that interacts with environment objects. The bottom part of the figure captures the *Environment Model*, which includes an explicit environment that contains a set of environment objects (that includes agents) and their relationships. The environment objects are governed by processes that implement specific environmental principles. *Interactions* are defined by the intended effect of operations on environment objects.

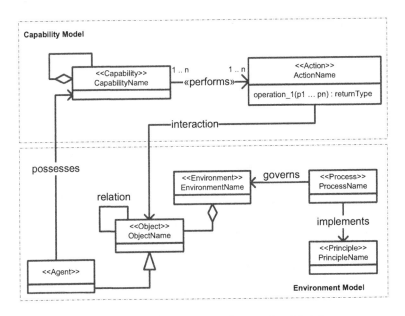

Fig. 2. Agent-Environment Interaction Model

Note that this general model captures all the items advocated by Ferber as described in Section 1. It also satisfies each of our specific requirements for an AEI Model: there is a unique entity called the environment, the environment consists of a set of objects that includes agents, it includes the notion of relations that may exist between objects in the environment, it defines a set of operations that agents may perform upon environment objects, and it captures the notion of laws that govern the effect of those operations on objects in the environment. The three main entities of our AEI Model are described in more detail in the following sub-sections.

3.1   Environment Model

In order to define the actions that an agent may perform upon then environment, it is critical that we understand exactly what types of objects may be in the environment and the attributes of those objects. While environments have been widely touted as important in multiagent systems design, there is not a well accepted representation for them. Odell et. al. define the environment as the entity that provides the principles and processes for agents and objects to exist and communicate [6] while Russell and Norvig define an environment as an entity with which agents interact, with properties defined by concepts such as accessibility, determinism, dynamism, and continuity [9].

In our AEI model we use a simple Environment Model to model the objects upon which agents perform the basic actions of sensing and affecting the environment through interactions. Basically, the *Environment* is a container of *Objects*, which can include *Agents* situated in the environment. All the objects in the environment are affected by physical *Principles* that are implemented by *Processes* as depicted in Fig 3. Objects are defined simply via a name and a set of attributes. Here, environment objects are actually more closely related to object-oriented classes or types than true object instances.

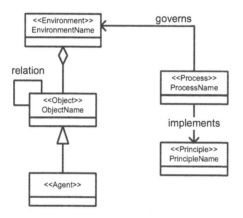

Fig. 3. Simple Environment Model

Fig 4 shows an example Environment Model for a Weapons of Mass Destruction Search (WMD) cooperative robotic search system. In this model, we are concerned with modeling the types of objects that can be found while doing a search of an area (office building, etc.) for suspicious boxes that can be classified as possible chemical, nuclear, or biological weapons based on signatures produced by the weapons. All objects in the environment have a location within the environment as well as a size (which we abstractly identify using a type PhysicalDimension). Robots also have four additional attributes: add, q, R, and G. The *add* attribute represents the address of the robot for communication purposes while the *q* attribute represents the message queue of incoming messages. As we will see later, the communication capability requires both these attribute values for proper operation. The *R* and *G* attributes represent the current set of roles and goals assigned to the robot. There are four types of inert objects:

doors, inert boxes, chairs, and tables. Each of these has a zero values for the rad, bio, and chem attributes. Finally, there are the three types of weapons that can exist: RadWeapons, BioWeapons, and ChemWeapons. Each of the weapon types are boxes. However, the exact type of weapon (or whether the box is inert) can be determined only by using special sensors mounted on specific robots.

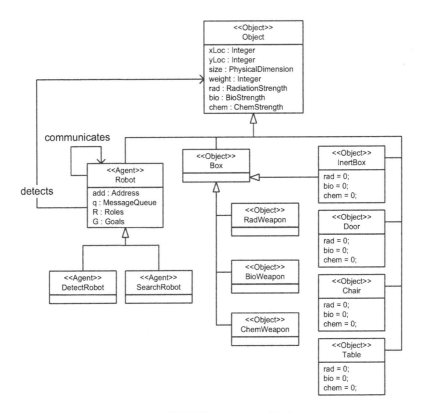

Fig. 4. WMD Environment Model

There are two relationships shown between objects in the Environment Model. The *communicates* relation is shown between two Robots. The communicates relation is critical in allowing Robots to use their communication capability (as described in Section 3.2) to send and receive messages. The *detects* relation is shown between Robots and all other objects in the environment (including other Robots). The detects relation allows Robots to use their Search and Pickup capabilities (see Section 3.2) to detect objects in the environment.

Besides identifying objects and attributes, it is also important to identify the principles and processes that govern the environment. For instance, in detecting radiation, there is the well known principle that the amount of radiation intercepted varies as the square of the distance between the source and the sensor. Thus, we must define a process that determines the amount of radiation detected at any location in the environment. To do this, we must add the amount of radiation produced by all radiation sources in the environment, regardless of how little they add to the total. Thus, the process that is in play can be defined by the following equation.

$$radiation(x, y) = \sum_{\forall o:Box} \frac{o.rad}{\sqrt{(o.x - x)^2 + (o.y - y)^2}}$$

The WMD Environment Model is developed using traditional domain modeling or domain analysis techniques common to most object oriented development methodologies. Essentially, the goal of the domain modeling is to capture the objects, relationships, and behaviors that define the domain [8]. For our purposes, the domain is the environment of the multiagent system under development. A good Environment Model is critical in the definition of the interactions between the capabilities and the environment objects as the precise definition of the operations is based on the object attributes.

3.2   Capability Model

As defined by Russell and Norvig, an agent is anything that can sense and perform actions upon its environment [9]. As described above, most multiagent systems methodologies represent these sensors and effectors in some way, either implicitly or explicitly. In our AEI Model, we abstract the notion of sensors and effectors as agent *capabilities*. To keep in line with our O-MaSE definition, we assume capabilities can be either hardware or software based capabilities.

In our AEI Model, we represent the sensors, effectors, or a combination of both as *capabilities*. A capability can be defined at different levels of abstraction like sense, move, jump, etc. The *Jump* capability can be accomplished by sensing an obstacle and then passing (moving) over it. We define *Capability* as an entity that can *perform* one or more *actions* (e.g. sense or move) and can be composed of other sub-capabilities.

An *Action* is defined as an entity that represents the agent's actual sensor or effector. Specification of the execution of an action is defined via a single accessible *operation*. Each action's operation has a set of preconditions that determine whether or not the operation can be executed. If the preconditions hold, the operation may be executed. If the preconditions do not hold, the operation may not be executed. Operations also have a set of post-conditions that specify the desired state of the world after completion of the operation. However, because operations are assumed to be performed in a dynamic environment with external influences, the post-condition do not guarantee that the desired state will hold. In reality, the processes that implement the environment principles determine the actual state of the world after an operation is performed. For instance, if a robot performs an operation to move forward one meter, the robot may or may not actually move exactly one meter. Wheel slippage and wind conditions are environmental processes that help determine exactly how far the robot will actually move. When such environmental processes are expected by the agent, the agent may predict its own performance or at least sense to determine the exact result of its operations.

The Capability Model provides support for reusability and modularity by encapsulating each sensor and effector operation individually in actions. Our model also provides support for constructing a capability using other capabilities, which we call a *composed* capability. We depict our Capability Model in Fig 5. By defining capabilities in terms of other capabilities as well as atomic actions, the model is very flexible and allows designers to capture sensor and effector operations at a continuum of granularity levels based on the application or designer preference.

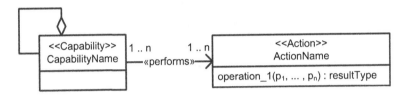

Fig. 5. Capability Model

The flexibility of capability definition using this model is shown in the following examples. In the example shown in Fig 6, the Search capability shows an agent's capability to scan and detect items in a particular location as a single high level action, SearchLocation. This level of abstraction may be appropriate during the initial stages of analysis or when the agent is using a predefined package that provides higher level services.

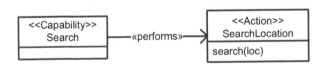

Fig. 6. Search Capability Example

In the second example shown in Fig 7, the PickUp capability is shown as being carried out by performing three lower level actions: Detect, Grab, and Lift. By defining actions at a lower level than that shown in Fig 6, the definitions of the actions in Fig 7 could be more easily reused when defining other capabilities such as Search (which could be defined using Detect) or Transport (which could use all three along with a Move action). Clearly, the level of abstraction or refinement should be left to the designer and, thus, our model allows a wide variety of choices.

Another feature of our Capability Model is the ability to capture the capability of an agent to send and receive messages in a single, consistent style. Fig 8 shows a simple definition of the Communicate capability, which is carried out by

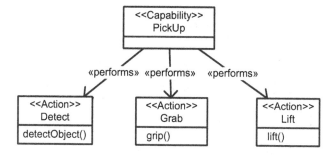

Fig. 7. Carry Capability Example

performing one of three actions: P2PTransmit, Broadcast or Receive. While most multiagent modeling techniques use special notation for sending and receiving of messages, they are actually special forms of actions. By allowing designers to specify communications in the same way as other actions, it actually allows the designer to specify exactly how communication can be performed.

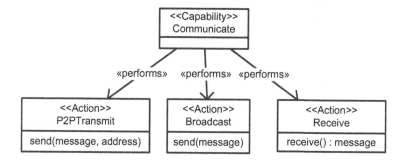

Fig. 8. Communication Capability Example

The AEI Model also allows the designer to create new capabilities out of existing capabilities. Thus, in Fig 9, the *Rescue* capability is an example of a composed capability that uses the previous defined capabilities of Search, Pickup, and Communicate. In essence, the Rescue capability has access to all the actions defined as part of the Search, Pickup, and Communicate capabilities.

Complete specification of the Capability Model requires defining pre- and post-conditions for each of the operations. These pre- and post-conditions completely and unambiguously define the interactions between agent capabilities and environment objects, which are defined in the next section.

3.3   Interactions

By executing an operation defined in an action, an agent can sense or manipulate its environment. If this action is to sense, the agent receives information

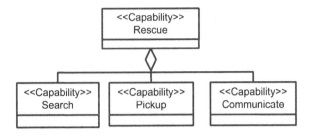

Fig. 9. Composed Rescue Capability Example

regarding the environment. If the action modifies an object in the environment, the environment will change and the agent representation of the environment will change as well.

As described above, each operation is defined by a pre-condition that determines whether or not the action can be executed and a post-condition that specifies the desired state of the world after the operation is performed. Again, the post-condition does not specify the *actual* state of the world after the operation is performed, but only the *desired* state since the environment is governed by the principles and processes defined in the Environment Model.

An example of the specification of an interaction via operation pre- and post-conditions is shown below in the definition of the send(message, address) operation from the P2PTransmit action. For consistency, the notation used is UML's Object Constraint Language (OCL).

P2PTransmit: send(message, address)
Pre: not(address = null)
Post: self.possesses.communicates->select(add = address).q->includes(message)

The semantics for this send operation state that if the address given as a parameter is not null, then the message (also given as a parameter) is added to the message queue (q) of the agent whose add parameter is equal to the address parameter. Since 'self' refers to the capability, the reference 'self.possesses' follows the possesses relation between capabilities and the agents that possess them. Thus 'self.possesses.communicates' refers to the set of agents with which the agent possessing the P2PTransmit capability can communicate.

3.4   AEI Model and O-MaSE

The AEI Model fits nicely into the O-MaSE metamodel due to the fact that O-MaSE already possesses the main concepts used in our AEI Model. While capabilities and actions existed in the original O-MaSE metamodel, their relationship had to be adjusted slightly to fit the AEI Model. The integration of the AEI Model into the O-MaSE metamodel is shown Fig 10; the bold lines represent the new/modified entities and relations. First, we had to allow capabilities to be composed of lower level capabilities. Next we had to change the semantics of capabilities being either a plan or an action. To maintain the semantics of the AEI Model presented, we have also added the constraint that capabilities may be composed of either a single plan or a set of lower level capabilities and actions. The Domain Model is used to capture the AEI Environment Model. We added the concept of environmental properties as a component of the domain model, where an Environmental Property specifies the principles and processes that govern the environment. We also added the ability for agents to be represented as environment objects.

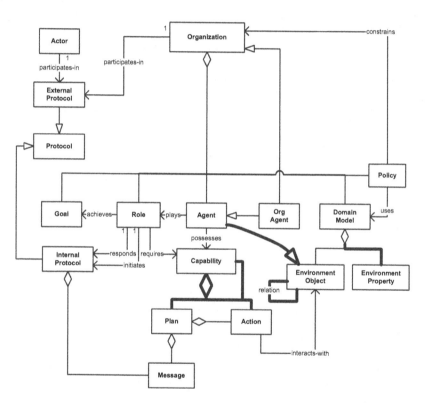

Fig. 10. O-MaSE Metamodel Extended with AEI Concepts

4   Example

To illustrate the use of the AEI Model integrated into the O-MaSE methodology, we chose to model a Weapon of Mass Destruction (WMD) Search system as an example of a cooperative robotic agent system. The goal for the robot team is to search a specified area for possible chemical, radioactive or biological weapons and remove such weapons once they have been positively identified. Each of the robots on the team have multiple capabilities that allow them to sense various weapon types, navigate, and locate themselves using Global Positioning System (GPS), and transport the weapons to a safe location.

Based on this system description, we defined an O-MaSE Agent Model in Fig 11. In our current notation, we annotate agents with the "Agent" keyword and capabilities by the "Capability" keyword. A base robot has three capabilities: Communication, GPS, and Move. SearchRobots have a Sonar capability to aid in searching while the RemovalRobots are equipped with Transport capabilities for removing any identified WMD objects. Finally, there are three types of DetectRobots: BioDetectRobots, ChemDetectRobots, and RadDetectRobots. All the DetectRobots are equipped with the capability to detect a specific type of WMD: BioDetector, ChemDetector, or a RadDetector. The filled-headed arrows between agents represent protocols used by the robots. The *divideArea* protocol is used at system initialization to determine which SearchRobots will be assigned which specific areas to search. When a SearchRobot detects a suspicious object, it uses the *detection* protocol to find an appropriate DetectRobot to investigate. If a positive detection is made by the DetectRobot, the SearchRobot uses the *positive* protocol to find an available RemovalRobot to remove the WMD object.

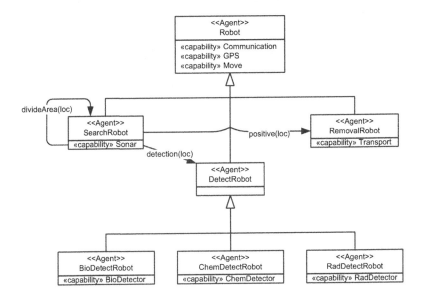

Fig. 11. WMD Agent Model

To complete the AEI model, we modeled the WMD environment using an O-MaSE Domain Model (as shown in Fig 4) and defined the set of capabilities to sense and manipulate that environment in the O-MaSE Capability Model as shown in Fig 12. As discussed previously, the level of abstraction for each capability may be different. For example, the *Communication* capability is implemented by two actions, P2PTransmit and Receive. The model also includes

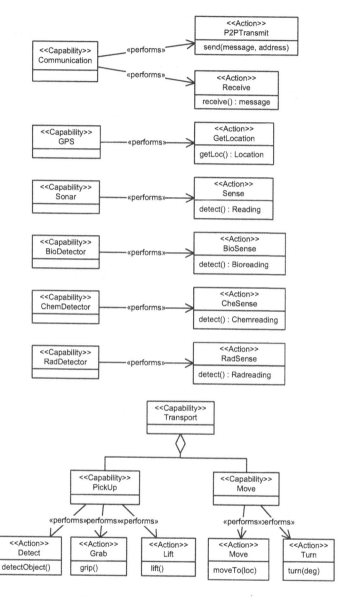

Fig. 12. WMD Capability Model

a composed capability *Transport* that uses the Pickup and Move capabilities. Each base capability is implemented by actions that interact directly with the objects in the environments.

Assuming the pre- and post-conditions for each operation are defined, the agent designer may use the operations to design the agent plans. A simple (algorithmic) plan for the ChemDetectRobot is shown below. It uses the Communication, GPS,

Move, and ChemDetector capabilities and their associated actions to define the plan. For simplicity, we describe the plan using a simple pseudo code approach. The notation used to access the operations assumes that names are unique and follows the form *CapabilityName.ActionName.OperationName*.

ChemDetector Plan

```
loop
  m = Communication.Receive.receive()
  if (m.performative = ''possible'')
    Communication.P2PTransmit.send(acknowledge(loc), m.sender)
    repeat
      Move.Move.moveTo(loc)
      currentLoc = GPS.GetLocation.getLoc()
    until (currentLoc = loc)
    result = ChemDetector.CheSense.detect()
    if (result = positive)
      Communication.P2PTransmit.send(positive(loc),m.sender)
    else
      Communication.P2PTransmit.send(negative(loc),m.sender)
    end if
  end if
end loop
```

When the ChemDetector robot receives a *possible* message, it sends an acknowledge message and then moves to the location specified. Once at the appropriate location, the robot uses its chemical sensor and returns the result, either positive or negative.

5   Conclusion and Future Work

In this paper we have described an approach for modeling a multiagent system's interactions with its environment. The key concepts in our approach were capabilities (and the actions they perform) and a model of the environment. We defined a set of requirements for an Agent Interaction Model based on Ferber's definition of a multiagent system. We suggest that our AEI Model captures all these requirements since it contains a unique entity called the environment (requirement 1) and that is modeled as a set of objects/agents (requirement 2) and a set of relations between those objects/agents (requirement 3). Through a set of capabilities possessed by the agents, the agents have access to a set of operations that they may perform upon environment objects (requirement 4) whose effect are governed by environmental laws (requirement 5).

We showed how our AEI Model could be integrated into the O-MaSE methodology with only slight modifications to the O-MaSE metamodel. Finally, we presented a WMD Search simulation system design using O-MaSE and the AEI

Model. We showed how the model captured the relationship between the agent's capabilities and their affect on the environment and how to use those definitions to model low-level agent plans.

It is our contention that all multiagent systems methodologies should provide a robust way to define the interaction of agents with their environments. While most methodologies provide some mechanism for describing these details, most do not provide a sufficient modeling capability. Thus, we believe that integrating the concepts of our AEI Model, or elements thereof, into existing methodologies is not only possible, but would be a positive step toward more complete system models.

Finally, we are working to fully integrate our AEI Model into the O-MaSE methodology and into agentTool III (aT^3) [2]. We are continuing to evolve O-MaSE to provide a flexible methodology that can be used to develop both traditional and organization-based systems. A long term goal is to provide a tailorable methodology that is fully supported by automated tools. aT^{3}is being developed as an Eclipse plug-in that will give the agent system designer unprecedented flexibility while providing enhanced verification capabilities between models. Eventually, aT^{3}will provide predictive performance metrics to allow the designer to make intelligent tradeoffs and will generate code for FIPA compliant frameworks. As defined in this paper, the AEI Model is a key step in fully defining the design of agents to the point where a higher degree of low-level code generation is possible.

References

1. DeLoach, S.A. Engineering Organization-based Multiagent Systems. LNCS Vol. 3914, Springer, (2006) 109-125
2. DeLoach, S.A. Multiagent & Cooperative Robotics Laboratory. "agentTool III Home Page," http://macr.cis.ksu.edu/projects/agentTool/agentool3.htm (2006)
3. DeLoach, S.A., Mark F. Wood and Clint H. Sparkman, Multiagent Systems Engineering, The International Journal of Software Engineering and Knowledge Engineering, 11(3) (2001) 231-258
4. Ferber, J. Multi-Agent Systems - An Introduction to Distributed Artificial Intelligence. Addison-Wesley, Harlow (1999)
5. MESSAGE: Methodology for Engineering Systems of Software Agents. Deliverable 1. Initial Methodology. EURESCOM Project P907-GI (2000)
6. Odell, J., Parunak, H., Fleischer, M., Bruckner, S. Modeling Agents and their Environments. LNCS Vol. 2585, Springer (2002) 16-31
7. Padgham, L. and Winikoff, M. Prometheus: A Methodology for Developing Intelligent Agents. LNCS Vol. 2585, Springer (2003) 174-185
8. Pressman, R. Software Engineering: A Practitioner's Approach (6 ed.), McGraw-Hill (2004)
9. Russell, S. and Norvig, P. Artificial Intelligence: A Modern Approach. Prentice Hall; 2nd ed. (2002)

10. Weyns, D., Parunak, H., Michel, F., Holvet, T., and Ferber, J. Environments for Multiagent Systems State-of-the-Art and Research Challenges. LNAI Vol. 3373, Springer (2005) 1-47
11. Wooldridge, M. Jennings, N. and Kinny, D. The Gaia methodology for agent-oriented analysis and design. Journal of Autonomous Agents and Multi-Agent Systems, 3(3), (2000) 285-312
12. Zambonelli, F., Jennings, N. R., and Wooldridge, M.J. Developing Multiagent Systems: The Gaia methodology. In ACM Transaction on Software Engineering Methodology 12(3), (2003) 317-370

Allocating Goals to Agent Roles
During MAS Requirements Engineering

Ivan J. Jureta[1], Stéphane Faulkner[1], and Pierre-Yves Schobbens[2]

[1] Information Management Research Unit (IMRU), University of Namur,
8 Rempart de la Vierge, B-5000 Namur, Belgium
iju@info.fundp.ac.be, stephane.faulkner@fundp.ac.be
[2] Institut d'Informatique, University of Namur,
8 Rempart de la Vierge, B-5000 Namur, Belgium
pys@info.fundp.ac.be

Abstract. Allocation of goal responsibilities to agent roles in Multi-Agent Systems (MAS) influence the degree to which these systems satisfy nonfunctional requirements. This paper proposes a systematic approach that starts from nonfunctional requirements identification and moves towards agent role definition guided by the degree of nonfunctional requirements satisfaction. The approach relies on goal-dependencies to allow potential MAS vulnerabilities to be studied. In contrast to related work where organizational patterns are imposed on MAS, roles are constructed first, allowing MAS organizational structures to emerge from role definitions.

1 Introduction

Requirements engineering is concerned with the identification of goals to be achieved by an information system (IS), the operationalization of these into the specification of IS services and constraints, the identification of resources required to perform those services, the assignment of responsibilities for the resulting requirements to agents, such as humans, devices and software.

At an abstract level, MAS are conceptualized as organizations of autonomous, collaborative, and goal-driven software components [45]. Flexibility, modularity, and robustness are some of the qualities hoped from MAS (e.g., [45,14]), making them an attractive choice for a range of applications, such as peer-to-peer computing, electronic commerce, etc.

There is widespread agreement that nonfunctional requirements need to be considered early in any IS development process (e.g., [8,12,26,38]) in order to assist reasoning about alternative system structures. While various approaches have been proposed to transform nonfunctional requirements into functional system characteristics during system development (e.g., [33,15,20,35,22,2,9]), the specific issue of using nonfunctional requirements to allocate goals to agent roles during the RE step of MAS development has received limited attention, and no systematic approach has been proposed. In this context, this paper proposes a preliminary approach to allocating goals to agent roles. It is situated within the

L. Padgham and F. Zambonelli (Eds.): AOSE 2006, LNCS 4405, pp. 19–34, 2007.

RE step of MAS development process and builds on widely accepted techniques for Goal-Oriented RE (GORE). The organizational MAS engineering metaphor is adopted, leading to the allocation of goals to roles instead of agents, in order to allow encapsulation and modularity nonfunctional requirements to be adequately addressed [45].

The proposed goal allocation approach advances the state of the art in three ways: (i) A systematic approach that starts with the identification of nonfunctional requirements and progressively moves towards the generation of and selection between alternative MAS role structures is proposed. It allows the choice of goal allocation to agent roles to be justified in relation to the identified nonfunctional requirements. (ii) A novel type of dependency relationship between goals is used to support the generation of, and selection between, alternative MAS role structures. (iii) Heuristics for generating and selecting alternative goal-to-role allocations are proposed.

Because the first step of the approach reuses the accepted goal analysis techniques, there are no obstacles to integrating it into existing MAS Goal-Oriented Requirements Engineering (GORE) frameworks.

2   Related Work

Within the RE field, GORE frameworks (e.g., [38,40]) have been shown as useful when engineering MAS requirements (e.g., [6] and related).

In GORE research, the NFR framework [33,8] has been the first to propose a representation language for nonfunctional requirements and to suggest a method for relating them to functional requirements. It has been adapted in Tropos, an agent-oriented development methodology [6], to deal with nonfunctional requirements in agent systems. In Tropos, goals are allocated to roles or agents through dependency links that indicate the need of an agent (the depender) to collaborate with another agent (the dependee) in order to achieve a goal, to have a task executed, or a resource provided. Tropos has recently been extended with additional modeling concepts and techniques specifically aimed at analyzing security nonfunctional requirements (see, e.g., [28,30,31,32]). Tropos assumes that agents and their goals are given. In [6], the selection of a MAS role structure consists in instantiating one of the predefined patterns of organizational structure (such as structure-in-five, pyramid, joint-venture, etc.). Using the qualitative reasoning techniques from the NFR framework, a pattern is selected by comparing the degree to which each alternative pattern satisfies the identified MAS nonfunctional requirements. The roles and their interdependencies are thus predefined (i.e., an organizational structure is selected and roles in that structure are instantiated), whereas the approach proposed here constructs roles first, allowing the organizational structure to appear from role definitions. In this respect, the latter approach seems less rigid for tailoring the MAS structure to nonfunctional requirements. It is guided by the goal dependency relationship to help the engineer to allocate interdependent goal pairs to roles so as to internalize or externalize the dependencies.

The Tropos security-specific approach [27] considers the allocation of goal achievement responsibilities to agents or roles by estimating the trustworthiness between collaborating agents. Trustworthiness is conceptualized as a characteristic of the collaborator agent and is estimated at system operation time by the agent requiring the collaboration. As trustworthiness is a characteristic inherent to individual agents, and not roles, a cautious approach has been adopted in this paper: the existence of trust is not assumed during the definition of MAS organizational structures through the allocation of goals to roles.

A formal approach has been proposed in [26] to support decision-making in the context of comparison and choice of alternative goal refinements that result in alternative system structures. The approach consists of enriching goal refinement models with a probabilistic layer for reasoning about partial goal satisfaction. Being focused on the analysis of alternative goal refinements, the selection of alternative allocations of goals to agent roles is not considered. The approach from [26] can be combined with the one proposed in [24], as they share the same conceptual foundations. A systematic technique is proposed in [24] (for more details, see, [25]) to support the process of goal refinement in the aim of generating alternative agents and responsibility assignments for goal achievement. It consists of checking goal realizability against the capabilities of system agents to monitor and/or control state variables restricted by the goals. Specific refinement tactics are given to facilitate the search for agents and agent capabilities, and for refining goals until they are realizable by single agents. While [24] is similar in motivation to this paper, the approach differs in the following respects: (i) There is no distinction between agents and agent roles in [24]. This hampers encapsulation and modularity for large MAS [45]. (ii) [45] use only refinement between goals. Below, we propose goal-dependency to allow new forms of analysis.

The MaSE methodology [42] supports security nonfunctional requirements at RE time by identifying negative use cases. The RE step (analysis phase) of the methodology involves goal identification, use case generation for goal achievement, and agent role definition. The RE step in MaSE relies on diagrammatic notation accompanied by textual descriptions, and is consequently of limited use when precise traceability is required. Goal allocation to roles is not treated in a systematic manner and no heuristics are provided. Similar remarks are relevant for the MESSAGE [5] MAS development methodology.

Our goal-to-role allocation approach complements the techniques discussed here. Our approach can be combined to [6] and [32] to introduce an additional technique to generate and choose between alternative agent roles, while relying on a formal nonfunctional requirements representation. It can be added to [24] and [25] to introduce the role concept in their process and account for the possibility of alternative agent role definitions, allowing encapsulation and modularity nonfunctional requirements to be addressed more adequately.

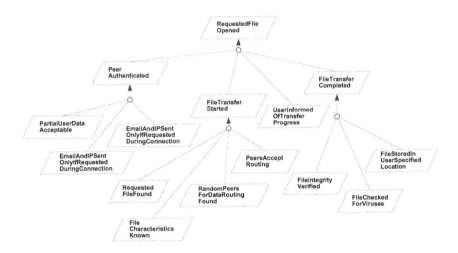

Fig. 1. Section of a goal tree for the P2P case study

3   A Process for Allocating Goals to Agent Roles

The proposed goal to role allocation approach consists of three steps described in the following subsections. Application of the suggested techniques is illustrated with examples of peer-to-peer MAS requirements discussed informally in [16] and [27].

3.1   Create a Consistent Goal Tree Containing Precise Requirements

This step uses well-known discovery techniques to identify a set of nonfunctional and functional requirements, modeled as goals. For illustration, we have used the KAOS framework [10], [39]. Fig. 1 shows a section of the goal tree built for the P2P MAS case study. The top goal, RequestedFileOpened is specified as follows:

> **Goal:** Achieve [RequestedFileOpened]
> **Definition:** Every remote file requested by the user should be opened
>   within at most 10 minutes.
> **FormalDef:** $\forall rf : File; p : Peer; Requested(rf, p) \land Remote(rf, p)$
> $\Rightarrow \Diamond_{\leq 10min} Opened(fl, p)$

3.2   Identify Goal Dependencies

Given a goal tree considered consistent and complete, dependency relationships can be defined between goals. This section first overviews the dependency conceptualization commonly used in the MAS RE literature. The possibility of employing another useful dependency type at the MAS RE step is discussed. Finally, tactics for finding and checking the completeness of the identified, so-called *goal-dependencies* are proposed.

Dependencies Between Agents. In MAS RE, the following definition of a dependency relationship has been adopted in i* [44], Tropos [6], GRL [29], and REF [13]:

> "A dependency link is a directed link that goes from the depender to the dependee; it can connect an agent to a hard or soft goal, a task, a resource, or vice-versa. In particular, an agent is linked to a goal, a task or a resource when it depends, in some way, on that goal to be achieved, that task to be performed or that resource to be provided; a goal/task/resource is linked to an agent when it depends on that agent to be achieved/performed/provided." [13]

The goal-to-role allocation approach presented in this paper relies on another type of dependency: *goal-dependencies*. Goal-dependencies are studied *before* knowing which agents will be responsible for goal achievement, whereas agent-dependencies are identified from system agent intentions *after* the agents are known. While agent-dependencies allow easier characterization of *existing* (e.g., organizational) conditions, the goal-dependencies are used to define new roles.

Dependencies Between Goals. In Fig. 1, the goal FileTransferStarted is refined into four other goals. As discussed in [38], many goal link types have been proposed to relate goals with each other, or with other elements of the requirements models: (i) *Refinement links* of two kinds have been suggested. *AND-refinements* relate a goal to a set of sub-goals (the set if called a goal refinement), meaning that achieving all sub-goals in the refinement is sufficient for satisfying the parent (or refined) goal. *OR-refinement* links a goal to alternative refinements. The achievement one of the refinements is sufficient to satisfy the refined goal [11]. (ii) In NFR [33], weaker versions of refinement links relate nonfunctional goals and functional goals. The notion of goal satisficing has been introduced, and contribution links express that sub-goals are expected to contribute to the parent goal.

After constructing a refinement of a goal FileTransferStarted, the requirements engineer knows that the achievement of the sub-goals is sufficient for the refined goal to be achieved. But refinement links do not indicate the sequence in which the sub-goals need to be achieved in order for the parent goal to be achieved. This information is encoded in temporal logic in the KAOS [25] and Formal Tropos [17] frameworks. But we believe it is worth making it more explicit, since it will allow specific tools and techniques to be used, and it may be easier to identify sub-goals by considering the sequence of activities for (parent) goal achievement [34]. The usual method to refine goals asks *how can a parent goal be achieved?* The natural answer to this question describes the sequencing of activities.

We propose thus a new type of inter-goal relationship, named goal-dependency. Formally, a goal g_2 depends on g_1 when:

$$\neg g_1 \Rightarrow \neg g_2 \mathbf{W} g_1$$

The classical temporal operator $\mathbf{W}$ is read "unless" (e.g., [25]), and means that the condition on its left stays true unless the condition on its right becomes true. Intuitively, this condition means that g_2 cannot be achieved unless g_1 is achieved.

Identification of Goal-Dependencies. Consider the two goals below. The first formalizes the condition for a file transfer to be started in the case-study P2P application, the second the condition for a requested file to be considered as found.

Goal: RequestedFileFound

Definition: When the file has been requested and at least one peer p_x having and sharing the file is found, the peer p_1 that requested the file knows that the file is found, and the routing peers are found.

FormalDef: $\forall p_1 : Peer; fl : File; rID : RequestID; p_1.req = fl \wedge (\exists p_x : Peer;$
$$p_x \in P \wedge p_1 \neq p_x \wedge fl \in p_x.file\_list \wedge Share(p_x, fl, rID))$$
$$\Rightarrow Found(fl, rID)$$

Goal: RandomPeersForDataRoutingFound

Definition: The n random peers for data routing are found when n routing peers are found and each peer confirms availability.

FormalDef: $\forall p_s, p_r : Peer; fl : File; rID : RequestID; Found(fl, rID) \wedge$
$$Sender(p_s, fl, rID) \wedge Receiver(p_r, fl, rID) \wedge$$
$$@(\exists p_1, \dots, p_n : Peer; \{p_s, p_r\} \cap \{p_1, \dots, p_n\} = \emptyset$$
$$\wedge \diamond_{\leq 5s} Available(p_1, rID) \wedge \dots \wedge \diamond_{\leq 5s} Available(p_n, rID))$$
$$\Rightarrow \diamond RoutingPeers = \{p_1, \dots, p_n\}$$

The existence of predicates that constrain values of the same MAS properties within different goals indicates that there may be a goal-dependency between the two goals. In the example, the property constrained in both goals concerns MAS behavior related to file transfers. It is a goal-dependency, since they have to be executed in this sequence. Notice that the refinement relationships cannot be used to determine the sequence between these goals as they are brother sub-goals.

Applying the reasoning described above, it can be seen that the property $Found(fl, rID)$ appears in both RandomPeersForDataRoutingFound and RequestedFileFound goals' specifications. Domain/solution knowledge allows affirming that a file first needs to be found before searching for random peers that will be used to route the file. It is thus assumed that there is a goal-dependency in which the achievement of RandomPeersForDataRoutingFound depends on the achievement of RequestedFileFound goals. To accept the reasoning above allows a goal-dependency identification technique to be proposed:

– (I1) If there is at least one MAS property, constrained in predicates that occur in formal specifications of two goals g1 and g2, then there is a goal-dependency between them. The direction of this goal-dependency is undetermined.
– (I2) If temporal operators in formal specifications of goals in a goal-dependency make it possible to establish the sequence of achievement of one in relation to the other goal, then the goal-dependency relationship between them is directed from the goal whose achievement precedes the other goal's achievement.

- (I3) If the goal-dependency direction cannot be determined using (I2), then domain/solution knowledge can be used to make an assumption and choose the goal in the goal-dependency whose achievement precedes that of the other goal.

Information about the temporal sequence of achievement of goals involved in the goal-dependency can only be extracted from explicit temporal operators of the predicate which constrain the MAS property giving rise to a goal-dependency. If there are no temporal operators associated with at least one of the predicates that constrain the relevant property, domain/solution knowledge will be the foundation for determining the goal-dependency direction. If neither (I2) nor (I3) allow the goal-dependency direction to be determined, then the direction remains undetermined. In the example above, there are few temporal operators in the goal specifications that allow (I2) to be useful. However, experience and the wide use of P2P applications allow the requirements engineer to make a reasonable assumption that a requested file first needs to be found before searching for routing peers (hence, (I3) is used).

The goal-dependency in the example can be specified with:

Goal-Dependency: FindFileThenSearchForRoutingPeers
Definition: Search for routing peers after the file to be transferred is found.
Involves: RequestedFileFound, RandomPeersForDataRoutingFound.
Direction: RandomPeersForDataRoutingFound **DependsOn** RequestedFileFound.
CommonProperties: $Found(fl, rID)$.

The proposed goal-dependency identification approach has some desirable characteristics: (i) Undirected goal-dependencies can be found automatically between all goals in the goal tree, as the goals' formal specifications contain all the necessary information. (ii) The second step, (I2) may indicate the need for rewriting goal specifications in order to make them more precise. In the example above, although it was not possible to determine dependency direction due to few temporal operators in the specifications, the direction was established from domain knowledge. It may be beneficial in such cases to strengthen the formal specifications by introducing domain knowledge assumptions. In the example, the specification of RequestedFileFound could be modified by replacing $Found(fl, rID)$ with $\circ Found(fl, rID)$, and writing $@Found(fl, rID)$ instead of $Found(fl, rID)$ in RandomPeersForDataRoutingFound. More precise specifications derived from acceptable/verifiable domain assumptions arguably lead to higher quality requirements, further facilitating the identification of potential inconsistencies in the form of additional obstacles and conflicts.

The goal-dependency identification process often leads to the possibility of specifying a large number of goal-dependencies. To make the goal-dependency set readable, we remove those that are deducible by transitivity, giving its Hesse diagram.

Completeness of the Goal-Dependency Set. The condition for dependency existence ($\neg g_1 \Rightarrow \neg g_2 \mathbf{W} g_1$) can be used to verify the completeness of the goal-dependency set provided that system histories can be generated using e.g., model checking techniques. An informal, but practical, completeness criterion is that each goal in the goal tree is involved in at least one goal-dependency. Any goal that does not fulfill this condition is outside of the overall process that is to be realized by the MAS.

Linking Goal-Dependencies to MAS Nonfunctional Requirements. The aim of relating individual goal-dependencies to MAS nonfunctional requirements is to know the type of vulnerability that is generated by each goal-dependency. Similarly to the notion of vulnerability suggested in the context of agent-dependencies [44], goal-dependencies generate potential vulnerability of MAS: When a goal being depended upon is not achieved, the goal that depends on it will not be achieved. Consequently, failure of a goal may lead to the failure of the future MAS to operate according to the desired quality level.

Recall that Step 1 of the proposed process involved, by application of the approach for reasoning about partial goal satisfaction [26], the identification of quality variables and their associated objective functions (to indicate whether the value of the variables should be maximized or minimized). For example, the quality variable NumberOfRoutingPeers is relevant for the RandomPeersFor-DataRoutingFound goal. Following [26] the specification given below can be written. That specification enriches the original goal specification with information about two quality variables that measure the degree of goal achievement. A quality variable can be conceptualized as kind of metric for measuring the degree to which a goal is achieved, whereas the sample space gives information on the case sample used to calculate probability values. The NumberOfRoutingPeers variable indicates that the probability of having at least two routing peers needs to be maximized, with a target value of 80%, while it is currently estimated at 30%. The second variable measures the probability of receiving a response from each peer regarding its availability for routing within a certain time frame.

Goal: RandomPeersForDataRoutingFound
Definition: The n random peers for data routing are found when n routing peers are found and each peer confirms availability.
Objective Functions:

Name	Def	Modal	Target	Current
HighNumRoutPeers	P(NoRoutPeers > 2) Max	80%	30%	
LowAvailRespTime	P(AvailRespT < 1s) Min	70%	40%	

Quality Variables:
   NumberOfRoutingPeers: *Natural*
   Sample space: set of routing peer numbers
   Def: number of peers that are used to route data between the sender and the receiver peers
   AvailabilityResponseTime: *Time*
   Sample space: set of routing availability responses
   Def: time from the request for availability confirmation until the reception of the response

   ...

In terms of system *nonfunctional requirements* (i.e., security, privacy, safety, usability, reliability, etc. - see e.g., [18,19,33]), the achievement of the above goal can be said to affect privacy and performance. In case the number of peers is small, it becomes easier to trace the entire route between the sender and the receiver, consequently allowing malicious users to obtain access to private peer information [16]. Performance is affected in that, the more peers are used to route data, the less it is likely that the performance in terms of availability response time will be low. Consequently, the degree to which the goal is achieved affects the degree to which the above qualities are satisfied. As goal-dependencies are identified from properties common to goal pairs, each goal-dependency can be associated with a MAS quality, provided that the members of the dependency's CommonProperties attribute can be related to a quality variable. In the example, if the RandomPeersForDataRoutingFound goal is involved in a directed or undirected goal-dependency that arises from the common property RoutingPeers, it can be inferred that this goal-dependency can be related to the degree to which privacy is satisfied in the MAS. In case this same goal is involved in a goal-dependency arising from the common property $Available(pi, rID)$, the system performance is the quality to which this goal-dependency is related. The number of qualities to which a goal-dependency can be related is not restricted.

Relating goal-dependencies to nonfunctional requirements using common properties and quality variables allows taxonomy of system vulnerabilities to be proposed for the engineered MAS. If a goal-dependency is related to performance, this goal-dependency is said to generate a *performance vulnerability*. Rich vulnerability taxonomies can be built from existing work in nonfunctional requirements analysis, such as [3], or standards (e.g., [18,19]). To make explicit the specific vulnerability generated by a goal-dependency, the attribute Vulnerability is added to the goal-dependency specification template. For example:

Goal-Dependency: FindFileThenSearchForRoutingPeers
Definition: Search for routing peers after the file to be transferred is found.
Involves: RequestedFileFound, RandomPeersForDataRoutingFound.
Direction: RandomPeersForDataRoutingFound **DependsOn** RequestedFileFound.
CommonProperties: $Found(fl, rID)$.
Vulnerability: Reliability.

Before the vulnerabilities can be used to generate and select between alternative goal to role allocations, the vulnerabilities need to be identified. This can be realized using the following process. For each goal:

- (VI1) Identify properties in the goal's formal specification whose values affect that goal's quality variables.
- (VI2) For each property identified in (VI1), check if there are goal-dependencies to which this property gives rise, and which involve the goal.
- (VI3) For each quality variable in the goal, identify system quality whose degree of satisfaction is measured by that quality variable.

For each goal-dependency involving the goal, indicate vulnerabilities by combining properties found in (VI2) with qualities found in (VI3) to which each property can be related.

3.3 Generate and Select Between Alternative Goal-to-Role Allocations

The purpose of Step 3 is to generate and explore alternative allocations of goals to roles. Each allocation is a set of agent roles, such that each role is allocated a set of goals. The achievement of allocated goals becomes the responsibility of the agent that is selected to occupy the role. Choosing agents to occupy the defined roles is not treated in this paper.

Allocating Goals to Roles Instead of Agents. Allocating responsibility for goal achievement directly to agents does not allow encapsulation and modularity nonfunctional requirements to be addressed satisfactorily when specifying requirements for large MAS. As suggested in [45], as soon as the complexity of MAS increases, modularity and encapsulation principles require MAS to be composed of agent roles. An agent can therefore play one or more roles to achieve goals within multiple and different agent organizations. In order to benefit from the *organizational* metaphor [45], it is necessary to ensure the separation of agents' action execution characteristics from its expected behavior within MAS organizations.

In the Gaia MAS development framework ([45,46]), a role is modeled as a set of responsibilities and permissions. Responsibilities are represented as protocols (i.e. activities that require interaction with other agents) that the role needs to execute, while role's permissions specify resources that the role can access and under which conditions. At a more abstract level, Gaia responsibilities can be seen as resulting from MAS goal operationalizations, involving, among other, the identification of agent capabilities and actions that are required for the goal to be achieved. Based on the role concept in Gaia, a restrictive way of conceptualizing a role is to consider it as being a set of MAS goals. While this is one of the many facets of the role concept used in MAS engineering, it may be sufficient to restrict the analysis during the RE step at this aspect of role only. Responsibilities and permissions could be derived from goals specifications later in the MAS development process. If the proposed goal-to-role allocation approach is to be used as the first requirements step in, e.g., Gaia, there are no barriers in enriching the suggested conceptualization with additional facets relevant for methodology-specific analyses.

The role conceptualization is consequently not fixed in the proposed allocation approach. It is up to the requirements engineer to choose the degree of expressivity of role by including its various facets (e.g., goals, permissions, etc.). The goal-to-role allocation approach does necessitate that the role be characterized *at least* as being a set of goals. Otherwise, alternative allocations cannot be studied.

Generate Alternative Roles. An alternative goal-to-role allocation is a set of roles such that all goals in the goal tree are allocated to at least one role. Using information about vulnerabilities, it can be shown that each allocation satisfies to a different degree the MAS qualities. Consequently, the ultimate purpose of generating alternative allocations is to choose one that is considered as the most adequate by the MAS RE project stakeholders.

Background. An essential and recurring question in the MAS development methodologies is whether to assign some responsibility (often represented as a goal) to a single agent, or to design the MAS so that the responsibility is fulfilled through interaction between two or more agents. Claims have been made that the former structure may increase security and/or robustness, while the later may be more flexible. In [42], no advice is given to the user of the MaSE methodology. Although responsibilities are assigned in the case studies discussed in, e.g., [27,32], discussions on why the proposed responsibility assignments have been chosen are missing. As suggested in the overview of related work, the assignment problem is addressed in a systematic way only in [6], where predefined MAS organizational structures are instantiated to determine the responsibility assignments in specific MAS. The patterns in [6] are based on responsibility assignment structures observed often in human organizations. However, there is doubt as to the adequacy of imposing a human organizational structure, elaborated historically in human organizations to fully-automated or partially-automated organizations of humans and agents subjected to different constraints than classical human organizations. In contrast, the approach proposed in this paper favors the creation of a structure by relying on an understanding of key parameters and trade-offs that need to be made when designing roles, instead of fitting a predefined structure to a set of goals.

Internalization vs. Externalization. In economics and organization sciences, most of the analysis of distributing work between economic agents (such as, e.g., entire firms) has focused on the question of whether to realize activities internally, or to assign their responsibility to external agents (e.g., [7,43,36]).

In terms specific to the allocation approach proposed in this paper, the internalization decision results in a goal-dependency that is under the responsibility of a single role, i.e., the role contains both goals involved in the dependency (Fig. 2). Whether a goal-dependency is internalized or externalized will result in a different degree of MAS nonfunctional requirements satisfaction. For example, the externalization of a dependency may require interaction between distinct agents. This in turn could lead to worse response rates of the MAS, security issues resulting from the possibility of interception of sensitive data communicated between the agents, etc. Consequently, it is assumed in the context of this paper, that a key parameter to consider when designing roles in MAS is whether to externalize or internalize goal-dependencies within roles. This is particularly relevant in the face of the long tradition economics and organization science preoccupation with internalization and externalization decisions, and when the organizational metaphor is adopted during MAS development.

Conclusions from seminal works in economics and organization science can be a valuable source of inspiration for justifying goal to role allocation decisions. The following motives can be used to argue for/against internalization decisions in the context of MAS development. Motives to internalize a goal-dependency (marked with "I") can be:

- (I-a) According to [7], it is the aim of exploiting *economies of speed* that pushes firms towards internalizing activities. Because firm throughput depends on

Fig. 2. Internalized goal-dependency (left) and externalized goal-dependency (right)

uninterrupted flows of material and payments, precise planning and control is of paramount importance. As internalization implies that larger parts of the firm's environment are under the influence of its management, it could be the strategy of choice for exploiting economies of speed [37]. A parallel can be made with the need for speed in MAS operation (or, more generally performance): To favor performance optimization in MAS, it is beneficial to internalize goal-dependencies, as the agent occupying the role will need to have capabilities allowing a larger part of MAS to be under its control.

- (I-b) Internalization can reduce *transaction costs* (e.g., [43]), including the costs of finding, selling, negotiating, contracting, monitoring, and resolving disputes with other firms. Although it may be argued that transactions between MAS agents have no cost, this may not be the case if cost includes the impact of goal-dependency failure on the degree of MAS qualities satisfaction. Transaction cost between agents may be considered a function of vulnerabilities generated by the goal-dependency that is externalized and involves transaction between agent roles. To avoid the "cost" of the vulnerabilities, internalization may be the tactic of choice.

- (I-c) In relation to the motives (I-a) and (I-b), if a transaction between firms involves *repeated interaction*, it may be better to internalize that transaction [43]. If two goals in a goal-dependency are likely to be achieved frequently during MAS operation, it may be beneficial to internalize that dependency. This allows, e.g., a role to be defined so that it can be occupied only by agents specialized in achieving the two goals, resulting in reduced vulnerability for qualities to which the internalized goal-dependency is related.

- (I-d) According to [1], internalization is a means to *access and protect knowledge* available in other parts of the industry value chain, in order to ensure advantage over competitors. A MAS reinterpretation can be that data leaks or malicious access to data passed in order to achieve two goals in a goal-dependency may be avoided, or at least their probability reduced, if the goal-dependency is internalized.

Motives to externalize a goal-dependency (marked with "E"):

- (E-a) Internalization carries a *commitment to a particular way of doing business* [4], leading to lower flexibility of the firm in the face of changing environment conditions. Building MAS using complex roles requires very specific agents to be available to occupy the roles. In open MAS, where existing and new agents may enter and exit, increased internalization of goal-dependencies commits MAS to a particular way of functioning that may rapidly become obsolete.

	Quality 1	Quality 2	Quality 3	Quality 4
Goal dependency 1	++ +	-- +	- ++	- +
Goal dependency 2	- ++	- +	++ +	-- +

Fig. 3. An example of how to record alternative role definitions

- (E-b) *Growth in the extent of the markets* reduces the incentives to internalize comparatively to externalizing activities through markets [23]. When designing MAS roles, it is relevant to consider externalizing goal-dependencies if this can allow the definition of roles that can be occupied by a wide variety of generic agents. This may facilitate changing role occupancy during MAS operation, allowing, e.g., to replace dysfunctional agents by other available agents.
- (E-c) *Standardization of transactions* (and contracts in particular) reduces the uncertainty a firm faces when externalizing activities (e.g., [23,37]). In other words, the more predictable the transaction, the more likely it is to be externalized. In MAS, some goal-dependencies, if externalized may involve interactions that are standardized, that is, widely used patterns may exist to codify interactions. Vulnerabilities that appear in such goal-dependencies may be considered as having a limited impact.

The above considerations need to be perceived as starting points for discussion when choosing a goal-to-role allocation. They serve to justify decisions when generating alternative allocations.

A Process to Generate and Select Roles. The process described below can be used to generate alternative sets of potential MAS agent roles. The process starts by generating an initial allocation. Then, alternatives are created by changing the initial role set. For each goal-dependency in the goal tree:

- (GAR1) Identify the vulnerabilities generated by that goal-dependency.
- (GAR2) Discuss whether internalization or externalization would lead to increasing or reducing the probability of the vulnerability to occur. Base justifications on motives for internalizing or externalizing discussed above.
- (GAR3) Decide whether to internalize or externalize the goal-dependency.

Although the application of the process above results in a single set of roles, information about potential alternatives can be recorded during the application of the process. Consider Fig. 3 as an example of how decisions can be recorded during the application of the identification process. Each cell in the table is at the intersection of a goal-dependency and a MAS quality, and is separated in an upper and lower part. The upper part of a cell represents the impact of the decision to *internalize* a goal-dependency on the degree to which the concerned quality is satisfied in the MAS. The lower part of a cell represents the same information for the decision to *externalize* the goal-dependency. Each part of a cell may contain one of four symbols: $(++)$ to indicate that the decision supports strongly and favorably the satisfaction of the concerned quality, $(+)$ to indicate somewhat favorable support, $(-)$ to indicate somewhat unfavorable support, and $(\tilde{-})$ to indicate strong unfavorable support. If the goal-dependency is unrelated to the quality (i.e., it does not generate a vulnerability for that quality), the cell is left blank.

Alternative roles can be constructed by choosing, in each non-blank cell, one cell part to indicate that the concerned goal-dependency needs to be internalized or externalized. As the table contains all possible individual alternatives (i.e., all possible internalizations and externalizations of goal-dependencies), it contains sufficient information to construct any alternative goal-to-role allocation.

While qualitative reasoning techniques, such as the one used to construct and interpret Fig. 3 have their limitations (notably in terms of accuracy [26]), they are accessible and are an adequate choice when too little information is available to provide quantitative motives (as opposed to qualitative ones proposed above).

4   Conclusions and Future Work

A systematic approach for allocating goals to agent roles during the RE step of the MAS development process is proposed. A novel type of inter-goal link, the *goal-dependency*, a type of the dependency relationship, serves two purposes in the approach. First, it is used to reason about the sequence of goal achievement in MAS, adding valuable information to classical goal refinement and contribution links. Second, each goal-dependency can be related, through goal quality variables and the value of the goal-dependency's CommonProperties attribute, to information about nonfunctional requirements of the MAS, to allow MAS vulnerabilities to be identified, classified for analysis, and used for agent role definition.

Two additional parameters for organizational design discussed in organizational sciences are the allocation of decision rights and the grouping of work in subunits of an organization. Further work is needed to study the tools and methods for integrating these factors in the process of designing MAS organizations. The proposed qualitative reasoning technique can be extended to integrate quantitative data. The use of goal-dependencies in the analysis of the timed operation of MAS during the RE step will also be addressed.

References

1. Afuah, A.: Dynamic boundaries of the firm: Are firms better off being vertically integrated in the face of a technological change? *Academy of Management Journal* 44, 6 (2001) 1211-1228.
2. Al-Naeem, T., Gorton, I., Ali Babar, M., Rabhi, F., Benatallah, B.: A Quality-Driven Systematic Approach for Architecting Distributed Software Applications. *Proc. Int. Conf. Softw. Eng.*, 2005.

3. Anton, A., Earp, J., A. Reese, A.: Analyzing Website Privacy Requirements Using a Privacy Goal Taxonomy. *Proc. IEEE Int. Req. Eng. Conf. RE'02*, 2002, 23-31.
4. Buzzel, R. D.: Is vertical integration profitable? *Harvard Business Rev.* (Jan.-Feb. 1983).
5. Caire, G., Coulier, W., Garijo, F., Gomez, J., Pavon, J., Leal, F., Chaainho, P., Kearney, P., Stark, J., Evans, R., Massonet, P.: Agent-Oriented analysis using message/uml. *Proc. 2nd Int. Worksh. Agent-Oriented Softw. Eng.*, LNCS 2222, 2002.
6. Castro, J., Kolp, M., Mylopoulos, J.: Towards requirements-driven information systems engineering: the Tropos project. *Inf. Sys.*, 27, 6 (2002) 365-389.
7. Chandler, A.: *The Visible Hand - The Managerial Revolution in American Business*. Cambridge, MA: Belknap Press, 1977.
8. Chung, L., Nixon, B., Yu, E., Mylopoulos, J.: *Non-Functional Requirements in Software Engineering*. Kluwer Publishing, 2000.
9. Cleland-Huang, J., Settimi, R., BenKhadra, O., Berezhanskaya, E., Christina, S. Goal-Centric Traceability for Managing Non-Functional Requirements. *Proc. Int. Conf. Softw. Eng.*, 2005.
10. Dardenne, A., van Lamsweerde, A., Fickas S.: Goal-directed requirements acquisition. *Sc. Comp. Prog.*, 20 (1993) 3-50.
11. Darimont, R., Van Lamsweerde, A.: Formal Refinement Patterns for Goal-Driven Requirements Elaboration. *Proc. 4th ACM SIGSOFT Symp. Found. of Softw. Eng. FSE4*, 1996, 179-190.
12. Devanbu, P.T., Stubblebine, S.: Software Engineering for Security: a Roadmap. *Proc. 22nd Int. Conf. on Softw. Eng.*, 2000.
13. Donzelli, P. A goal-driven and agent-based requirements engineering framework. *Req. Eng.*, 9 (2004) 16-39.
14. Faulkner, S., Kolp, M., Mouratidis, H., and Giorgini, P.: Delegation Mechanisms for Agent Architectural Design. *Proc. 4th Joint conf. Auton. Ag. Multi-Ag. Syst.*, 2005.
15. Franch, X.: Systematic Formulation of Non-Functional Characteristics of Software. *Proc. Int. Conf. on Req. Eng. RE'98*, 1998.
16. Friedman, A., Camp, L. J.: Peer-to-Peer Security. In Bidgoli, H. (Ed.) *The Handbook of Information Security*. J.Wiley&Sons, 2005.
17. Fuxman, A., Liu, L., Mylopoulos, J., Pistore, M., Roveri, M., Traverso, P.: Specifying and Analyzing Early Requirements in Tropos. *Req. Eng.*, 9, 2 (2004) 132-150.
18. IEEE Computer Society: *IEEE Standard for a Software Quality Metrics Methodology*. IEEE Std. 1061-1992, New York, 1992.
19. ISO: *ISO/IEC Standards 9126 - Information Technology - Software Product Evaluation*. ISO, 1991.
20. Issarny, V., Bidan, C., Saridakis, T.: Achieving middleware customization in a configuration-based development environment: experience with the Aster prototype. *Proc. 4th Int. Conf. Config. Distr. Syst.*, 1998.
21. Keller, A., Blumenthal, U., Kar, G.: Classification and Computation of Dependencies for Distributed Management. *Proc. 5th Int. Conf. Comp. Comm. ISCC*, 2000.
22. Landes, D. Studer, R.: The Treatment of Non-Functional Requirements in MIKE. *Proc. 5th Eur. Softw. Eng. Conf.*, 1995.
23. Langlois, R. N.: The vanishing hand: the changing dynamics of industrial capitalism. *Ind. and Corp. Change*, 12, 2 (2002) 351-385.
24. Letier, E., van Lamsweerde, A.: Agent-Based Tactics for Goal-Oriented Requirements Elaboration. *Proc. Int. Conf. Softw. Eng.*, 2002.

25. Letier, E.: *Reasoning about Agents in Goal-Oriented Requirements Engineering.* Ph.D. Thesis, Univ. of Louvain, 2001.
26. Letier, E., van Lamsweerde, A.: Reasoning about Partial Goal Satisfaction for Requirements and Design Engineering. *Proc. SIGSOFT'04/FSE-12*, 2004.
27. Liu, L., Yu, E., Mylopoulos, J.: Analyzing Security Requirements as Relationships Among Strategic Actors. *Proc. 2nd Symp. on Req. Eng. Info. Security SREIS'02*, 2002.
28. Liu, L., Yu, E., and Mylopoulos, J. Security and Privacy Requirements Analysis within a Social Setting. *Proc. Int. Conf. on Req. Eng.*, 2003.
29. Liu, L., and Yu, E. Designing information systems in social context: a goal and scenario modeling approach. *Info. Syst.*, 29 (2004).
30. Mouratidis, H., Giorgini, P., Manson, G., Philp, I.: A natural extension of Tropos methodology for modelling security. *Proc. of the Agent Oriented Meth. Worksh. OOPSLA*, 2002.
31. Mouratidis, H., Giorgini, P., Manson, G.: Modelling Secure Multiagent Systems. *Proc. Auton. Ag. Multi-Ag. Syst.*, 2005.
32. Mouratidis, H., Giorgini, P., and Manson, G. When security meets software engineering: a case of modelling secure information systems. *Info. Syst.*, 2005. (To Appear.)
33. Mylopoulos, J., Chung, L., and Nixon, B. Representing and Using Nonfunctional Requirements: A Process-Oriented Approach. *IEEE Trans. on Softw. Eng.*, 18, 6 (1992) 483-497.
34. Rolland, C., Souveyet, C., and Ben Achour, C. Guiding Goal Modelling Using Scenarios. *IEEE Trans. Softw. Eng.* (Dec. 1998).
35. Rosa, N.S., Cunha, R.F., Justo, G.R.R.: ProcessNFL: A Language for Describing Non-Functional Properties. *Proc. 35th Hawaii Int. Conf. Syst. Sci.*, 2002.
36. Rubin, P. *Managing Business Transactions.* NY: Free Press, 1990.
37. Sturgeon, T. J.: Modular production networks: a new American model of industrial organization. *Ind. Corp. Change* 11, 3 (2002).
38. van Lamsweerde, A.: Goal-Oriented Requirements Engineering: A Guided Tour. *Proc. 5th IEEE Int. Symp. Req. Eng.*, 2001.
39. van Lamsweerde, A. Letier, E.: Handling Obstacles in Goal-Oriented Requirements Engineering. *IEEE Trans. Softw. Eng.*, 26, 10 (Oct. 2000) 978-1005.
40. van Lamsweerde, A. Goal-Oriented Requirements Enginering: A Roundtrip from Research to Practice. *Proc. 8th IEEE Int. Symp. on Req. Eng.*, 2004.
41. van Lamsweerde, A., Darimont, R., Letier, E.: Managing Conflicts in Goal-driven Requirements Engineering. *IEEE Trans. Softw. Eng.*, 24, 11 (1998) 908-926.
42. DeLoach, S.A., Wood, M., Sparkman, C.: Multiagent system engineering. *Int. J. Softw. Eng. Knowl. Eng.*, 11, 3 (2001) 231-258.
43. Williamson, O. *The Economic Institutions of Capitalism.* NY: Free Press, 1985.
44. Yu, E. *Modeling Strategic Relationships for Process Reengineering.* Ph.D. Th., Univ. of Toronto, 1995.
45. Wooldridge, M., Jennings, N.R., Kinny, D.: The Gaia methodology for agent-oriented analysis and design. *J. Auton. Ag. M.-Ag. Syst.*, 3, 3 (2000) 285-312.
46. Zambonelli, F., Jennings, N.R., and Wooldridge, M.: Developing Multiagent Systems: The Gaia Methodology. *ACM Trans. on Softw. Eng. and Meth.*, 12, 3 (2003) 317-370.

An Aspect-Oriented Modeling Framework for Multi-Agent Systems Design

Alessandro Garcia[1], Christina Chavez[2], and Ricardo Choren[3]

[1] Computing Department, Lancaster University, UK
garciaa@comp.lancs.ac.uk
[2] Computing Department, Federal University of Bahia, Brazil
flach@dcc.ufba.br
[3] Computer Engineering Department, Military Institute of Engineering, Brazil
choren@de9.ime.eb.br

Abstract. A number of concerns in multi-agent system (MAS)design have a crosscutting impact on agent-oriented models. These concerns inherently affect several system agents and their internal modeling elements, such as actions and goals. Examples of crosscutting concerns in MAS design encompass both internal and systemic properties, such as learning, mobility, error handling, and security. Without an explicit modeling of such MAS properties, designers can not properly communicate and reason about them and their broadly-scoped effects. This paper presents a meta-modeling framework for supporting the modular representation of crosscutting concerns in agent-oriented design. The framework is centered on the notion of aspects to describe these concerns. It also defines new composition op-erators to enable the specification on how aspects affect the agent goals and ac-tions. The proposed framework is a result of our previous experience in both using aspect-oriented techniques for MAS design and implementation, and integrating aspect-oriented abstractions in an agent-oriented modeling language, called ANote.

1 Introduction

MAS developers usually face a number of concerns which have a crosscutting impact on agent-oriented design artifacts, such as goal models and agent models [2,15,16,30,36,2,18]. A crosscutting concern at MAS design is any broadly-scoped concern that cannot be modularly captured with the conventional agent-oriented modeling abstractions and composition mechanisms [18]. For example, the learning concern is composed of a number of specific goals and actions, which systematically crosscut the goal hierarchies and actions descriptions associated with several agents in an application. Other examples of crosscutting MAS concerns are widely-scoped properties, such as mobility, error handling, and security.

The problem is that these concerns consistently cut across the modularity of several MAS modeling elements, such as agents, goals, actions, and plans. Very often, the crosscutting property of such design concerns remains either implicit or is described in informal ways leading to reduced uniformity, impeding traceability between higher-level models and implementations, and hindering detailed design

L. Padgham and F. Zambonelli (Eds.): AOSE 2006, LNCS 4405, pp. 35–50, 2007.

and implementation decisions. Hence there is a pressing need for the conception of a modeling framework that provides MAS designers with proper support for the modular representation and reasoning [23] of crosscutting MAS concerns.

In fact, there is a growing number of modeling extensions dealing with cross-cutting concerns in multi-agent systems [7,21,27,28,37]. However, each of them introduces a plethora of extensions to the underlying modeling language that are targeted at supporting one specific agency concern, such as mobility [21], coordination [27], or autonomy [9]. It makes more evident the inadequacy of conventional agent-oriented design languages [8,29,34,38] and respective abstractions to cope with the crosscutting nature of some MAS concerns. As a result, their crosscutting effects are inevitably spanned over the resulting agent-oriented design artifacts. To encompass all crosscutting MAS concerns, it is important to describe generic abstractions and to devise new composition rules.

The notion of aspects [1,13,22] looks promising for handling crosscutting MAS concerns in early phases of the software lifecycle. Aspect-Oriented Software Development (AOSD) is an emerging development paradigm aimed at promoting improved separation of concerns by introducing a new modular unit, called aspect. However, the existing aspect-oriented modeling approaches have been limited to the object-oriented and component-oriented paradigms. Moreover, AOSD has being only systematically investigated to cope with the modularity of traditional crosscutting concerns, such as distribution [24], persistence [24,25], exception handling [12], and some design patterns [3,20]. Our previous work has investigated the interplay of AOSD and agent-oriented software engineering, but it has focused on different contexts other than agent-oriented design and modeling, including architecture design [17,30,19,32], detailed design [14,15], and implementation [10,30,36,26]. In other recent work [18], we have enhanced ANote, a specific agent-oriented modeling language, with aspect-oriented notation.

In this context, this paper presents a meta-modeling framework to enable the modular representation of broadly-scoped concerns in agent-oriented design modeling. Our framework blends core concepts from AOSD with recurring abstractions of agent-oriented design. Our meta-modeling approach enriches agent-oriented modeling with aspectual composition mechanisms in order to promote MAS decompositions with superior modularity. The proposed framework is agnostic to specific agent-oriented modeling languages, and relates its aspectual concepts to fundamental agent-oriented design elements, such as agents, actions, and goals. The proposed framework is centered on: (i) the notion of aspects to describe these concerns, and (ii) new composition mechanisms to capture how MAS aspects affect the agent goals and actions.

The paper is organized as follows. Section 2 illustrates crosscutting concerns in agent-oriented modeling in terms of an example, and shows the inability of existing abstractions and composition rules to support their separation. Section 3 presents our aspect-oriented framework for agent-oriented design and modeling. Section 4 describes the applicability of the concept of aspects in agent-oriented design according to our approach. Section 5 discusses related work. Section 6 presents concluding remarks.

2   Crosscutting Concerns in Agent-Oriented Goal Modeling

This section presents some examples of crosscutting concerns in agent-oriented design modeling. Section 2.1 presents the main concerns associated with our running example. Section 2.2 illustrates and discusses some typical examples of crosscutting concerns in MASs in terms of our case study. Section 2.3 shows the consequences of not having explicit support for the modularization of crosscutting concerns in agent-oriented design models.

2.1   The Expert Committee Example

The Expert Committee (EC) is a multi-agent application that supports the management of the reviewing process for research conferences. The EC system encompasses three types of software agents: (i) information agents, (ii) user agents, and (iii) the manager agent. Figures 1 and 2 show a partial design representation for the EC system [15] specified with the ANote modeling language [21]. ANote defines modeling views that allow for the expression of a MAS design from seven different perspectives: goal, agent, environment, scenario, action, interaction and organization. For instance, the goal view diagram (Figure 1) provides the identification of the hierarchy that outlines the system goals. In this diagram, complex goals can be functionally decomposed into more granular goals until the designer reaches the desired level of goals (functionalities) to distribute among the agents. These two diagrams support the representation of the agents, goals and contexts respectively. A context is a scenario that indicates how agents should achieve goals.

Figure 1 illustrates some goals associated with the information and user agents respectively. Information agents goals are managing the system information that is mainly stored in a database, and providing information to the other system agents and users as requested. User agents are software assistants that represent system users in reviewing processes. Their basic functionalities are to infer and to keep information about the users' research interests and participations in scientific events.

2.2   Modularity Issues in Goal Models

Designers are able to successfully use agent-oriented abstractions and composition mechanisms to represent several system concerns in a modular fashion. For example, the goal composition rules *and*, *or* and *xor* allow for consistently specifying how goals and sub-goals are combined to realize a given concern. The "finding information" and "reviewing papers" concerns, for instance, can be smoothly captured in separate goal hierarchies, as illustrated in Figure 1.

However, we can notice in Figures 1 and 2 that there are some concerns which cannot be represented in a modular way across the design views. Learning and

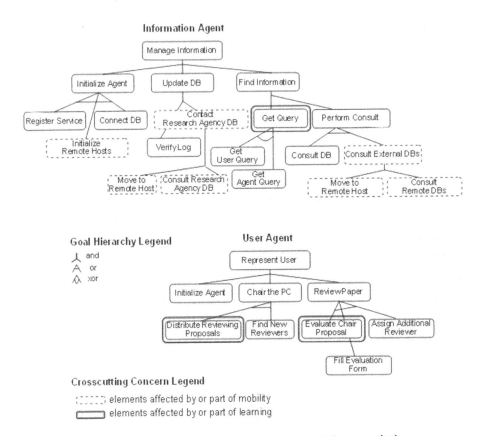

Fig. 1. Crosscutting Concerns in ANote Goal Diagram [18]

mobility are two examples of crosscutting concerns in the agent-oriented design of the EC system. The set of goals, which is part of and affected by these broadly-scoped concerns, is spread over the agent-oriented design. The set of goals for a specific crosscutting concern is surrounded by dotted rectangles in Figure 1. The mobility concern consists of goals that crosscut distinct goal hierarchies, and of actions intermingled with diverse scenarios. A similar problem happens with the learning-specific goals and actions. These two concerns have a huge impact on the agent structure and behavior since they cut through the primary modularity of goal hierarchies representing other agent concerns.

The crosscutting manifestation leads to two major problems at the agent-oriented design level: scattering and tangling [35]. Scattering in agent-oriented models is the manifestation of design elements that belong to one specific concern, over several modeling units referred to other MAS concerns. For example, the mobility-related goals are scattered over multiple goal hierarchies, such as the ones under the goals "Perform Consult" and "Update DB" (Figure 1).

Goal	Perform Consult
Agent	Information Agent
Precondition	Local DB is available Remote environments are available
Actions	1. process the query 2. consult DB 3. gather consult details 4. decide whether moving or not 5. notify manager agent 6. get remote permissions to move 7. move to remote environments 8. consult external DBs 9. return home 10. return result 11. gather user feedback 12. process information using ML strategies 13. adapt user/agent preferences
Interactions	Manager Agent

Goal	Evaluate Chair Proposal
Agent	User Agent
Precondition	Chair sent the reviewing proposal
Actions	1. receive the proposal 2. process the proposal 3. propose a decision to the user 3. get confirmation from the user 4. gather decision and proposal details 5. process information using ML strategies 6. adapt user preferences 7. return final decision to the chair
Interactions	User Agent

Fig. 2. Crosscutting Concerns in ANote Scenario Diagrams [18]

Tangling in agent-oriented models is the mix of multiple concerns together in the same modeling elements. For instance, tangling is evident in the "Perform Consult" scenario since it is realizing mobility-related and learning-related actions in addition to its primary actions of performing the consult.

2.3   Side Effects on MAS Design Modularity

Existing agent-oriented modeling abstractions and composition mechanisms do not provide proper support to isolate crosscutting MAS concerns as exemplified in Figures 1 and 2. This brings a number of substantial design pitfalls relative to modularity breakdowns, as described below.

Hindering of modular and compositional reasoning. Tangling and scattering of MAS concerns hinder both modular and compositional reasoning at the design stage. Developers are unable to reason about a concern while looking only at its description, including its core goals and actions, and its structural and behavioral implications in terms of other MAS concerns. Hence its analysis inevitably forces developers to consider all the design artifacts in an ad hoc manner. For example, the designers treating the learning and mobility concerns in Figure 1 need to consult the goals associated with all other design concerns across the different views.

Replication of agent-oriented design elements. Replication of goals (and their actions) in the agent-oriented design is another side effect of tangling and scattering. Replication in turn decreases the system understandability, reusability and evolvability. For instance, the mobility-specific goal "Move to Remote Host" is duplicated in the goal view diagrams due to its crosscutting relationships with the goals "Update DB" and "Find Information".

Essential information missing. Without appropriate abstractions and composition mechanisms for crosscutting concerns in agent-oriented models, MAS designers are not able to locally express the structural and behavioral implications of a given broadly-scoped MAS concern in several design elements and views. The result is that design information is irrecoverable just because the lack of support for properly specifying them. For example, the learning concern (Figure 2) would clearly have a goal "Learn User Preferences" associated with it, which influences at least two goals: "Get Query" and "Evaluate Chair Proposal". As the designer does not have support to describe this crosscutting impact of a learning-specific goal, such important design information has been lost and such goal is not appearing in the design models. Even if the designers use the standard abstractions and composition rules of the underlying modeling languages to register such information, the learning-specific goal would end up being scattered over two or more goal hierarchies.

Reduced evolvability and reuse opportunities. Tangling and scattering are two of the main anti-reuse and anti-evolution factors in the MAS software lifecycle. For example, it is not easy to understand, in the EC system design, which agent types are mobile and which have learning abilities. In addition, the goals associated with learning and mobility concerns are not coherently documented in a single modular unit so that they can be easily reused in other design contexts. Also, if the designers need to evolve the system and introduce changes related to the mobility and learning properties, the evolution process will be cumbersome as those concerns are intermingled in the system design.

3 An Aspect-Oriented Modeling Framework for MAS Design

This section describes our approach to address the need for supporting the modular representation of crosscutting concerns in agent-oriented design. We present a meta-modeling framework that enriches agent-oriented models with aspects, which are the design first-class units to overcome tangling and scattering of concerns. The proposed framework is a result of our previous experience in both using aspect-oriented techniques for MAS design and implementation [14,15,30,36], and integrating aspect-oriented abstractions in an agent-oriented modeling language, called ANote [18]. The proposed framework is independent of specific agent-oriented modeling languages, and is composed of 3 models: the Agent Model, the Aspect Model and the Composition Model. We use entity-relationship diagrams to illustrate each conceptual model in terms of entity sets and relations over these sets.

3.1   The Agent Model

The *Agent Model* is a conceptual meta-model for agent-based system modeling. The model presented here comprises a set of fundamental agent-oriented design elements, such as agents, actions, and goals. Figure 3 summarizes the agent model. An Agent is the module that is able to perform actions; it is the main abstraction of the agent paradigm. An action is a computation that results in a change in the state of an agent. An agent acts in the system in order to achieve a goal. While executing actions, an agent can interact with other agents. A goal is a system objective, and it defines a state that must be achieved by one or more agents. The execution of one or more actions allows for the achievement of a goal. A goal can be of different categories that are organized into a specialization hierarchy. This means that goals can be decomposed into several alternative combinations of sub-goals.

Fig. 3. The Core Agent Model: Agents, Goals, and Actions

3.2   The Aspect Model

The *Aspect Model* is a conceptual framework for AOSD [5,6] that subsumes concepts, relationships and properties for supporting the design of aspect-oriented modeling languages. These elements are organized around three interrelated conceptual models: (i) the component model, (ii) the join point model and (iii) the core model (Figure 4). As a generic conceptual framework, the aspect model needs to be instantiated in order to be used [5]. This means that the designer of a new aspect-oriented language must adopt a component model, a suitable joint point model, and appropriate structure and semantics for the core model concepts (aspect and crosscutting).

In our meta-modeling framework, the adopted component model is the agent model described above and join points are elements related to the structure or the behavior of agent models, referenced and possibly affected by an aspect. The join point model represents a conceptual framework that describes the kinds of join points of interest and the associated restrictions for their use. Agents, Goals and Actions are defined as join points, that is, locations in agent models that can be affected by aspects.

The core model represents a conceptual framework used for describing aspects and crosscutting. An aspect is a first-class, nameable entity that provides modular representation for a crosscutting concern and localizes both (a) the specification of (sets of) join points, and (b) the enhancements to be combined at the specified join points. The enhancements may add new structure and behavior to agents, goals and actions, refine or replace existing behavior. The kinds of enhancements depend on the kind of component model adopted. For the agent model, enhancements are goal-like and action-like elements; aspects modularize crosscutting goals and crosscutting actions.

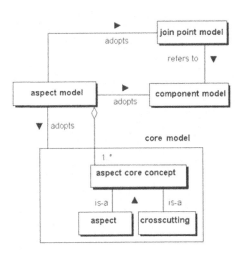

Fig. 4. The Aspect Model

Crosscutting denotes the generic composition mechanism used to compose aspects and agents, enhancing them at the designated join points (Figure 5). Aspects crosscut one or more agents, possibly affecting their structure and behavior at those well-defined join points. A join point can be associated with an agent, a goal, an action, or even an entire plan. The next section discusses the different composition operators to capture crosscutting structures and behaviors in MAS designs.

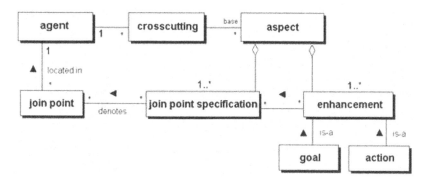

Fig. 5. An Aspect Model for an Agent Model

3.3   The Composition Model

The *Composition Model* is a conceptual framework that provides semantics description of the crosscutting composition mechanism. In other words, this model characterizes the possible ways aspects may affect agents, their goals, and actions. Currently, our composition model organizes crosscutting operations according to three categories or dimensions (Figure 6): aspect-agent, goal-goal and goal-action composition. Table 1 presents the semantics description and the possible crosscutting operations for each composition category.

Fig. 6. Crosscutting dimensions for the Agent Model

Aspect-Agent crosscutting composition basically adds a new goal G to Agent A. For example, the mobility concern in the EC system design (Section 2.1) is an example of aspect that introduces the mobility-specific goals "Move to Remote Host" and "Consult Research Agency DB" in the goal hierarchy of Information Agent. Goal-Action crosscutting composition supports the addition of a new Action to some Goal G. The other two categories are further detailed in Table 2.

Table 1. Composition Model: crosscutting categories semantics and operations

Category	Description	Operations
Aspect-Agent	Aspect X introduces Goal G (and related set of Actions) into Agent A	introduce
Goal-Goal	Goal G1 of Aspect X is composed with Goal G2 of Agent A (possibly giving a new Goal G in A)	merge, replace, AND, OR, XOR
Goal-Action	Aspect X introduces Action α into Goal G (of Agent A)	introduce
Action-Action	Action α1 of Aspect X is composed with Action α2 (of Goal G, Agent A)	merge-before, merge-after, replace

The Goal-Goal composition style combines an aspect goal G1 with an existing agent goal G2. For example, the goal "Learn User Preferences" associated with the learning concern in the EC system (Section 2.1) needs to be composed with goals of Information Agent and User Agent, such "Get Query" and "Evaluate Chair Proposal". The "merge" operation describes well this kind of goal-goal composition since the learning aspect enhances the goals of querying the DB and evaluating the chair proposal without changing the semantics of the state to be reached (the agent goals).

Figure 7 presents a diagrammatic representation of merge semantics between Goals. Note that the learning-specific goal "Learn User Preferences" has been omitted in the EC design (Figure 2) because the lack of support of the modeling notation to express such aspectual influence of the learning concern (Section 2.3).

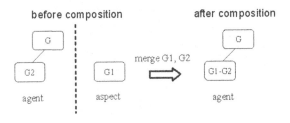

Fig. 7. Goal-Goal composition: Merge

4 Discussions

The Aspect Model abstracts from the kinds of component an aspect affects. In [6], the Aspect Model was instantiated with the UML object model to provide an aspect-oriented conceptual framework for object-oriented design and modeling. Furthermore, the Aspect Model can be instantiated with different agent models and sets of agent-oriented abstractions. The applicability of the concept of aspects in agent-oriented design, and the usability of our modeling approach [18]

Table 2. Crosscutting semantics for Goal-Goal and Action-Action composition

Kind	Operation	Semantics
GOAL-GOAL CROSSCUTTING	X.G1 AND A.G2	Goal G1 of Aspect X is AND-ed with Goal G2 of Agent A
	X.G1 OR A.G2	Goal G1 of Aspect X is OR-ed with Goal G2 of Agent A
	X.G1 XOR A.G2	Goal G1 of Aspect X is XOR-ed with Goal G2 of Agent A
	X.G1 MERGE A. G2	Goal G1 of Aspect X is merged with Goal G2 of Agent A
	X.G1 REPLACE A. G2	Goal G1 of Aspect X replaces Goal G2 of Agent A
ACTION-ACTION CROSSCUTTING	X.α1 MERGE A.α2	Action α1 of Aspect X is merged before Action α2 of Agent A (within Goal G)
	A.α2 MERGE X.α1	Action α1 of Aspect X is merged after Action α2 of Agent A (within Goal G)
	X.α1 REPLACE A. α2	Action α1 of Aspect X replaces Action α2 of Agent A (within Goal G)

have been evaluated in different contexts and with respect to different modeling criteria as the ones described in the subsections below. Section 4.1 discusses integrability and extensibility issues, while Section 4.2 focuses on design knowledge management, evolvability, and reusability.

4.1 Integrability and Extensibility

As presented in Section 3.1, We have used the meta-modeling framework to introduce aspect-oriented capabilities in the ANote modeling language, which was straightforward [18]. In fact, we did not experience particular conflicts while integrating the aspect-oriented meta-model and the ANote meta-model. During this integration process, we observed that additional join points were necessary to be defined due to particularities of the ANotes agent model. For example, a certain precondition can be also part of a crosscutting behavior in ANote models.

The precondition "Remote Environments are Available" in Figure 2 is part of the mobility concern. Hence, preconditions need to be also defined as join points in the aspect-oriented meta-model for the ANote language. The accommodation of crosscutting pre-conditions and other join points in the extended ANote meta-model was a smooth step, as our Aspect Model is flexible enough. It supports this extensibility through a chain of associated meta-abstractions, such as "join point" and "enhancement", and a comprehensive set of composition styles under the "crosscutting" concept.

4.2 Design Knowledge Management, Evolvability, and Reusability

We have also assessed the aspect-oriented modeling approach in three case studies. These MASs encompassed different characteristics, different degrees of complexity, and diverse domains: the Expert Committee system (Section 2.1), a system for the Trading Agent Competition [33], and a portal development management system [14,15]. The design of these systems encompassed different crosscutting concerns in their agent-oriented models, including adaptation, mobility, learning, and proactive autonomy.

In fact, we were able to explicitly model the implications of these broadly-scoped MAS properties in the same way we model the basic MAS behaviors. This externalized better the knowledge present in the agent-oriented design process, and provided an improved basis for further evolution and reuse. For example, the learning-specific goals and its synergistic relationships with other system goals have been better captured based in our aspect-oriented notation [18]. These aspectual goals have been lost in the "non-aspectized" agent-oriented models (Section 2.3).

5 Related Work

Existing approaches that aim to provide an unifying conceptual framework for AOSD are tightly coupled to the object-oriented paradigm and the modularization problems related to its main abstractions and composition mechanisms. As far as we know, our work is the only aspect-oriented conceptual framework that is agnostic to the base component model and that can be easily instantiated to deal with different sets of abstractions, including agent abstractions.

Since our conceptual framework is the base for enhancing the ANote modeling language with aspect-oriented notation [18], we also discuss some related work that deals with existing modeling languages and methodologies (Section 5.1), and modeling extensions to address specific concerns (Section 5.2). The list of related work here is not intended to be exhaustive. We have focused on the ones we believe have explicit links with our aspect-oriented modeling framework. As elucidated below, what makes our approach distinct from all these approaches is the expressiveness and precision with which it allows capturing and describing crosscutting concerns at the agent-oriented design stage.

5.1 Modeling Languages and Methodologies

Tropos provides to some extent abstractions for expressing crosscutting concerns [4]. However, the focus is on the representation of inter-goal influences in the early and late requirements development phases. It provides a very-high level set of abstractions (goals and soft-goals), which allow the description of positive and negative contributions between goals representing functional and non-functional MAS properties. Soft goals can be viewed as MAS aspects at the requirements level. Although the goal models could be refined in late development stages, Tropos does not provide a complete composition framework to design stages as described in our framework.

As pointed out in Section 2, crosscutting relationships naturally emerge in agent-oriented modeling beyond inter-goal relationships and, as a result, more concrete composition rules are required. In fact, we believer our agent-oriented design framework is complementary to the Tropos notations. Soft goals at the requirement levels can be easily traced backward and forward from our aspect-oriented agent models (Section 3.1)

Another approach that shows interesting aspect-oriented ideas in the modeling language is [9]. This approach focuses on representing the system-to-be according to several different perspectives; each one of them promoting an abstract representation of the system. Nevertheless, it only sketches the characteristics of an autonomy perspective for MAS specification. In addition, it does not address a comprehensive concern-independent composition framework for modularizing crosscutting structure and behavior in agent-oriented design.

5.2   Specific Extensions

Several other approaches try to develop extensions and notations that focus on specific concerns for MAS development, which are typically crosscutting. For example, the work on [28] reports on a secure architectural description language (ADL) for MAS. It focuses on the provision of ADL constructs to specify security issues in MAS architectures. The specification of security issues is however entangled to the core components of a MAS architecture. Another work, presented by Weiss [37], intends to capture autonomy in agent roles using a formal schema called RNS (standing for "Roles, Norms, and Sanctions") which allows for a specification of an agents autonomy. It deals only with autonomy and it is mostly concerned with providing a formal schema to describe it, i.e. it is not focused on how autonomy crosscuts other agent functionalities.

Some graphical notations have also been extended to cope with specific crosscutting concerns. For instance, the work reported in [21] demonstrates how Activity Diagrams in UML 2.0 can be readily used to model dynamic behaviors of mobile agent systems and point out why they are effective for them from its underlying computational model.

In our point of view, the growing number of modeling approaches dealing with specific crosscutting concerns in agent-oriented systems denotes that there is a pressing need to define a generic aspect-oriented metamodel and associated notation that provide support for their proper specification. To encompass all crosscutting MAS concerns, it is important to describe generic abstractions and to devise composition rules, as proposed in this paper. The existing AOSD approaches have been limited to the object-oriented and component-oriented paradigms. Our previous contributions have focused in other development phases other than agent-oriented design.

6   Conclusions

This paper is a first attempt to systematically tame broadly-scoped concerns in agent-oriented design modeling. Many internal agent properties and systemic properties in the design of MAS are typically crosscutting, and they need to be handled as such. No matter what kind of decomposition and abstractions the agent-based software developers arc relying on; there are always MAS concerns that crosscut the boundaries of other concerns. As discussed here, widely-scoped properties can bring deeper problems to the designers; they can even be scattered and tangled in more than one design view, as it is the case for the learning and mobility concerns. Because a clear separation of concerns is a main tenet in software engineering, the lack of modularization support for those concerns generates undesirable burdens on agent-oriented design reuse and evolution.

The contributions of this paper were the following. We described a comprehensive list of problems associated with the non-modularized handling of crosscutting concerns in agent-oriented modeling. To address those problems, we have proposed an aspect-oriented framework for agent-oriented modeling. Our previous work [18] is an example of aspect-oriented notation, which instantiates our proposed modeling framework by integrating it into the ANote language [9]. Since our work is a first step towards enhancing agent-oriented design models with aspects, we cannot guarantee that our set of composition operators is necessarily complete. Our goal here was to provide a core meta-modeling framework to support the central abstractions and composition mechanisms. Further case studies are necessary to evaluate the coverage degree of our composition operators.

Acknowledgments. Alessandro is supported by European Commission as part of the grant IST-2-004349: European Network of Excellence on Aspect-Oriented Software Development (AOSD-Europe), 2004-2008. This work has been also partially supported by CNPq-Brazil under grant No. 479395/2004-7 for Christina.

References

1. AOSD Steering Committee: aosd.net main page. http://aosd.net/ (2006)
2. Bergenti, F., Gleizes, M.-P., Zambonelli, F. (eds.): Methodologies and Software Engineering for Agent Systems: The Agent-Oriented Software Engineering Handbook, volume 11. Springer-Verlag, Berlin Heidelberg New York (2004)
3. Cacho, N., Sant'Anna, C., Figueiredo, E., Garcia, A., Batista, T., Lucena, C.: Composing Design Patterns: A Scalability Study of Aspect-Oriented Programming. In: Proc. of the 5th International Conference on Aspect-Oriented Software Development (2006)
4. Castro, J., Kolp, M., Mylopoulos, J.: Towards Requirements-Driven Information Systems Engineering: the Tropos Project. Information Systems **27(6)**, (2002) 365-389
5. Chavez, C., Lucena, C.: A Theory of Aspects for Aspect-Oriented Development. In: Proc. 17th Brazilian Symposium on Software Engineering (2003) 130–145
6. Chavez, C.: A Model-Driven Approach to Aspect-Oriented Design. PhD Thesis, Computer Science Department, PUC-Rio (2004)

7. Cheong, C., Winikoff, M.: Hermes: Designing Goal-Oriented Agent Interactions. In: Proc. of the 6th International Workshop on Agent-Oriented Software Engineering (2005)
8. Choren, R., Lucena, C.: Modeling Multi-agent Systems with ANote. Journal of Software and Systems Modeling **4(3)**, (2005) 199–208
9. Cossentino, M., Zambonelli, F.: Agent Design from the Autonomy Perspective. In: Nickles, M., Rovatsos, M., Weiss, G. (eds.): Agents and Computational Autonomy: Potential, Risks and Solutions. LNCS, Vol. 2969. Springer-Verlag, Berlin Heidelberg New York (2004) 140–150
10. D'Hondt, M., Gybels, K., Jonckers, V.: Seamless Integration of Rule-Based Knowledge and Object-Oriented Functionality with Linguistic Symbiosis. In: Proc. of the 2004 ACM Symposium on Applied Computing (2004) 1328–1335
11. Dijkstra, E.: A Discipline of Programming. Prentice Hall, Englewood Cliffs (1976)
12. Filho, F., Cacho, N., Ferreira, R., Figueiredo, E., Garcia, A, Rubira, C.: Exceptions and As-pects: the Devil is in the Details. In: Proc. of the 14th International Conference on Foundations on Software Engineering (2004)
13. Filman, R., Elrad, T., Clarke, S., Aksit, M.: Aspect-Oriented Software Development. Addison-Wesley (2004)
14. Garcia, A., Sant'Anna, C., Chavez, C., Silva, V., Lucena, C., von Staa, A.: Separation of Con-cerns in Multi-Agent Systems: An Empirical Study. In: Software Engineering for Multi-Agent Systems II. LNCS, Vol. 2940. Springer-Verlag, Berlin Heidelberg New York (2004) 49–72
15. Garcia, A., Lucena, C., Cowan, D.: Agents in Object-Oriented Software Engineering. Software: Practice and Experience **34(3)** (2004) 489-521
16. Garcia, A., Kulesza, U., Sant'Anna, C., Chavez, C., Lucena, C.: Aspects in Agent-Oriented Software Engineering: Lessons Learned. In: Proc. of the 6th International Workshop on Agent-Oriented Software Engineering (2005)
17. Garcia, A., Kulesza, U., Lucena, C.: Aspectizing Multi-Agent Systems: From Architecture to Implementation. In: Software Engineering for Multi-Agent Systems III. LNCS, Vol. 3390. Springer-Verlag, Berlin Heidelberg New York (2005) 121–143
18. Garcia, A., Chavez, C., Choren, R.: Enhancing Agent-Oriented Models with Aspects. In: Proc. of the 5th International Conference on Autonomous Agents and MultiAgent Systems (2006)
19. Garcia, A., Lucena, C.: Taming Heterogeneous Agent Architectures with Aspects. Commmunications of the ACM, October 2006. (to appear)
20. Garcia, A., Sant'Anna, C., Figueiredo, E., Kulesza, U., Lucena, C., Staa, A.: Modularizing Design Patterns with Aspects: A Quantitative Study. Transactions on Aspect-Oriented Software Development. LNCS. Springer-Verlag, Berlin Heidelberg New York (2006) 36–74
21. Kang, M. et al: Modelling Mobile Agent Applications in UML 2.0 Activity Diagrams. In: Proc. of 3rd SELMAS Workshop at ICSE 2004 (2004) 104–111
22. Kiczales, G. et al: Aspect-Oriented Programming. In: Akcsit, M., Matsuoka, S. (eds.): Proc. European Conference on Object-Oriented Programming. LNCS, Vol. 1241. Springer-Verlag, Berlin Heidelberg New York (1997) 220–242
23. Kiczales, G., Mezini, M.: Aspect-Oriented Programming and Modular Reasoning. In: Proc. of the 27th International Conference on Software Engineering (2005) 49–58
24. Kulesza, U., SantAnna, C., Garcia, A., Coelho, R., von Staa, A., Lucena, C.: Quantifying the Effects of Aspect-Oriented Programming: A Maintenance Study. In: Proc. of the 9th International Conference on Software Maintenance (2006)

25. Kulesza, U., Alves, V., Garcia, A., Lucena, C., Borba, P.: Improving Extensibility of Object-Oriented Frameworks with Aspect-Oriented Programming. In: Proc. of the 9th International Conference on Software Reuse (2006)

26. Lobato, C., Garcia, A., Lucena, C., Romanovsky, A.: A Modular Implementation Framework for Code Mobility. In: Proc. 3rd IEE Mobility Conference (2006)

27. Mallya, A.U., Singh, M.P.: Incorporating Commitment Protocols into Tropos. In: Proc. of the 6th International Workshop on Agent-Oriented Software Engineering (2005)

28. Mouratidis, H. et al: A Secure Architectural Description Language for Agent Systems. In: Proc. of 4th Intl. Conference on Autonomous Agents and Multiagent Systems (2005) 578–585

29. Odell, J., Parunak, H., Bauer, B.: Extending UML for Agents. In: Proc. of the Agent-Oriented Information Systems Workshop at AAAI 2000 (2000) 3-17

30. Pace, A., Trilnik, F., Campo, M.: Assisting the Development of Aspect-based MAS using the SmartWeaver Approach. In: Garcia, A.F., Lucena, C.J.P., Zambonelli, F., Omicini, A., Castro, J. (eds.): Software Engineering for Multi-Agent Systems. LNCS, Vol. 2603. Springer-Verlag, Berlin Heidelberg New York (2003) 165–181

31. Parnas, D.: On the Criteria to Be Used in Decomposing Systems into Modules. Communications of the ACM **15(12)** (1972) 1053–1058

32. SantAnna, C., Lobato, C., Garcia, A., Kulesza, U., Chavez, C, Lucena, C.: On the Quantitative Asessment of Modular Multiagent Architectures. In: Proc. of Net.ObjectDays.06 (2006) (to appear)

33. SICS AB: Trading Agent Competition. http://www.sics.se/tac/page.php?id=1 (2006)

34. Silva, V., Lucena, C.: From a Conceptual Framework for Agents and Objects to a Multi-Agent System Modeling Language. Journal of Autonomous Agents and Multi-Agent **9(1–2)** (2004) 145–189

35. Tarr, P., Ossher, H., Harrison, W., Sutton Jr., S.M.: N Degrees of Separation: Multi-Dimensional Separation of Concerns. In: Proc. 21st International Conference on Software Engineering (1999) 107–119

36. Ubayashi, N., Tamai, T.: Separation of Concerns in Mobile Agent Applications. In: Third International Conference REFLECTION 2001. LNCS, Vol. 2192. Springer-Verlag, Berlin Heidelberg New York (2001) 89–109

37. Weiss, G., Rovatsos, M., Nickles, M.: Capturing Agent Autonomy in Roles and XML. In: Proc. Intl. Conference on Autonomous Agents and Multiagent Systems (2003) 105–112

38. Zambonelli, F., Jennings, N., Wooldridge, M.: Developing multiagent systems: The Gaia methodology. ACM Transactions on Software Engineering and Methodology **12(3)** (2003) 417–470

Extending UML Sequence Diagrams to Model Agent Mobility

Mario Kusek and Gordan Jezic

University of Zagreb
Faculty of Electrical Engineering and Computing
Department of Telecommunications
Unska 3, HR-10000 Zagreb, Croatia
{mario.kusek, gordan.jezic}@fer.hr

Abstract. This paper presents a proposal for modeling agent mobility with UML sequence diagrams. The notations used to model agent mobility are focused on capturing agent creation, mobility paths and current agent location. Four approaches are described and compared according to their clarity, the space needed for graphics and their expression of mobility. In a case study, the most suitable solution of the proposed notations for the given scenario is elaborated.

1 Introduction

Agent concepts and mobile software agents have become part of the system and service architecture of new generation networks. Application areas include the use of the agents in the operation and management of networks, systems and services. This is where agents mobility offers important advantages [1]. In current environments, where a large number of nodes exist, agents perform actions and migrate through the network changing their locations. In some cases, migration from node to node can be a permanent event and location changing can be done frequently. Our goal is to successfully model such a dynamic environment with a good representation of agent mobility and execution paths.

There are several notations and types of diagrams available for modeling agent mobility. UML (Unified Modeling Language) has played the most dominant role in graphical notation in the past several years. Its major advantage is its expressiveness [2]. UML has proven to be very useful in describing various aspects of behaviour, but in some cases offers limited support for modeling mobility. Namely, it is difficult to use UML diagrams to describe some useful parameters included in agent migration, such as agent creation, migration/execution paths and current agent location. These mobility parameters have not yet been fully addressed in current UML sequence diagrams, or by other existing modeling languages FIPA [3], AUML [4] or AML [5]. Not one of these modeling languages give an overall view of agent roaming and execution paths [6].

In this paper, we propose four graphical notations for modeling agent mobility. The notations are extensions of UML sequence diagrams and will be referred to as the stereotyped mobility diagram, the swimlaned mobility diagram, the state

L. Padgham and F. Zambonelli (Eds.): AOSE 2006, LNCS 4405, pp. 51–63, 2007.

representation mobility diagram, and the frame fragment mobility diagram [7, 8]. The proposed approaches are compared with respect to their clarity regarding agent creation, migration path and current agent location, and the space required for graphics. Examples with a different number of agents and nodes will be considered. In a case study, we evaluate and compare all the proposed notations for a given price searcher scenario.

The paper is organized as follows: Section 2 presents related work. Section 3 elaborates modeling agent mobility using UML sequence diagrams and proposes four new graphical notations for this problem. Section 4 gives a case study of a price searcher scenario in which one of the proposed notations is elaborated. Section 5 concludes the paper.

2   Related Work

There exist several diagrams and approaches to modeling mobility available in literature. The following are specialized for agent mobility: FIPA modeling area - deployment and mobility [4], extending activity diagrams to model mobile systems [9], modeling mobile agent applications with UML 2.0 Activity Diagrams [10], sequence diagram for mobility [11], and Agent Modeling Language (AML) [5].

AUML (Agent UML) supports the modeling of agent mobility with deployment and activity diagrams [4]. AUML deployment diagrams can depict the reason an agent moves to a different node and the location to where it moves. AUML activity diagrams can express agent timing, i.e. when the mobile agent has to move. Nodes in the activity diagram model agents plans while transitions model events. The time a mobile agent can move from one node to the next is determined by a condition indicated on the transition that leads to the end point (Figure 1).

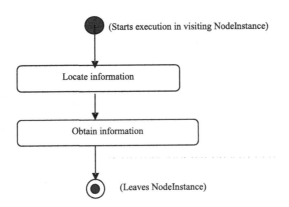

Fig. 1. Mobility using AUML Activity Diagram

This notation does not depict agent migration paths which give an overall view of agent migration. An agent migration path can be extracted from various diagrams such as that in Figure 1.

UML is the standard graphical notation used for modeling object–oriented software. Extensions of UML activity diagrams for modeling agent mobility are presented in [9]. The authors introduced into UML the concepts of location, mobile objects, mobile locations, move actions and clone actions. Two notations of mobility in activity diagrams are presented. The first notation is responsibility centered and focuses on who is performing an action and is based on the standard notation for activity diagrams. The second notation is location centered and focuses on where an action is performed, and how activities change this relation (Figure 2). In Figure 2 we can see that the source of the move action is the object–flow state "Hubert" which is an instance of Passenger. Its location is represented by the value of attribute "atLoc". The value is initially set to "MUC" which represents an airport. The target of the move action is marked with stereotype <<become>> and is directed to the object–flow state "Hubert" with a new attribute value (the "atLoc" value becomes "LH123" which represents a plane). Like the previously suggested notation, this approach does not show agent migration paths either.

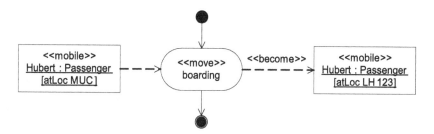

Fig. 2. The move action in UML

In [10], the authors propose an extension of activity diagrams in UML 2.0. A new stereotype <<Host>> with parameter is introduced for a swimlane, which represents an agent location with a unique name (address) as a parameter in order to capture the mobility of agents. Agent communication and cloning are also defined by existing model elements with a rule for subactivities. An agent movement from location "host1" to "host2" is represented by using the "Go" activity (Figure 3). This diagram gives a clear representation of agent migration paths, but timing and message exchanges are not shown.

A notation for modeling agent mobility based on UML sequence diagrams is used in [11]. The author presents Sequence Diagrams for Mobility (SDM), which are an extension of UML sequence diagrams for modeling mobile objects, the interaction between objects and the network topology of nested objects. These diagrams can not be represented with UML 2.0.

Agent Modeling Language (AML) [5] defines metaclasses used to model structural and behavioral aspects of entity mobility. Movement is depicted with a UML dependency relationship with the stereotype <<move>> (Figure 4) and is used in the deployment diagram. MobilityAction (Figure 4a) is used to model the mobility action of entity and MoveAction is used to model the action that results in the removal of an entity from its current hosting location [12]. This is used in the activity diagram (Figure 4b). Neither representation depicts agent mobility paths.

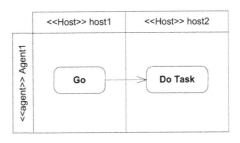

Fig. 3. "Go" action in UML 2.0

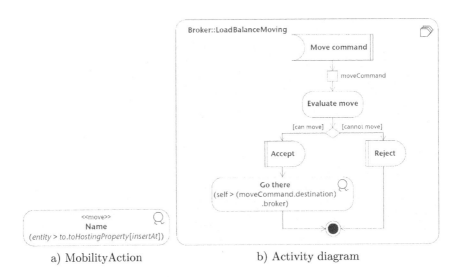

a) MobilityAction   b) Activity diagram

Fig. 4. Mobility in AML

All these modeling languages are very useful and are often used in practice, but they do not provide an overall view of agent roaming and migration paths, so in some cases offer limited support for modeling mobility. We propose four graphical notations for modeling agent mobility. These notations are focused on capturing agent creation, mobility paths and current agent location. These notations should have a clearer representation of the mentioned features than existing approaches.

3   Modeling Agent Mobility with Sequence Diagrams

In this section we propose four approaches to modeling agent mobility developed by extending UML sequence diagrams. Our notations are focused on capturing three basic mobility elements which are useful in analyzing mobile agent system behaviour. These elements are:

- Current agent location,
- Agent mobility paths, and
- Agent creation.

The notations will also be evaluated according to the number of agents and nodes involved in the system. For evaluation purposes, we consider the following example. An agent a1 located at node n1 migrates to node n2 and creates agent a2 at node n1, a3 at n2, and a4 at n3. The proposed approaches are compared with respect to:

- The clarity of the notation, and
- The space required for graphics depending on the given number of nodes.

The four notations proposed will be referred to as the stereotyped mobility diagram, the swimlaned mobility diagram, the state representation mobility diagram, and the frame fragment mobility diagram. A description of each follows.

3.1   The Stereotyped Mobility Diagram

In the stereotyped mobility diagram we introduce the following three stereotypes: <<at>>, <<move>> and <<new>> (Figure 5). An agent is represented with stereotype <<agent>>. An agent is initially located at node n1 which is indicated with a message with stereotype <<at>>. The agent then migrates from this location to the location at node n2, which is indicated with message stereotype <<move>>. Each agent can create a new one which is indirectly done by sending a message to the node where the new agent is to be created. This is indicated with message *new* (Figure 5). In other words, agent location at a node is indicated with one stereotyped message, while its migration to another node is indicated with another one.

This notation of mobility is similar to that described in [11]. Mobility here is shown as the change of the state of an object as it moves from one location to another. An agent moves by sending stereotyped messages to the node where it wants to go. This representation clearly depicts agent mobility paths, agent creation and current agent location. The downsides of this notation include the following. For each node there is an object which represents the node and it is not clear when an agent leaves the node. In the case of large number of nodes, the diagram is useless.

3.2   The Swimlaned Mobility Diagram

In the swimlaned mobility diagram (Figure 6), a node is represented by a swimlane with stereotype <<node>>. A swimlane represents the execution at a

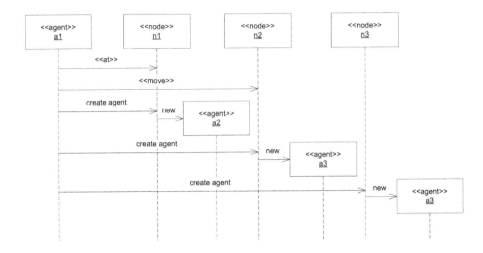

Fig. 5. The Stereotyped Mobility Diagram

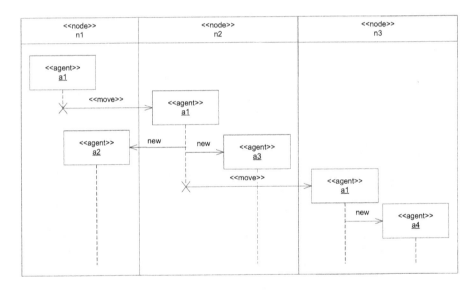

Fig. 6. The Swimlaned Mobility Diagram

specified node. Agent migration from one node to another is indicated by a message with stereotype <<move>>. In such a case, the lifeline of the agent at the source node is terminated and a new representation at the destination node is created. The agent continues its execution in the new swimlane. The creation of a new agent is indicated with message new inside of a certain swimlane which means that the agent is created at this node.

In other words, a swimlane represents a node and an agent migrates in the same way as in the approach using stereotyped mobility diagrams, except that it terminates at the source node and is created again at the destination node. The diagram has a clear representation of mobility, agents current locations and agent creation. The diagram gives a clear representation regarding activity on particular node and agents located on it. This notation requires less space for graphics than the stereotyped diagram, but in the case of a large number of nodes it is also useless.

3.3   The State Representation Mobility Diagram

The idea for the state representation mobility diagram is taken from [11] where mobility is indicated with the change of the state of a moving agent. In the state representation diagram (Figure 7), mobility is represented with state elements in the sequence diagram as specified by the UML 2.0 specification [2]. The first state element starts with "at node" and the rest is the node name where the agent is located. When an agent moves from one node to another, a new state represents

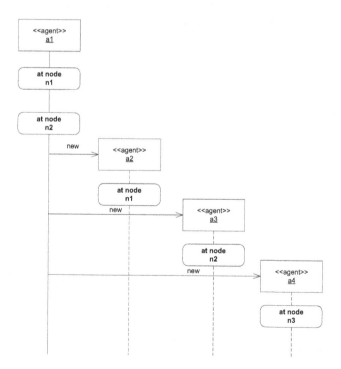

Fig. 7. The State Representation Mobility Diagram

this movement. The creation of new agent is indicated with the message new. After creation, the agents state indicates its location at a specified node.

This diagram is very similar to the classical UML sequence diagram. It is a good solution for the notation of agent mobility in a multi–agent system with a large number of nodes. The diagram gives a clear representation of agent creation and current agent location. A shortcoming of this approach is poor representation of migration and execution paths, and poor representation of agent location on particular nodes. This diagram requires less space for graphics due to its vertical representation than those previously described. It is suitable for modeling agent systems with large number of nodes.

An example from practice is the Sniffer agent [13] in the Jade agent platform [14]. It enables the monitoring of message exchanges between agents. A tool uses sequence diagrams for representation of agent communication. Using the presented state representation mobility diagram, it is possible to model a mobility component of the agents in order to analyze and debug a multi–agent system.

3.4   The Frame Fragment Mobility Diagram

The frame fragment mobility diagram depicts agent mobility with frame fragments in a sequence diagram (Figure 8). Each frame fragment, with interaction operation node, represents the execution on a node. Agent mobility is represented by entering the next fragment.

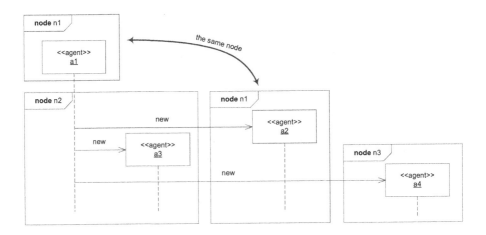

Fig. 8. The Frame Fragment Mobility Diagram

The diagram gives a clear representation of agent creation, current agent locations, and migration and execution paths. The notation is suitable for systems with a large number of nodes. The representation of mobility is clearer and requires less space for graphics than the state representation mobility diagram.

A potential problem is that in some cases it is not possible to order agents in such a way that one frame fragment can represent all the agents at a certain node.

4   Case Study: A Simple Price Searcher

After describing and comparing the proposed approaches for modeling agent mobility, suppose an agent system with three network nodes (Home, Host1 and Host2), two stationary agents (Store1 and Store 2 agents) and a mobile agent (Searcher agent) (Figure 9). On Host1 and Host2 reside Store1 and Store2 agents responsible for providing pricelists. The Searcher agent is created on the Home node. Its input parameters are the list of nodes and the item (price list).

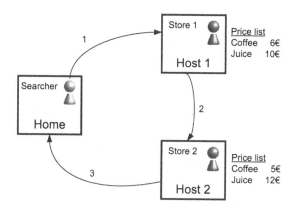

Fig. 9. The price searcher scenario

The Searcher agent migrates from the Home node to the Host1 node and requests the price list from the Store1 agent. The Store1 agent responds with the entire pricelist. The Searcher extracts the price for the item specified and migrates to the next node (Host2). After visiting all nodes in the network, the Searcher agent returns to the Home node and informs the user of its obtained results, i.e. where and at what price it found the specified item.

The agent system consists of three network nodes and a mobile agent. Because of the small number of nodes and only one agent involved in the system, it is possible to model the system with the stereotyped or swimlaned mobility diagrams. The stereotyped mobility diagram is simple and the diagram offers a clear representation of agent creation, current location, execution and mobility paths (Figure 10).

Figure 11 presents the swimlaned mobility diagram for this scenario. Information regarding activity on particular node is clearer A potential problem may be caused by agents returning to the same node after migration. Namely, such agents are shown as two entities (agents) in one swimlane which may be confusing.

Figure 12 presents the scenario modeled with the state representation (Figure 12a) and the frame fragment mobility diagrams (Figure 12b). These

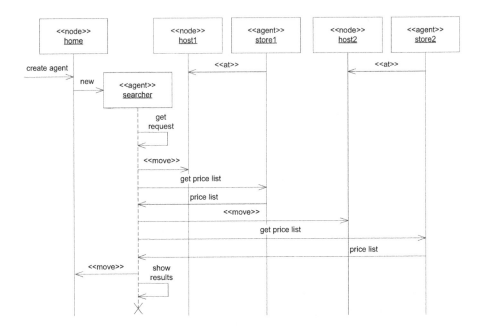

Fig. 10. The stereotyped mobility diagram for the scenario

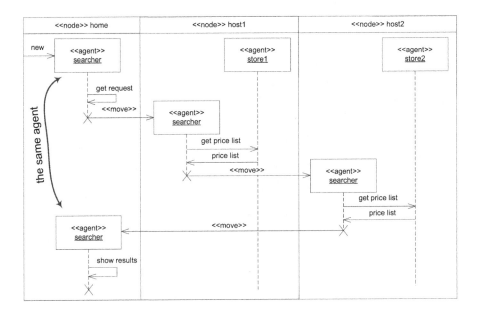

Fig. 11. The swimlaned mobility diagram for the scenario

notations need less space and have a clearer representation of agent creation and current agent location. The main shortcoming of these notations is their representation of migration paths for agents returning to nodes at which they were previously located. Furthermore, it is not clear which agents are placed on which nodes.

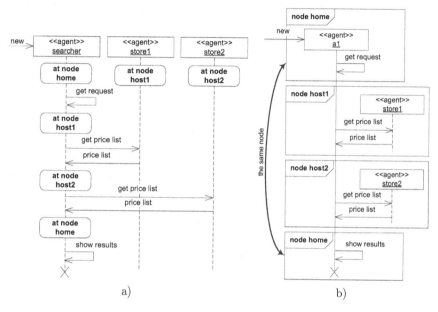

Fig. 12. The state representation (a) and frame fragment mobility diagrams (b) for the scenario

We feel the stereotyped mobility diagram is the most suitable solution for the given scenario. It provides a clear notation of the given scenario in which there is a small number of agents and nodes, only one agent is mobile and all communication is performed locally.

5   Conclusion

The motivation for this paper was to model agent mobility, focusing on capturing agent creation, migration paths and current agent location since these parameters have not yet been fully addressed in existing modeling languages. Four approaches were proposed and their corresponding advantages and drawbacks were compared according to their clarity, the space needed for graphics and their representation of mobility.

The stereotyped mobility diagram gives an overall view of nodes and agent mobility paths. The swimlaned mobility diagram gives a clear representation of agent mobility, current locations and creation. Both stereotyped and swimlaned mobility diagrams clearly represent agent execution and mobility paths, but they are not suitable for modeling the systems with a large number of nodes and agents. In state representation mobility diagrams, mobility is represented by changing the state of a moving agent. In frame fragment mobility diagrams, each frame fragment of a sequence diagram represents the execution at a node. The state representation and frame fragment mobility diagrams have poorer representations of migration and execution paths. These diagrams are suitable for modeling multi–agent systems with mobile agents and a large number of nodes. An advantage of these approaches is a better overall view of agent roaming and current agent location, but in some cases it is not possible to order agents in such a way that one frame fragment can represent all the agents at a certain node.

It is difficult to say which notation is best since that depends on which aspect of the representation we wish to focus on. Each notation has its advanatages and disadvantages for particular conditions which differ with respect to the number of nodes and agents in the system, the nature of changing locations (migration frequency; migrating to the same/different locations), creating agents (on the same node; remotely on other nodes), and communication (with an agent at the same node; remotely with agents at other nodes). However, it is still possible to draw some general conclusions. Namely, all the notations have good representations of mobility paths, current agent location and agent creation. Although the stereotype mobility diagram is "the simpliest" and the swimlaned mobility diagram has the best representation from a node activity, both are suitable only for a small number of nodes. For a large number of nodes, the frame fragment mobility diagram is better than the state representation mobility diagram in most cases, except for cases where agents return to nodes at which they were previously located.

Future work will include investigation of modeling agent mobility in different UML diagrams. The result of that work will be a UML profile for modeling agent mobility.

References

[1] Braun, P., Rossak, W.R.: Mobile Agents: Basic Concepts, Mobility Models, and the Tracy Toolkit. Morgan Kaufmann (2004)
[2] OMG: Unified modeling language: version 2.0 (UML 2.0), final adopted specification. Technical report, OMG (2003) Available online at: http://www.uml.org/#UML2.0.
[3] FIPA Modeling TC: FIPA modeling area: Deployment and mobility. Technical report, FIPA (2003) Available online at: http://www.auml.org/auml/documents/DeploymentMobility.zip.
[4] Odell, J., van D. Parunak, H., Bauer, B.: Extending UML for agents. Available online at: http://www.jamesodell.com/ExtendingUML.pdf (2000)
[5] Cervenka, R., Trencansky, I.: Agent modeling language, language specification, version 0.9. Technical report, Whitestein Technologies AG (2004) Available online at: http://www.whitestein.com/resources/aml/wt_AMLSpecification_v0.9.pdf.
[6] Bergenti, F., Gleizes, M.P., Zambonelli, F.: Methodologies and Software Engineering for Agent Systems: The Agent-Oriented Software Engineering Handbook. Kluwer Academic Publishers (2004)

[7] Cossentino, M., Bernon, C., Pavon, J.: Modelling and meta–modelling issues in agent oriented software engineering: The agentlink AOSE TFG approach. Available online at: http://www.pa.icar.cnr.it/~cossentino/al3tf2/docs/aosetfg_report.pdf (2005)

[8] Kusek, M., Jezic, G.: Modeling agent mobility with UML sequence diagram. Technical report, University of Zagreb, Faculty of Electrical Engineering and Computing (2005) presented at Agentlink III AOSE TFG2 – Ljubljana, Slovenia, Available online at: http://www.pa.icar.cnr.it/~cossentino/al3tf2/docs/kusek_ppt.ppt.

[9] Baumeister, H., Koch, N., Kosiuczenko, P., Wirsing, M.: Extending activity diagrams to model mobile systems. In Aksit, M., Mezini, M., Unland, R., eds.: Lecture Notes in Computer Science – LNCS. Volume 2591. Springer Verlag, Erfurt, Gremany (2003) 278–293 Objects, Components, Architectures, Services, and Applications for a Networked World. International Conference NetObjectDays, NODe 2002, Available online at: http://www.pst.informatik.uni-uenchen.de/baumeist/publications/netobjectdays2002.pdf.

[10] Kang, M., Wang, L., Taguchi, K.: Modelling mobile agent applications in UML 2.0 activity diagrams. Available online at: http://www.auml.org/auml/supplements/UML2-AD.pdf (2004)

[11] Kosiuczenko, P.: Sequence diagrams for mobility. In: Lecture Notes in Computer Science – LNCS. Volume 2784. Springer Verlag, Finland (2002) 147–158 In Proc. of Advanced Conceptual Modeling Technique (Er) '02, Available online at: http://www.pst.informatik.uni-muenchen.de/personen/kosiucze/SDM.pdf.

[12] Cervenka, R., Trecansky, I., Calisri, M., Greenwood, D.: AML: Agent modeling language toward industry-grade agent based modeling. In Odell, J., et al., eds.: Lecture Notes in Computer Science – LNCS. Volume 3382. Springer Verlag (2005) 31–46 Agent–Oriented Software Engineering 2004 (AOSE 2004).

[13] CSELT, Computer Engineering Group of the University of Parma: JADE Sniffer Agent. (2003) Available online at: http://jade.tilab.com/doc/tools/sniffer/index.html.

[14] CSELT, Computer Engineering Group of the University of Parma: Java Agent DEvelopment Framework (JADE). (2003) Available online at: http://jade.tilab.com/.

Applying the Governance Framework Technique to Promote Maintainability in Open Multi-Agent Systems

Gustavo Carvalho[1], Carlos J.P. de Lucena[1], Rodrigo Paes[1],
Ricardo Choren[2], and Jean-Pierre Briot[3]

[1] PUC-Rio - Marqus de So Vicente 225,
4 Andar RDC - Gvea RJ, Brazil
{guga,lucena,rbp}@inf.puc-rio.br
[2] SE/8 - IME
Pa Gen Tibrcio 80 - Praia Vermelha,
RJ, Brazil
choren@de9.ime.eb.br
[3] LIP6, Université Pierre et Marie Curie (Paris 6)
8 rue du Capitaine Scott, 75015 Paris, France
Jean-Pierre.Briot@lip6.fr

Abstract. Governance means that specifications are enforced dynamically at application runtime. Governance framework is a technique to design and implement an extensible interaction specification for a family of open systems. This specification can be refined for particular applications. We based this proposal on object-oriented framework concepts and adapted them for distributed agents and interactions. A governance framework structures the extensions of open system instances as variations in interactions among agents, defined as templates. Templates are used to gather core implementation and extension points. Extension points are "hooks" that will be customized to implement an instance of the governance framework. During framework instantiation, templates are refined to concrete interaction specification. As a proof of concept experiment, in this paper we propose a framework for instantiating supply chain management applications as open systems.

Keywords: Interaction protocol, Reuse, Law-enforcement.

1 Introduction

Nowadays, software permeates every aspect of our society, and it is increasingly becoming a distributed and open asset. Distribution means that it is possible to integrate different software solutions from different sources or machines and they work cooperatively to achieve system requirements. Openness is crucial for software. Open systems are software systems in which autonomous distributed components interact and may enter and leave the environment at their will [10]. Auction systems and virtual enterprises are examples of such open and

L. Padgham and F. Zambonelli (Eds.): AOSE 2006, LNCS 4405, pp. 64–83, 2007.

distributed applications [19]. Software agent technology is considered a promising approach for the development of open system applications [19].

The specification of open multi-agent systems (open MAS) includes the definition of agent roles and any other restrictions that the environment imposes on an agent to enter and participate in conversations. Agents will only be permitted to interact if they conform to the specification of the open MAS. Since open system components are often autonomous, sometimes they behave unpredictably and unforeseen situations arise. Taming this uncertainty is a key issue for open software development. The establishment of laws over interaction specification and their enforcement over software agents create a boundary of tolerated autonomous behavior and can be used to foster the development of reliable systems.

In open software systems, rules that enforce the relationships between agents are not always fully understood early in the development life cycle. Still, many more rules are not applied because of the lack of system support for changing specifications or the complexity of the specifications. Inspired by object-oriented frameworks [9], governance frameworks are proposed to deal with this complexity, reifying proven software designs and implementations in order to reduce the cost and improve the quality of software.

Since software systems need to be customized according to different purposes and peculiarities, it should be possible to express evolution as variations related to interactions of open systems and to components that inhabit the environment. Following this hypothesis, we propose to design open systems using extension points [5] to annotate interaction specification and using laws to customize the agents' expected behavior. We argue that some specification elements can be reused and that some predefined "hooks" can be refined to develop a set of open MAS applications in a specific domain.

We are proposing governance frameworks based on some object-oriented framework concepts [9]. This approach provides the necessary modelling capabilities for constructing reusable implementations of open systems. Governance frameworks may demonstrate in practice the ability to apply enforcement (or, when needed, to relax enforcement) for both complex and changing specifications. Besides customizations, the compliance of the system to the specification must continue to be analyzed by a mechanism that governs the laws of interactions in open MAS. We use the XMLaw description language [16] to map the specification of interaction rules into a governance mechanism. The purpose of governance frameworks is to provide an approach to support the development of governance mechanisms.

A proof of concept prototype has been developed based on the specification of the Trading Agent Competition - Supply Chain Management (TAC SCM) [2, 8, 18]. In this example, we discuss how the changes to the laws of open MAS applications can be represented as templates that structurally "hook" the extension points into the interaction protocol. The goal of this study is to approach the TAC SCM structure by considering it an open system and, through the analysis of its specifications, we aim to learn about how to extend the interaction specification and compliance verification in open system applications. The main purpose of the current investigation is not to contribute to TAC SCM evolution as a realistic open system for B2B trading, but rather to show that it is possible to specify and develop open software systems using extension points.

The contributions of this paper are threefold. First, we jointly apply variations and laws to specify, implement and maintain extension points in open systems. Second, we support the implementation of these variations using a law-governed mechanism. Third, we specified and implemented a governance framework for supply chain management applications based on TAC-SCM's specifications.

The organization of this paper is as follows. Section 2 briefly describes the law-governed mechanism. In Section 3, we discuss the governance framework approach as a means to design open system for extensions. Section 4 maps the variations identified in TAC-SCM's editions into a governance framework for supply chain management. Section 5 partly describes two instances of the TAC SCM using our approach. Related work is described in Section 6. Finally, we describe our conclusions in Section 7.

2   Governing Interactions in Open Systems

Software agents in open MAS are heterogeneous, i.e., the development is done without a centralized control, possibly by different parties, with different purposes and preferences. The only restriction an open MAS imposes is that the agents communicate through a common language. In this work we assume that every agent developer may have an a priori access to the open system specification, including protocol descriptions and interaction laws and that agents communicate using ACL.

Law-governed architectures are designed to guarantee that the specifications will be obeyed. We developed an infrastructure that includes a modification

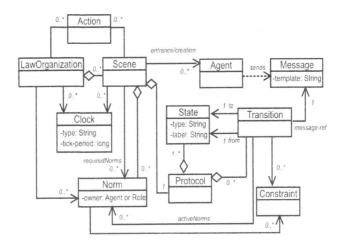

Fig. 1. Conceptual Model of XMLaw

of a basic communication infrastructure [4] that is provided to agent developers. This architecture intercepts messages and interprets the laws previously described. Whenever necessary, a software support [17] permits extending this basic infrastructure to fulfill open system requirements or interoperability concerns regarding law monitoring. In this paper, we use the description language XMLaw [16] to represent the interaction rules of an open system specification. XMLaw (Fig.1) specifies interaction protocols using time restrictions, norms, or even time sensitive norms.

Those elements are represented in an XML structure like (Listing 1.1). The composition and interrelationship among elements is done by events. One law element can generate events to signal something to other elements. Other elements can sense events for many purposes - for instance, activating or deactivating themselves.

```
<Laws>
 <LawOrganization id="..." name="...">
  <Scene id="..." time-to-live="...">
   <Creators>...</Creators>
   <Entrance>
     <Participant role="..." limit="..."/>
   </Entrance>
   <Messages>...</Messages>
   <Protocol>
     <States> ... </States>
     <Transitions>...</Transitions>
   </Protocol>
   <Norms>... </Norms>
   <Clocks>...</Clocks>
   <Actions>...</Actions>
  </Scene>
 </LawOrganization>
</Laws>
```

Listing 1.1. XMLaw structure

2.1 Refinement Operators to Specify Laws in Open Multi-Agent Systems

To design the interaction laws of open MAS to facilitate extensions to deal with changing requirements, it is necessary to have an instrument to specify which law elements can be customized and so described as extension points. The extension points are a means of representing knowledge about the place where modifications and enhancements in laws can be made. In our context, it is useful to permit the inclusion of norms, constraints and actions into a pre-defined law specification.

XMLaw [16] has two elements that can be easily plugged into the specification of interaction laws: actions and constraints. Actions are used to plug services into open systems. Services are domain specific functionalities that can be triggered while the mediator monitors agents' interactions. The first attempt to define extension points was deferring the definition of the class implementation [5]. We enhanced this notion with the proposal of refinements operators in XMLaw [6]. Below, we explain how the interaction specification with extension points can be prepared to further refinements. The examples below detail laws applied on sales that are customized according to the period of the year (e.g. discounts are given in summer and winter). The action giveDiscount (Listing 1.2) will calculate and apply the discount and the constraint badClient (Listing 1.3) restricts discounts to this kind of client.

```
<Actions>
   <Action id="giveDiscount">
   <Element ref="payment"
      event-type="transition_activation"/>
   </Action>
</Actions>
```

Listing 1.2. Action hook

```
<Constraints>
   <Constraint id="badClient"/>
</Constraints>
```

Listing 1.3. Constraint hook

The abstract attribute defines when a law element is not completely implemented. If no value for the abstract attribute is determined, the element is a concrete one (default abstract = "false"). If the law designer wants to specify that a law element needs some refinements to be used he has to explicitly specify the attribute abstract with the value true (abstract = "true"). If a law is defined as concrete, it cannot leave any element to be further refined; all elements must be fully implemented, otherwise, the interpreter will indicate an error. An abstract operator can define law elements with some gaps to be filled further (Listing 1.4). This is the extension point idea, defining clearly the context where the extensions are expected. Until now, we can defer the definition of the implementation of actions and constraints classes or the inclusion of any law element. Below, we structure the usage of the badClient constraint and giveDiscount action inside the permission Sale. If this permission active during the enforcement process, this discount action and verification constraint can be triggered.

```
<Permission id="Sale" abstract="true">
    <Owner>...</Owner>
    <Activations> ... </Activations>
    <Deactivations> ... </Deactivations>
    <Constraints>
        <Constraint id="badClient"/>
    </Constraints>
  <Actions>
   <Action id="ad" class="..." >...</Action>
       <Action id="giveDiscount">...</Action>
   </Actions>
</Permission>
```

Listing 1.4. Abstract operator

The completes attribute is an operator that is useful to fill the elements that were left unspecified when a law element was defined as abstract (Listing 1.5). It is a simple operator to realize extensions as it can just be used to define action and constraints class implementations. The completes operator turns an abstract element into a complete one and cannot leave any element unspecified unless it also redefines this element as an abstract one. The completes operator is limited to the definition of class implementations.

```
<Permission id="SummerSale" completes="Sale">
  <Constraint id="badClient" class="BadCustomers"/>
  <Action id="giveDiscount" class="Percentage10"/>
</Permission>
```

Listing 1.5. Completes operator

The extends attribute is a more powerful operator and it is similar to the specialization operation in object-oriented languages. Basically, an extends operator reuses the description of law elements and includes any modifications that are necessary to customize the law element to users' needs, including the redefinition of law elements. For example, this operator can include new activation references, new action elements, and new norm elements and can also superpose any element that was previously specified. The extends operator also turns an abstract element into a complete one and cannot leave any element unspecified unless it redefines this element as an abstract one (Listing 1.6).

```
<Permission id="WinterSale" extends="Sale">
  <Constraints>
    <Constraint id="badClient" class="BadPayers"/>
  </Constraints>
  <Actions>
    <Action id="giveDiscount" class="Percentage15"/>

    <Action id="giveSuperDiscount"
            class="ChristimasDiscount">
      <Element ref="christimas"
               event-type="clock_activation"/>
    </Action>
  </Actions>
</Permission>
```

Listing 1.6. Extends operator

3 Improving Governance Mechanism Maintainability

Suppose that it is possible to specify and implement the kernel of a general solution and this kernel can be customized to different purposes. In this kernel, you have the exact points that can be modified and enhanced. In our context, this approach can be used to derive a family of governance mechanisms that share a core specification and implementation. The customization is used for two purposes. First, different governance mechanisms can be derived for different purposes and application scenarios. Second, different versions of the same governance mechanism can be instantiated during its lifecycle. To realize this scenario, we propose to use some object-oriented framework concepts. An object-oriented framework is a reusable; semi-complete application that can be specialized to produce custom applications [9], i.e., it is a collection of abstract entities that encapsulate common algorithms of a family of applications [3].

In this work, we focus on understanding how interaction specification enhanced by laws can be designed to support extensions. A governance framework is an extensible design for building governance mechanisms for open MAS. A solution for open system development is achieved by relaxing the boundary between a framework (the common part of the family of applications) and its instantiations (the application-specific part). In a governance framework, certain laws of the open system are abstract, because they are left either unspecified or incompletely specified because they would expose details that would vary among particular executable implementations.

A governance framework is flexible by design. Flexibility works in opposition to the concept of static interaction specification or enforcement. In design time, customizability ensures the framework may receive new law elements or adapt the existing ones. For this purpose, a governance framework provides "hooks" for its instances; we define abstract definitions for interactions as templates. Governance functionalities that have specificities according to their applications are fully implemented later, but all common definitions and implementations are present in general specifications. The realization of abstract interactions is deferred to instantiation time.

In MAS, the collaboration structure defines the agent roles and their relationships. Roles are useful to specify general descriptions for agents' responsibilities in an organization [20] and they are bound to real software agents in open system execution. While playing roles, agents acquire the obligation to obey the law that is specified for their responsibilities and it is possible to enforce the laws prescribed in the protocol. Our main purpose is not to discuss how to structure the component reuse as agent roles [12, 20], which will be realized by external software agents. We intend to use an agent role at the design level as a means to describe agents' responsibilities.

Our main concern is over how agents interact in the open MAS. The interaction elements comprehend the specification of dynamical concerns of an open system. The interaction specification is composed of interaction laws and interaction protocols. Interaction protocols define the context and the sequence of messages of a conversation between agent roles. The fixed part of interaction specifications is called general interaction. General interactions (Fig. 2) can be derived by analyzing the application domain. If any interaction element is common to all intended instances, this element is attached to the core definition of the framework. Concerning interactions, the variability implies a more flexible protocol specification to include some alternatives and options to the design of a family of similar open MAS. Each interaction element in the open MAS is a potential extension point. The specification of interaction protocols can be made flexible enough to include new elements like norms, constraints and actions that define the desired behavior for the open MAS applications. Templates (Fig. 2) are part of the flexibility of the open MAS interactions [5]. In governance frameworks, templates are defined as "hooks" for elements of the interaction specification that will be refined during the governance mechanism instantiation.

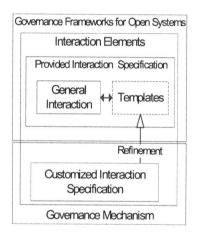

Fig. 2. Governance Framework Overview

Even with extension points, we still need to monitor the entire application; to gather information about its execution, and also to analyze the compliance of the system components with the desired behavior. This means that the governance mechanism must support this peculiarity.

4   Governance Framework for Open Supply Chain Management

An important characteristic of a good framework is that it provides mature runtime functionality and rules within the specific domain in which it is to be applied [9]. Hence, we based our proof of concept prototype on the specification of the TAC SCM [2, 8, 18]. The game rules have been updated over the last three years. This evolution was achieved by observing the behavior of different agents during the last editions and their consequences (e.g. interaction rules were defined to protect agents from malicious participants). In our prototype, each set of rules can be used to configure a different instance of a framework for instantiating governance mechanisms in open supply chain management domain.

In TAC SCM, assembler agents need to negotiate with supplier agents to buy components to produce PCs. A bank agent is used to monitor the progress of the agents. In the real TAC SCM architecture, there is a TAC Server that simulates the behavior of the suppliers, customers, and factories. We converted part of the simulation components present in TAC SCM to external agents or the open system's services of a prototypical version. We continue to have the TAC SCM Server, but this server aims to monitor and to analyze the compliance of agents' behavior to laws that were previously established.

Analyzing the variability of the negotiation between suppliers and assemblers over TAC SCM editions we depict the architecture below. The kernel of this framework is composed of a scene for negotiation, a scene for payment, the definition of interaction steps (transitions), states and messages, and a permission to restrict the offer values of an RFQ. The extension points that will be described here include the permission granted to assemblers to issue requests during one day (number of permitted requests and how to count them), the constraint to verify the date in which a request is valid, and the payment method implemented by actions inside the obligation.

4.1   Kernel Description

In the negotiation, assemblers buy supplies from suppliers to produce PCs. Besides these two roles, there is the bank role. There are six assembler agents that produce PCs participating in each TAC SCM instance. These participants interact with both suppliers and a bank agent. There are eight different supplier agents in each supply chain. Only one bank agent is responsible for managing payments accounts. The agent class diagram [7] (Fig. 3) depicts the roles, their relationships and their cardinalities.

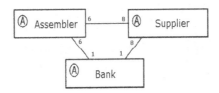

Fig. 3. Roles, relationships and cardinalities

We decided to organize this scenario in two scenes: one for the negotiation process between assemblers and suppliers, and the other for the payment involving the assembler and the bank agent. Listing 1.7 details the initial specification of the scene that represents the negotiation between the supplier and the assembler. Each negotiation scene is valid over the duration of the competition, which is 3300000ms (220 days x 15000ms). Listing 1.8 describes the payment process. We decided not to specify any time out to the payment scene and this is represented by the "infinity" value of the attribute time-to-live.

```
<Scene id="negotiation" time-to-live ="3300000">
   <Creators>
     <Creator role="assembler"/>
   </Creators>
   <Entrance>
     <Participant role="assembler" limit ="6"/>
     <Participant role="supplier" limit ="8"/>
   </Entrance>
</Scene>
```

Listing 1.7. Negotiation scene structure

```
<Scene id="payment" time-to-live="infinity">
   <Creators>
     <Creator role="any"/>
   </Creators>
   <Entrance>
     <Participant role="assembler" limit ="1"/>
     <Participant role="bank" limit ="1"/>
   </Entrance>
</Scene>
```

Listing 1.8. Payment scene structure

Analyzing the evolution of TAC SCM's requirements, we can observe evidences that interaction protocols have a core definition. In this specification we can also identify some extension points, which can be customized to provide different instances of the supply chain. The negotiation between assemblers and suppliers is related to the interaction between the assembler role and the bank role. Basically, a payment is made through a payment message sent by the assembler to the bank and the bank's reply with a confirmation response, represented by the receipt message ((Listing 1.9 and 1.10, Fig. 4). Fig. 4 is based on the interaction diagram [7].

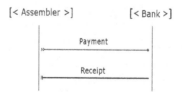

Fig. 4. Payment interaction

```
<Messages>
   <Message  id="payment"  template="..."/>
   <Message  id="receipt"  template="..."/>
</Messages>
```

Listing 1.9. Payment messages description

```
<Protocol>
   <States>
    <State  id="p1"  type="initial"/>
    <State  id="p2"  type="execution"/>
    <State  id="p3"  type="success"/>
   </States>
   <Transitions>
     <Transition  id="payingTransition"
        from="p1"  to="p2"  message-ref="payment"/>
     <Transition  id="paymentConcludedTrans"
        from="p2"  to="p3"  message-ref="receipt"/>
   </Transitions>
</Protocol>
```

Listing 1.10. Payment interaction protocol description

The negotiation between assemblers and suppliers is carried out in five steps, four messages (Fig. 5, (Listing 1.11) and six transitions. Below ((Listing 1.11 and 1.12), this scene is described in detail using XMLaw. Fig. 5 is based on the interaction diagram [7].

```
<Messages>
   <Message  id="rfq"       template="..."/>
   <Message  id="offer"     template="..."/>
   <Message  id="order"     template="..."/>
   <Message  id="delivery"  template="..."/>
</Messages>
```

Listing 1.11. Negotiation interaction protocol: messages

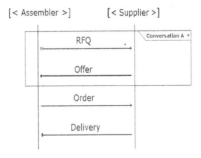

Fig. 5. Negotiation protocol diagram

```
<Protocol>
  <States>
    <State id="as1" type="initial"/>
    <State id="as2" type="execution"/>
    <State id="as3" type="execution"/>
    <State id="as4" type="execution">
    <State id="as5" type="success"/>
  </States>
  <Transitions>
    <Transition id="rfqTransition" from="as1"
      to="as2" message-ref="rfq">...</Transition>
    <Transition id="newRFQTransition" from="as2"
      to="as2" message-ref="rfq">...</Transition>
    <Transition id="otherRFQTransition" from="as3"
      to="as2" message-ref="rfq">...</Transition>
    <Transition id="offerTransition" from="as2"
      to="as3" message-ref="offer">...</Transition>
    <Transition id="orderTransition" from="as3"
      to="as4" message-ref="order"/>
    <Transition id="deliveryTransition" from="as4"
      to="as5" message-ref="delivery">...</Transition>
  </Transitions>
</Protocol>
```

Listing 1.12. Negotiation interaction protocol description

To further illustrate the use of general specifications, we identified the stable interaction laws in the last three editions of TAC SCM and we implemented it using XMLaw. This specification is reused in every instance of our governance framework. This law defines the relation between a request for quote (RFQ) sent by an assembler and an offer that will be sent by a supplier. Below, we briefly describe the specification according to [2,8, 18].

"On the following day of the arrival of a request for quotation, the supplier sends back to each agent an offer for each RFQ, containing the price, adjusted quantity, and due date. The supplier may respond by issuing up to two amended offers, each of which relaxes one of the two constraints, quantity and due date: (i) a partial offer is generated with the quantity of items relaxed; or (ii) an earliest complete offer is generated with the due date relaxed. Offers are received the day following the submission of RFQs, and the assembler must choose whether to accept them. In the case an agent attempts to order both the partial offer and the earliest complete offer, only the order that arrives earlier will be considered and the others will be ignored."

The implementation of this rule in XMLaw is illustrated in Listings 1.13 and 1.14. A permission was created to define a context in the conversation that is used to control when the offer message is valid, considering the information sent by an RFQ. For this purpose, two constraints were defined into the permission context, one determining the possible configurations of offer attributes that a supplier can send to an assembler, while the other constraint verifies if a valid offer message was generated - that is, if the offer was sent one day after the RFQ. This permission is only valid if both of the constraints are true. Below, we illustrate the offerTransition (Listing 1.13) and describe the permission RestrictOfferValues and its XMLaw specification (Listing 1.14).

```
<Transition id="offerTrabsition" from="as2"
   to="as3" message−ref="offer">
  <ActiveNorms>
      <Norm ref="RestrictOfferValues"/>
  </ActiveNorms>
</Transition>
```

Listing 1.13. General Transition Specification

```
<Permission id="RestrictOfferValues">
<Owner>Supplier</Owner>
 <Activations>
    <Element ref="rfqTransition" event−type="transition_activation"/>
 </Activations>
 <Deactivations>
   <Element ref="offerTransition" event−type="transition_activation"/>
 </Deactivations>
 <Actions>
  <Action id="keepRFQInfo" class="norm.actions.KeepRFQAction">
   <Element ref="rfqTransition" event−type="transition_activation"/>
  </Action>
 </Actions>
 <Constraints>
   <Constraint id="checkDates" class="norm.constraints.CheckValidDay"/>
   <Constraint id="checkAttributes" class="norm.constraints.
       CheckValidMessage"/>
 </Constraints>
</Permission>
```

Listing 1.14. General Norm specification

XMLaw includes the notion of context. Elements in the same context share the same local memory to share information, i.e., putting, getting and updating any value that is important for other law elements. Listing 1.14 depicts one example of context usage. The keepRFQInfo Action preserves the information present in the RFQ message to be later used by the checkAttributes and checkDates contraints.

4.2   Extension Point Descriptions

The constraint checkDueDate verifies if the date attribute is according to the restrictions imposed by the edition of the environment. It means that if the verification is not true the transition will not be fired. This constraint is associated with the transition rfqTransition and this transition is specified as abstract to clearly document the extension point. Listing 1.15 is an example of a template. In this example, we opted to keep the attribute class of the constraint check-DueDate not specified, that is, it will be set during framework instantiation.

```
<Transition id="rfqTransition" from="as1" to="as2"
            message-ref="rfq" abstract="true">
  <Constraints>
    <Constraint id="checkDueDate"/>
  </Constraints>
  <ActiveNorms>
    <Norm ref="AssemblerPermissionRFQ"/>
  </ActiveNorms>
</Transition>
```

Listing 1.15. Permission and Constraint over RFQ message Templates

According to TAC SCM specifications [2, 8, 18], every day each agent may send up to a maximum number of RFQs. But the precise number of RFQs has changed over the last editions of TAC SCM, so it is possible to defer this specification to instantiation time. We use a template for this purpose and we have created a permission to encapsulate this requirement (Listing 1.16); in the template some hooks will guide the specialization of an instance of this framework.

This permission is about the maximum number of requests for quotation that an assembler can submit to a supplier. To implement this sort of verification, the constraint checkCounter is associated with the permission AssemblerPermissionRFQ. It means that if the verification is not true the norm will not be valid, even if it is activated. The action ZeroCounter is defined under the permission AssemblerPermissionRFQ and it is triggered by a clock-tick every day, turning to zero the value of the counter of the number of requests issued by the assembler during this day. The other action orderID is activated by every transition transitionRFQ and is used to count the number of RFQs issued by the assembler, updating a local counter. Finally, a clock nextDay is used to mark the day period, and this mark is used to zero the counter of RFQs by the action ZeroCounter. In this paper, we do not describe the clock nextDay specification.

```
<Permission id="AssemblerPermissionRFQ" abstract="true">
  <Owner>Assembler</Owner>
  <Activations>
    <Element ref="negotiation" event-type="scene_creation"/>
  </Activations>
  <Deactivations>
    <Element ref="orderTransition" event-type="transition_activation
      "/>
  </Deactivations>
  <Constraints>
    <Constraint id="checkCounter"/>
  </Constraints>
  <Actions>
    <Action id="permissionRenew" class="tacscm.norm.actions.
      ZeroCounter">
      <Element ref="nextDay" event-type="clock_tick"/>
    </Action>
    <Action id="orderID">
      <Element ref="rfqTransition" event-type="transition_activation
        "/>
    </Action>
  </Actions>
</Permission>
```

Listing 1.16. Norm description Template

Another extension point is used to specify the relationship between orders and offers of the negotiation protocol. According to [2], agents confirm supplier offers by issuing orders. After that, an assembler has a commitment with a supplier, and this commitment is expressed as an obligation. It is expected that suppliers receive a payment for its components. But when they will receive the payment is not completely specified in this law. Another template specifies the structure of the ObligationToPay obligation (Listing 1.17), defining that it will be activated by an order message and it will be deactivated with the delivery of the components and also with the payment. A supplier will only deliver the product if the assembler has the obligation to pay for them (Listing 1.18). The assembler can only enter into the payment scene if it has an obligation to pay for the products (Listing 1.19). An assembler cannot enter into another negotiation if it has obligations that were not fulfilled (Listing 1.20).

```
<Obligation id="ObligationToPay" abstract="true">
  <Owner>Assembler</Owner>
  <Activations>
      <Element ref="orderTransition" event-type="transition_activation
          "/>
  </Activations>
  <Deactivations>
      <Element ref="payingTransition" event-type="transition_activation
          "/>
  </Deactivations>
</Obligation>
```

Listing 1.17. Obligation to pay

```
<Transition id="orderTransition" from="as3" to="as4" message-ref="
    order"/>
<Transition id="deliveryTransition" from="as4" to="as5" message-ref="
    delivery">
  <ActiveNorms>
    <Norm ref="ObligationToPay"/>
  </ActiveNorms>
</Transition>
```

Listing 1.18. Negotiation and Payment Scene

```
<Scene id="payment" time-to-live="infinity">
  <ActiveNorms>
    <Norm ref="ObligationToPay"/>
  </ActiveNorms>
  ...
</Scene>
```

Listing 1.19. Payment scene and ObligationToPay norm

```
<Scene id="negotiation" time-to-live="3300000">
  <DeActivatedNorms>
    <Norm ref="ObligationToPay"/>
  </DeActivatedNorms>
  ...
</Scene>
```

Listing 1.20. Negotiation scene and ObligationToPay norm

5   TAC SCM Editions as Framework's Instances

In this section, we present two examples of instantiations of the framework for open SCM, explaining the refinements proposed to the templates described above.

In TAC SCM 2004 and according to [2], a supplier will receive an assembler's payment after the delivery of components and at this time the cost of the order placed before will be fully charged. We implemented the payment as an action where the system forces the agent to pay the entire debit at the end of the negotiation (Listing 1.23). According to [2], on each day each agent may send up to ten RFQs to each supplier. An RFQ with DueDate beyond the end of the negotiation will not considered by the supplier. For this purpose, we implemented the constraint class ValidDate (Listing 1.21). The constraint class CounterLimit (Listing 1.22) checks if the local attribute for controlling the number of RFQs is below the limit of 10. The RFQCounter action increments the same attribute when receiving new messages of RFQ.

```
<Transition  id="rfq2004"  completes="rfqTransition">
  <Constraint  id="checkDueDate"
                class="constraints.ValidDate2004"/>
</Transition>
```

Listing 1.21. checkDueDate instance for TAC SCM 2004

```
<Permission  id="AssemblerPermissionRFQ2004"
              completes="AssemblerPermissionRFQ">
  <Constraint  id="checkCounter"
                class="constraint.CounterLimit"/>
  <Action  id="orderID"  class="norm.actions.RFQCounter">
</Permission>
```

Listing 1.22. Permission instance for TAC SCM 2004

```
<Obligation  id="ObligationToPay2004"  extends="ObligationToPay">
  <Actions>
    <Action  id="supplierPayment"
              class="actions.SupplierPayment100">
      <Element  ref="deliveryTransition"
                event-type="transition_activation"/>
    </Action>
  </Actions>
</Obligation>
```

Listing 1.23. Obligation instance for TAC SCM 2004

In TAC SCM 2005, suppliers wishing perhaps to protect themselves from defaults will bill agents immediately for a down payment on the cost of each order placed [8]. The remainder of the value of the order will be billed when the order is shipped. In 2005, the down payment ratio is 10.

```
<Transition id="rfq2005" completes="rfqTransition">
    <Constraint id="checkDueDate"
        class="constraints.ValidDate2005"/>
</Transition>
```

Listing 1.24. checkDueDate instance for TAC SCM 2005

```
<Permission id="AssemblerPermissionRFQ2005"
            completes="AssemblerPermissionRFQ">
    <Constraint id="checkCounter"
        class="constraint.CounterLimit2005"/>
    <Action id="orderID"
        class="norm.actions.RFQCounter2005"> ... </Action>
</Permission>
```

Listing 1.25. Permission instance for TAC SCM 2005

```
<Obligation id="ObligationToPay2005" extends="ObligationToPay">
    <Actions>
        <Action id="supplierDownPayment"
                class="actions.SupplierPayment10">
            <Element ref="orderTransition"
                    event-type="transition_activation"/>
        </Action>
        <Action id="supplierPayment"
                class="actions.SupplierPayment90">
            <Element ref="deliveryTransition"
                    event-type="transition_activation"/>
        </Action>
    </Actions>
</Obligation>
```

Listing 1.26. Obligation instance for TAC SCM 2005

6   Related Work

Ao and Minsky [1] propose an approach that enhances their Law Governed Interaction (LGI) with the concept of policy-hierarchy to support that different internal policies or laws are formulated independently of each other, achieving a flexibility support by this means. [1] consider confidentiality as a requirement for their solution. However, the extensions presented here intend to support the maintenance of governance mechanisms, rather than flexibility for the purpose of confidentiality.

Singh [15] proposes a customizable governance service, based on skeletons. His approach formally introduces traditional scheduling ideas into an environment of autonomous agents without requiring unnecessary control over their actions, or detailed knowledge of their designs. Skeletons are equivalent to state based machines and we could adapt and reuse their formal model focusing on the implementation of a family of applications. But [15] has its focus on building multi-agent systems instead of providing support for monitoring and enforcement purpose.

Below we describe some useful instruments to promote reuse; they can be seen as instruments for specifying extendable laws in governance frameworks. COSY

[11] views a protocol as an aggregation of primitive protocols. Each primitive protocol can be represented by a tree where each node corresponds to a particular situation and transitions correspond to possible messages an agent can either receive or send, i.e., the various interaction alternatives. In AgenTalk [14], protocols inherit from one another. They are described as scripts containing the various steps of a possible sequence of interactions. Koning and Huget [13] deal with the modeling of interaction protocols for multi-agent systems, outlining a component-based approach that improves flexibility, abstraction and protocol reuse.

7   Conclusions

In open MAS, in which components are autonomous and heterogeneous, governance is crucial. This paper presented an approach to augment reliability on customizable open systems. The approach is based on governing the interactions in the system. This is a non-intrusive method, allowing the independent development of the agents of the open system - they are only required to follow the protocols specified for the system.

The purpose of governance frameworks is to facilitate extensions on governance mechanisms for open systems. Interaction and roles are first order abstractions in open system specification reuse. Besides, it is possible to distinguish two kinds of interaction specification: fixed (stable) and flexible (extensible). The challenge to developers is to deliver a specification that identifies the aspects of the open MAS that will not change and cater the software to those areas. Stability is characterized by the interaction protocol and some general rules that are common to all open MAS instances. Extensions on interaction rules will impact the open MAS and the agents and extensions are specified. The main contribution of this work is to provide a technique to design software that evolves, therefore reducing maintenance efforts.

With this proposal we aim to improve the engineering of distributed systems, providing a customizable conformance verification mechanism. We are also targeting improvement in the quality of governance mechanisms of open systems; this will be achieved by facilitating the extension of governance mechanisms. We propose to use variations and laws to specify, implement and maintain extension points. We also support the implementation of these variations using a law-governed mechanism. The experiment showed that this is an interesting and promising approach; it improves the open system design by incorporating reliability aspects that can be customized according to application requirements and it improves maintainability. The application development experience showed us that it is possible to obtain benefits from the use of proper engineering concepts for its specification and construction. However, more experiments with real-life MAS applications are needed to evaluate and validate the proposed approach.

Acknowledgments. We gratefully acknowledge the financial support provided by the CNPq as part of individual grants and of the ESSMA project (552068/2002-0) and by CAPES as part of the EMACA Project (CAPES/COFECUB 482/05 PP 016/04).

References

1. Ao, X. and Minsky, N. Flexible Regulation of Distributed Coalitions. In Proc. of the 8th European Symposium on Research in Computer Security (ESORICS). Gjvik Norway, October, 2003.
2. Arunachalam, R; Sadeh, N; Eriksson, J; Finne, N; Janson, S. The Supply Chain Management Game for the Trading Agent Competition 2004. CMU-CS-04-107, July 2004
3. Batory, D; Cardone, R. and Smaragdakis, Y. "Object-Oriented Frameworks and ProductLines", 1st Software Product-Line Conference, Denver, Colorado, August 2000.
4. Bellifemine, F; Poggi, A; Rimassa, G. Jade: a fipa2000 compliant agent development environment, in: Proceedings 5th international conference on Autonomous agents, ACM Press, 2001, pp. 216-217
5. Carvalho, Gustavo; Paes, Rodrigo; Lucena, Carlos. Extensions on Interaction Laws in Open Multi-Agent Systems. In: First Workshop on Software Engineering for Agent-oriented Systems (SEAS 05), 19th Brazilian Symposium on Software Engineering. Uberlndia, Brasil
6. Carvalho, G.; Lucena, C.; Paes, R.; Briot, J.P.; Refinement Operators to Facilitate the Reuse of Interaction Laws in Open Multi-Agent Systems, International Workshop on Software Engineering for Large-scale Multi-Agent Systems (SELMAS'06), 5th, at ICSE 2006, Shanghai, China. In: Proceedings of the Fifth International Workshop on Software Engineering for Large-scale Multi-agent Systems, p. 75-82, May 21-22, 2006.
7. Choren, R. and Lucena, C.J.P. Modeling Multi-agent systems with ANote. Software and Systems Modeling 4(2), 2005, p. 199 - 208.
8. Collins, J; Arunachala,R; Sadeh,N; Eriksson,J; Finne,N; Janson,S. (2005) The Supply Chain Management Game for the 2005 Trading Agent Competition. CMU-ISRI-04-139.
9. Fayad, M; Schmidt, D.C.; Johnson, R.E. Building application frameworks : object-oriented foundations of framework design. ISBN 0471248754, New York: Wiley, 1999.
10. Fredriksson M. et al. First international workshop on theory and practice of open computational systems. In Proceedings of twelfth international workshop on Enabling technologies: Infrastructure for collaborative enterprises (WETICE), Workshop on Theory and practice of open computational systems (TAPOCS), pp. 355 - 358, IEEE Press, 2003.
11. Haddadi, A. Communication and Cooperation in Agent Systems: A Pragmatic Theory, volume 1056 of Lecture Notes in Computer Science. Springer Verlag, 1996.
12. Kendall, E. "Role Modeling for Agent Systems Analysis, Design and Implementation", IEEE Concurrency, 8(2):34-41, April-June 2000.
13. Koning, J.L. and Huget, M.P.. A component-based approach for modeling interaction protocols. In H. Kangassalo and E. Kawaguchi (eds) 10th European-Japanese Conference on Information Modeling and Knowledge Bases, Frontiers in Artificial Intelligence and Applications.IOS Press, 2000
14. Kuwabara, K; Ishida, T; and Osato, N. AgenTalk: Coordination protocol description for multiagent systems. In First International Conference on MultiAgent Systems (ICMAS-95), San Francisco, June 1995. AAAI Press. Poster.
15. Singh, M. P., "A Customizable Coordination Service for Autonomous Agents," Intelligent Agents IV: Agent Theories, Architectures, and Languages, Springer, Berlin, 1998, pp. 93-106.

16. Paes, R. B.; Carvalho G. R.; Lucena, C.J.P.; Alencar, P. S. C.; Almeida H.O.; Silva, V. T. Specifying Laws in Open Multi-Agent Systems. In: Agents, Norms and Institutions for Regulated Multi-agent Systems (ANIREM), AAMAS2005, 2005.
17. Paes, R.B; Lucena, C.J.P; Alencar, P.S.C. A Mechanism for Governing Agent Interaction in Open Multi-Agent Systems MCC n 30/05, Depto de Informtica, PUC-Rio, 31 p., 2005
18. Sadeh, N; Arunachalam, R; Eriksson, J; Finne, N; Janson, S. TAC-03: a supply-chain trading competition, AI Mag. 24 (1) 92-94, 2003.
19. Wooldridge, M; Weiss, G; Ciancarini, P. (Eds.) Agent-Oriented Software Engineering II, Second International Workshop, AOSE 2001, Montreal, Canada, May 29, 2001, Revised Papers and Invited Contributions, Vol. 2222 of Lecture Notes in Computer Science, Springer, 2002.
20. Yu, L; Schmid, B.F. "A conceptual framework for agent-oriented and role-based workflow modelling", the 1st International Workshop on Agent-Oriented Information Systems, Heidelberg, 1999.

Designing Institutional Multi-Agent Systems*

Carles Sierra[1], John Thangarajah[2], Lin Padgham[2], and Michael Winikoff[2]

[1] Artificial Intelligence Research Institute (IIIA)
Spanish Research Council (CSIC)
Catalonia, Spain
sierra@iiia.csic.es
[2] School of Computer Science and Information Technology,
RMIT University,
GPO Box 2476V, Melbourne, VIC 3001, Australia
{johthan, linpa, winikoff}@cs.rmit.edu.au

Abstract. The vision of agents working together on the Internet, in virtual organizations, is one that is increasingly common. However, one of the issues is the
regulation of the participating agents and their behaviour. A substantial body of
work exists that investigates agent societies and agent organizations, including
work on *electronic institutions*, such as *Islander* and *Ameli*. However, although
such work provides concrete tools for specifying and enacting institutions, there
is a lack of clear documented guidance to designers who are using these tools. In
this paper we describe a methodology for developing an institutional structure for
multi agent systems. This methodology captures the knowledge and experience
within the Islander group, and integrates it with the *Prometheus* methodology.

1 Introduction

The vision of agents working together on the Internet, in virtual organizations, is one
that is increasingly common. One of the issues however is the regulation of the participating agents and their behaviour. There is a substantial body of work that investigates
agent societies and agent organizations (for a review see [1]) and electronic institutions
(e.g. [2,3,4]). Methodologies for designing agent organizations such as OperA [5] have
been used for developing industrial systems, and there are various examples of implemented systems. However there is very limited support for developing such systems, in
terms of runtime platforms or design tools. One exception is the Islander design tool [6]
and the Ameli runtime platform [7]. Together these provide an environment for designing and developing electronic institutions. Currently there is no written methodology or
guidance on how to actually use these tools to develop electronic institutions, although
there is considerable experience developed within the Islander group. This paper provides a methodology for developing an institutional structure for multi agent systems,
capturing the knowledge and experience within the Islander group into a *Social Design*

* This work was supported by the Australian Research Council under grant LP0453486, in collaboration with Agent Oriented Software. We also thank the Australian Tourism Data Ware-
house for use of their tourism content in our agents. Carles Sierra is being supported by the
Spanish Web-I(2) project and the ARC Discovery Grant DP0557168.

L. Padgham and F. Zambonelli (Eds.): AOSE 2006, LNCS 4405, pp. 84–103, 2007.

phase, within a slightly modified version of the Prometheus methodology [8], a practical agent-oriented software engineering methodology that aims to be usable by software developers and undergraduate students.

Design tools play an extremely important part in supporting the development of complex systems. Consequently this Social Design phase has been developed specifically to work with the Islander design tool. As the area of methodological support for design and development of agent organizations, institutions and societies matures, it is likely that this would be generalized to provide an approach less dependent on the particular available toolset. However at this stage, we believe it is useful to provide a very concrete methodology that gives sufficient guidance to the developer that they can successfully develop a system.

The approach that we have taken is to use the Prometheus Design Tool (PDT[1]) [9] and a variant of the Prometheus methodology for doing the initial analysis and system specification. The system specified may include the Electronic Institution as a part of the system, or it may be the entire system. Using this initial design in PDT, the design of the Electronic Institution component is then carried out within the Islander tool, and the outcome of this provides information back into the Prometheus design process for those parts of the system that lie outside the actual Electronic Institution infrastructure.

In the rest of this paper we provide some background on Islander, and the view of Electronic Institutions that Islander and Ameli are designed to support. We then describe in detail the design process for developing an Electronic Institution, embedding this within the Prometheus methodology. In order to illustrate the design process in a concrete way, we take an example of an (very limited) Electronic Institution for travel bookings, and use this for illustration throughout the methodological description.

2   Background: ISLANDER

The idea behind Electronic Institutions (EIs) is to mirror the roles traditional institutions play in the establishment of "the rules of the game"– that is, the set of conventions that articulate agents' interactions. The essential roles EIs play are both descriptive and prescriptive: the institution makes the conventions explicit to participants, and it warrants their compliance. Development environments to realize Electronic Institutions involve a conceptual framework to describe agent interactions as well as an engineering framework to specify and deploy actual interaction environments. Work on such a development environment has been happening for some time within the Intelligent Agents Group at the Artificial Intelligence Research Institute of Spain [2,3,4,10]. Considerable experience in the deployment of applications as EIs (e.g. [11,12]) provide confidence in the validity of the approach.

EIs are socially-centered, and neutral with respect to the internals of the participating agents. They provide a regulated virtual environment where the relevant interactions among participating entities take place. The Electronic Institution provides an infrastructure which ensures, as well as specifies, legitimate interactions. In order to realize this infrastructure all interactions are considered to be speech acts, and any effect

---

[1] Freely available from www.cs.rmit.edu.au/pdt

on the shared environment is considered to happen only as a result of illocutions uttered by participating agents.

The Islander tool supports specification of an EI which is then executable using the Ameli runtime environment[2]. Conceptually there are four main areas to be specified using Islander, and we will describe each in turn. These are:

- **The Dialogical Framework** which specifies the roles within the particular domain and the ontology.
- **The Interaction Structure** which describes the scenes, the pattern of allowable interactions within each scene, and also the effect these interactions have within the shared environment.
- **The Performative Structure** which provides an overview of the connections between different scenes and possibly other (sub-)Performative structures, and the role-flow policies.
- **Norms and Constraints** which capture rules which will be enforced by the EI.

2.1   Dialogical Framework

A *role* defines a particular pattern of behaviour and all participants within an EI take on a particular role. For example, in an auction house there may be buyers and sellers. Participants may change their roles over time, for example an agent acting as a buyer at one point may act as a seller at another. It may also be the case that we restrict an agent from acting as a buyer and seller at the same time, this is done by specifying a particular relationship between roles called DSD (Dynamic Separation of Duties). A stronger version of this relationship, called SSD (Static Separation of Duties) prevents agents from playing two incompatible roles within an institution even if they are played at different times.

We also need to distinguish between internal and external roles. The internal roles define a set of roles that will be played by *staff* agents which correspond to employees in traditional institutions. Agents that are external to the institution cannot take on these roles and are restricted to external roles. When defining an EI we need to consider the roles that participants may take on, whether the roles are internal or external and the relationship between roles if any.

We need to settle on a common illocutory language that serves to tag all pertinent interactions, or more properly, the valid speech acts. Formally, we consider each interaction to be an illocutory formulae: $\iota(speaker, listener, \varphi, t)$. The speech acts that we use start with an illocutory particle (inform, request, accept, ...) that a *speaker* addresses to a *listener*, at time t, and the content φ of the illocution is expressed in some object language whose vocabulary is the EI's *ontology*. The *speaker* and *listener* are roles within the EI.

To fill in these formulae therefore, we need vocabulary and grammar, and we need to refer to speakers and listeners, actions and time. We call all this the *Dialogical Framework* because it includes all that is needed for agents to participate in admissible dialogues in a given EI. Two important aspects of the Dialogical Framework are the

---

[2] Further details about electronic institutions can be found at http://e-institutor.iiia.csic.es

Social Structure model which captures the roles and their relationships, and the *Ontology model* which defines the entities in the domain.

2.2 Interaction Structure

Interactions between agents are articulated through recurrent dialogues which we call *scenes*. Each scene follows some type of conversation protocol, that restricts the possible interactions between roles. Scenes also represent the context in which the uttered illocutions must be interpreted, as the same message may have different meanings in different contexts.

The protocol of a scene is specified by a directed graph whose nodes represent the different states of a dialogical interaction between roles (e.g. see figure 6). Each state indicates the agents that are allowed to enter or leave a particular scene. The transitions from one state to another are labeled with illocution schemata from the scene's dialogical framework (whose sender, receiver and content may contain variables) or timeouts. These transitions may also have constraints and actions attached. Constraints are used to restrict the paths that the scene execution can follow. For example, in an auction scene it is possible to specify as a constraint, that a buyer can only submit a bid that is greater than the previous bid. Actions are used to specify any updates to the shared state of the institution when a transition occurs.

At execution time agents interact by uttering grounded illocutions matching the specified illocution schemata, and so binding their variables to values, building up the *scene context*.

2.3 Performative Structure

Activities in an electronic institution are organized in a *performative structure* as the composition of multiple, distinct, and possibly concurrent, dialogical activities, each one involving different groups of agents playing different roles.

A performative structure can be seen as a network of scenes, whose connections are mediated by transitions. It determines the role-flow policy among the different scenes by showing *how* agents, depending on their roles, may move into different scenes (other conversations), and showing *when* new scenes (conversations) are created.

In all EIs we assume that there is always an initial and a final scene, which are the entry and exit points of the institution. Each scene can have multiple instances at run-time. An example is shown in figure 5 on page 96. Rounded rectangles depict scenes, and arcs between them indicate the paths that agents can take.

A Transition can be thought of as a gateway between scenes or as a change of conversation. When an agent leaves a particular scene, there are different transitions that could happen: An *Or* transition allows an agent to choose which target scene(s) to enter. An *And* transition forces agents to synchronize before progressing to different scenes together. The arc of a transition to a target scene is labeled with *new* if the scene is created for the first time, and *one, some* or *all* indicating if the agent enters one, some or all instances of the target scene type.

In each transition it is possible to also specify if an agent takes on a different role when entering a new scene. Hence the performative structure provides an overview of the path and roles taken up by an agent from the start to the end scene within an EI.

2.4   Norms and Commitments

The main purpose of an EI is to control the interactions between the participants and ensure that they all adhere to agreed rules.

Actions within an institution are speech acts. These speech acts create obligations or socially binding commitments whose fulfillment is ensured by the institution. We make such intended effects of commitments explicit through *normative rules*.

We define the predicate $uttered(s, w, i)$ that allow us to express the connection between illocutions and norms. It denotes that a grounded illocution unifying with the illocution scheme i has been uttered at state w of scene s (the state w is an optional element).

A normative rule is specified using the following three elements: (i) Antecedent: the actions that trigger the activation of the norm, expressed as a predicate defined above; (ii) Defeasible antecedent: the utterance which releases the agent from the obligations described in the consequent; also expressed as an $uttered$ predicate; and (iii) Consequent: the set of obligations. An obligation is expressed as $Obl(x, i, s)$, denoting that the agent bound to role x is obliged to utter i in scene s.

3   Designing Institutional MAS with Islander and Prometheus

In exploring how the design of an Islander EI is typically done, we have identified that it is useful to begin with a slight modification of the Prometheus System Specification phase.

This phase in Prometheus consists of a number of interleaving, iterative steps, to define goals, roles, scenarios and environmental interface in the form of actors, actions and percepts. These elements, as well as the *ontology*, then provide input to a new phase which we call the *Social Design* phase, where the EI can be specified in the Islander tool. Specifically, the roles are incorporated into Islander's social structure, the scenarios are used as a starting point for developing the performative structure and the interaction model, goals are used to help identify norms, and, of course, ontology elements identified in the system specification phase feed into developing the ontology in the Social Design phase (see figure 1).

Once the Electronic Institution has been designed, there is additional information which can be provided back into Prometheus' Architectural Design phase, in order to design the agents that will join the institution. The institution is used as a starting point for the design. Specifically, the social structure and the norms identified in the Social Design phase are used, in addition to the system interface and goals, in determining which agent types should exist; and the interaction model is used as a starting point for defining interaction protocols.

In order to illustrate the methodology in greater detail we use a simple example of an EI for making flight and hotel arrangements. In this EI, agents can make and accept flight and hotel bookings, including payment for these. The idea is that the EI provides a trusted interaction space in which agents can engage in these interactions with other agents.

The remainder of this section explains the design methodology in greater detail, using this example. Section 3.1 covers the System Specification phase, with particular focus on the changes that have been made to the existing phase in Prometheus. Section 3.2 covers in detail the (new) Social Design phase, and section 3.3 briefly indicates how the Architectural Design phase has been modified to make use of the information produced in the Social Design phase. The detailed design phase is unchanged and is not discussed in this paper.

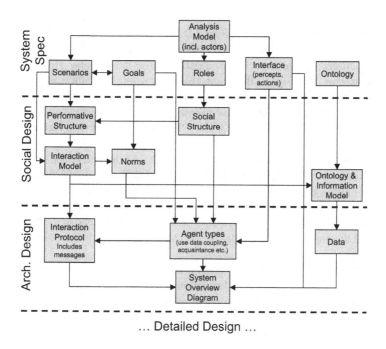

... Detailed Design ...

Fig. 1. Revised Methodology

3.1 System Specification

In order to appropriately use the Prometheus System Specification phase in conjunction with designing an electronic institution, there are a few changes that need to be made. In the standard Prometheus approach, we would start with identifying the actors, persons or entities, including software, that are external to the system, and that would interact with the system. In this case, the natural starting point is identification of the roles that will interact within the Electronic Institution. In our example these could be a Customer[3] role, a Travel Agent role, and a Banker role. These are external to the Institution, so one option could be to model them as Prometheus actors. However we choose

---

[3] We use san serif font to indicate names in the design. Due to limitations with the tool multi-word names do not have spaces in the figures (e.g. TravelAgent), but, for readability, do have spaces in the paper's text (e.g. Travel Agent).

to retain actors as the entities external to both the Institution and the software agents which we are designing. In our example, the actors may be Airline companies (with whom our electronic travel agent must eventually make a booking), Hotel proprietors, and Human customers.

Having identified the roles, (which will eventually be played by agents) we then identify the main scenarios for the EI. In this case we identify a Travel Booking scenario and a Payment scenario. The Customer and the Travel Agent roles are involved in the Travel Booking scenario, while the Bank and the Customer roles are involved in the payment scenario (called Pay Booking). The details of the interaction of the roles, with respect to the scenario is left until the Social Design phase.

If desired, we can identify the external actors that our roles will interact with, and the percepts or actions that we expect to be a part of those interactions. This information can then be used in the design of the agents that will be able to fill these roles. We identify that the Travel Agent role can be expected to have a booking action for interaction with the Airline and the Hotel proprietor. (We may later decide that we also want a confirmation percept from actor to Travel Agent). Similarly we identify a Request percept from the human customer to the agent that will play the Customer role, and an action to Provide Itinerary (again, further interaction may well be defined later).

We also add to the System Design phase a step to identify *soft goals* and to link these to particular entities if appropriate. In our example we identify three soft goals: reliable service provision; safe transactions; and ability to hold reservations for three days. The first of these we leave unattached, while safe transactions is attached to the Pay Booking scenario, and the ability to hold (unpaid) reservations is attached to the Travel Booking scenario.

The resulting analysis overview diagram is shown in figure 2. Boxes with stick figures denote either roles or actors (the distinction is indicated in the name), large squares denote soft goals, and arrows-like icons (with the indication "scenario") denote scenarios. Percepts are star-bursts, and actions are arrows (e.g. Provide Itinerary).

Having identified the roles and the main scenarios, we then further develop both the goals and the scenarios.

Goals: Whereas in "classical" Prometheus, goals are all system goals, which will be eventually allocated to specific agents, here we distinguish between *three* types of goals: *individual* goals that are allocated to a role (and later to an agent type), *joint* goals that are achieved by a group of roles (eventually agents), and *social* goals, where the EI plays a part in ensuring that these goals are achieved.

In deciding what type a given goal should be we consider whether it belongs to a single role (so is probably an individual goal), or to multiple roles (in which case it is probably joint or social). If any of the roles that the goal is assigned to are institutional ("staff") roles, then it must by definition be a social goal. However, at this stage in the process we may not have enough information to determine whether a goal should be joint or social, and so we may defer this decision until the Social Design phase.

As in "classical" Prometheus, the identification of system goals goes hand in hand with identification of scenarios and scenario steps. Goals are refined by techniques such as asking 'how can we achieve this goal?' [13]; and refinement and abstraction, along

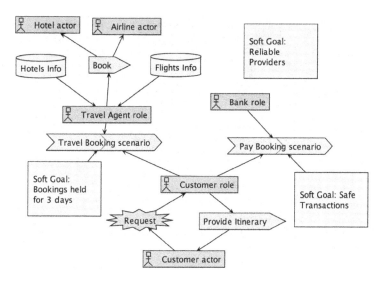

Fig. 2. Analysis diagram

with combining similar subgoals that arise in different parts of the system, eventually leads to a well developed goal hierarchy.

In addition to the individual/joint/social distinction, we have also introduced *soft goals* and the Goal Overview Diagram has been extended to show these. Soft goals are (optionally) linked to goals and provide information on the desired properties of the system. This information is captured explicitly so that it can be used later to develop constraints (in scenes) or norms (see section 3.2).

For example, figure 3 shows the goal overview diagram for the travel agent example. It shows that the high-level goal Travel Booking is a joint goal, as are its three child goals (Find Flights, Find Hotels and Make Booking). However, the sub-goals of Pay Booking are clearly individual goals.

Scenarios: Prometheus scenarios, which are identified for each actor that will interact with the system, contain steps (which can be *goals, percepts actions* or *sub-scenarios*). In modelling scenarios within EIs it is natural to think of these scenario steps conceptually as *joint activities* involving some number of agents. Joint activities in our example would be Make Booking, Pay Booking, etc. The details that need to be recorded for a joint activity (name, roles, goal, and relevant data) are the same as for a scenario but without any steps. Consequently, rather than introduce joint activity as a new step type, we simply allow the steps of a scenario to be optional. A minor change is that we allow the goal in the scenario descriptor to be a set of goals, interpreted as a conjunction, rather than a single goal. Figure 4 depicts the Travel Booking scenario with joint activities (scenarios) as the steps[4].

---

[4] Note that this scenario uses the roles of Hotel Provider and Flight Provider instead of the more general super-role Travel Agent.

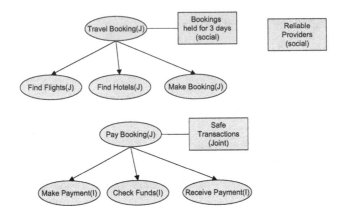

Fig. 3. Goal Overview Diagram. Ovals denote goals, and rectangles denote soft goals.

Scenario: Travel Booking
Goal(s): Travel Booking
Steps:

#	Type	Name	Role(s)	Data used	Data produced
1	Scenario	Find Flights	Flight Provider Customer	Flights Info	
2	Scenario	Find Hotels	Hotels Provider Customer	Hotels Info	
3	Scenario	Make Booking	Flight Provider Customer	Flights Info	Bookings
4	Scenario	Make Booking	Hotels Provider Customer	Hotels Info	Bookings
5	Scenario	Pay Booking	Bank, Customer	Bookings	Bookings, Flights Info
6	Scenario	Pay Booking	Bank, Customer	Bookings	Bookings, Hotels Info

Fig. 4. Example Scenario

Roles and Ontology: In standard Prometheus roles are identified by grouping goals (along with percepts and actions) into clusters and identifying a role that would manage these goals. Here we have already identified some roles in the analysis overview diagram. The clustering of goals may identify additional roles. In our example we identify the additional roles of Flight Provider, Hotel Provider, and payer. We then extend the standard Prometheus process to consider and capture sub-role relationships. In our example we identify Flight Provider and Hotel Provider as sub-types of Travel Agent. The exclusion relationships between roles (static separation of duties (SSD), and dynamic separation of duties (DSD)), required by Islander, is however left until the Social Design phase.

In addition to the roles played by agents entering the Electronic Institution, Islander has a concept of *internal roles* which are played by staff agents, and are part of managing the infrastructure of the EI. We do not necessarily identify these internal roles during the System Specification phase, as they are typically introduced during the Social

Design phase, where consideration is given to managing the infrastructure functions of the EI. If some such roles are identified at this stage, they should be marked as internal.

During scenario specification there is identification of data used and produced, which is the start of ontology definition, and is defined as such. In our example we identified Flight Info, Hotel Info and Booking as three necessary items in the ontology, and made some initial decisions about fields required.

Summary of Modifications to Prometheus: There are five modifications to the standard Prometheus process in order to have a process which facilitates and feeds into the Social Design phase done in Islander. These are:

(a) The analysis overview diagram was changed to capture roles (that would be taken on by agents entering the EI) as well as the actors external to the system, and also to include soft goals.
(b) A role hierarchy is developed, if appropriate. Also a distinction is introduced between internal roles ("staff" roles of the EI) and external roles (to be taken on by agents operating within the EI).
(c) Steps are made optional in a scenario to allow use of scenarios for modelling joint activities.
(d) The goal overview diagram is extended to allow soft-goals to be captured, and to allow different types of goals to be distinguished.
(e) Identification of data in scenario steps is extended to a preliminary ontology development activity.

3.2   Social Design

The social design phase, specifying the details of the Electronic Institution (completed using the Islander tool), takes input from the Prometheus based system specification. We structure this phase as eight separate steps. Note that, as with all system design and development, these are iterative rather than strictly sequential. The steps, along with the part of Islander that is addressed in each step, are as follows:

1. Develop the social structure (roles and relationships)
   Social Structure model (in the Dialogical Framework)
2. List scenes with participating roles (input to step 3)
3. Develop the performative structure (network of scenes) and initial flow
   Performative structure model
4. For each scene, define the interaction structure: basic conversation stages, and flow of conversation
   Interaction Structure
5. Develop the ontology (influenced by interaction model)
   Ontology Model (in the Dialogical Framework)
6. Define the information model, actions and constraints
   Interaction Model
7. Identify and specify norms
   Norms and Commitments Model
8. Check that all social goals have been achieved

In particular, steps 4-6 are performed for each scenario and are very iterative. We have presented them as distinct steps for two reasons. Firstly, because the steps are concerned with different parts of Islander (e.g. steps 4 and 5 are concerned with the interaction model and the ontology model respectively). Secondly, because the sequencing of the steps can vary: one possibility is to perform steps 4-6 for one scene, then perform them for the next scene, and so on; but it is also possible to perform steps 4 and 5 for each scene in sequence, and only then continue with step 6.

The rest of this section describes these steps in detail, with reference to our travel example.

Step 1: Develop the Social Structure (Roles and Relationships). In this (simple) step we refine the roles identified in the system specification phase by adding further relationship information.

We begin by simply transcribing the roles that have been identified in the previous phase. In our example these are Travel Agent, Customer, Bank, Flight Provider and Hotel Provider. We then add any additional roles we recognize as being necessary internal roles (though these may well be added later when considering norms), and further develop the role structure if desired. In our example we decide to introduce an internal Reliability Monitor role to maintain information about providers in order to support the soft goal of "Reliable Providers".

Finally, we consider and specify exclusivity relationships: which roles cannot be filled by the same agent. As discussed in section 2, Islander defines both a static and a dynamic separation of duties. In our example, it is fairly clear that the Reliability Monitor should be separate from the provider or consumer of the service that is being monitored, and so we add an SSD (Static) relationship between the Reliability Monitor and the Travel Agent, and between the Reliability Monitor role and the Customer role.

Step 2: List Scenes with Participating Roles. Having refined the roles that exist in the institution, the next step is to define the scenes that these roles will participate in. A good starting point for identifying scenes is to take the joint activities (sub-scenarios) that are the steps of scenarios in the previous phase. (These are primarily scenarios that have no sub-scenario steps.) It is also useful to consider whether certain scenarios can be generalized into a common scenario type which permits two or more of the existing scenarios to be merged. There are certain commonly-used types, such as information seeking, that can often be used to do this generalization.

For example, looking at the scenario in figure 4, we have six sub-scenarios that could become scenes. In this case we decide that finding a flight and finding a hotel may have significant differences in the information that is exchanged, but that once information has been found, booking a hotel and booking a flight are likely to be similar enough that they can be merged into a more generic booking scene. Similarly, paying for a flight and paying for a hotel are merged into a payment scene. This gives us the following scenes: Hotel Info, Flight Info, Booking, and Payment. Additionally, Islander requires a starting and ending scene (respectively called Enter and Exit), and so these are added.

If the scenario structure is deeply nested, then it may be useful to use nested performative structures as a way of modeling the interaction in such a way that the complexity at each level is manageable.

When defining scenes, we need to think about a number of properties of scenes such as cardinalities (will there be one instance of the scene or many?), what triggers scene creation, and, where there are multiple scene instances, whether agents join all scene instances, one instance only, or some subset of the scene instances. For example, for the Hotel Info scene we choose to have one scene per Hotel Provider, with the Customer choosing to join some subset of the available scenes. Since there is one scene instance per Hotel Provider, it makes sense for new scene instances to be created when a Hotel Provider moves into the scene.

Finally, we need to consider whether multiple scenes may map to the same underlying scene type. In Islander, nodes in the performative structure are scenes, which are instances of scene types. Although often there is a one-to-one mapping between scenes and scene types, in some cases, multiple scenes map to the same scene type. For example, it may be possible to define a scene type Travel Info which both Hotel Info and Travel Info are instances of. However the message contents (as well as the roles) must be the same, if scenes are of the same type. As the information required about flights is quite different than that required for hotels we decide not to generalize to a Travel Info scene type as it would preclude us from having the flight/hotel specific structure in the messages.

Step 3: Develop the Performative Structure (Network of Scenes) and Initial Flow.
Having defined what scenes exist, based on the scenarios, we now develop the performative structure which shows how the scenes are linked up and how agents "flow" between the scenes. Additionally, we define which roles play parts in which scenes (initial information is based on the scenarios), and specify how many instances of the roles can take part in a scene instance. For example, one of the scenes is Flight Info. This scene involves the roles of Customer and Flight Provider, with potentially many Customers, but exactly one Flight Provider. We define the minimum number of Customer roles to be 0, and the maximum 1, while both minimum and maximum for the Flight Provider role are defined as 1.

In order to obtain the flows between scenes we can start by mapping the flow implied within our scenarios from the previous phase. We then visit each scene in turn to determine where else each agent might go, from that scene, other than what was captured in the scenario. In the particular scenario we had developed a Customer and Flight Provider start off (after entry) in the Flight Info scene. In the following step, the Customer is in the Hotel Info scene, implying that the Customer can move from Flight Info to Hotel Info. In generalizing we recognize that the customer can move back and forth between these two scenes, and could in fact come to either of them after the entry scene. Scenario variation descriptions from the system specification phase may provide information regarding additional flows. When specifying how a role can move between scenes, we must also consider whether they will go to one, some, or all instances of that scene. For example we have a Flight Info scene for each provider, so a Customer may well choose to go (simultaneously) to multiple scene instances. Therefore we choose *some* as the specification.

By default if a role can transition to multiple scenes, we use an OR connector. If there is only a single choice, we could make it either AND or OR. However we choose OR, in order to highlight any actual cases of AND which are more unusual.

As we define the flows it is sometimes necessary to introduce new roles. For example, in defining the flow into the Booking scene, we need the Customer to be able to be accompanied by either the Flight Provider (coming from the Flight Info scene), or the Hotel Provider (coming from the Hotel Info scene). As the flight and hotel providers will play the same role within the Booking scene, we need to introduce a new role, which each of them can transform into. We introduce the Booking Provider role, which is added to the role structure. We also introduce the role Payer at this stage for the Banking scene, which the Customer transforms into, as it is somewhat more generic.

As we develop the performative structure it sometimes becomes quite complex, in which case it can be advantageous to abstract a part of it and have nested performative structures. Figure 5 shows the performative structure developed for our example. It could be an option to abstract the structure between flightinfo, hotelinfo and booking into a sub-performative structure (which is actually the scenario structure identified at the top level in the analysis overview).

Step 4: for each Scene, Define the Interaction Structure. The next step involves development of the details of the interaction within a particular scene. The representation used here is a directed graph, which can be seen as an annotated finite state machine. Transitions between states are messages, with the contents defined according to the ontology model. Consequently there is substantial interaction with step 5, development of the ontology. Each state is also annotated with information as to which role types can enter ("+") or leave ("−") at that state. There is also a "stay-and-go" ("+−") annotation which allows an agent to simultaneously be in multiple scenes. For example, when a Flight Provider leaves a scene, with a Customer, in order to make a booking (in the Booking scene), it also stays within the Flight Info scene to attend to other customers.

Figure 6 shows the annotated states and message transitions for the Hotel Info scene in our example. There are some issues to determine in setting up when a Customer may leave the scene. If we wished to require that a Customer waited to receive the response to a request, before leaving, we would not allow them to leave at S1. However this would have the effect that no Customer would be able to leave while any Customer was awaiting

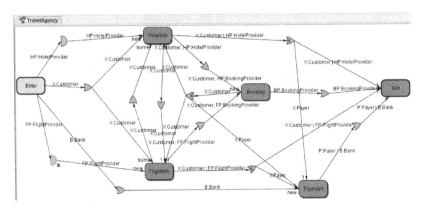

Fig. 5. Performative Structure (from Islander)

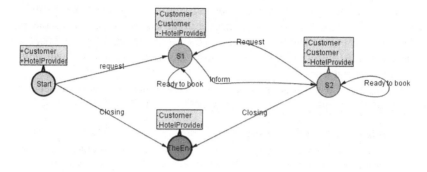

Fig. 6. Hotel Info Scene (from Islander)

a response. If finding information took some time, this could cause unnecessary delays. Consequently we allow a Customer to leave without waiting to receive a response, if desired. Customers tell Hotel Providers when they are ready to go and book so both can ask the infrastructure to leave and enact a booking scene. The scene ends when the Hotel Provider sends a closing message, as customers can come and go as desired.

Part of this step also involves defining the structure of the relevant messages, which is done in Islander by opening a message specification window, where we specify the illocutionary particle, sender, receiver, and message content. For example, the left-most *request* arc may be specified as being from a Customer to a Hotel Provider, and containing a location, desired check in and check out dates, and the class of hotel sought.

Step 5: Define the Ontology. There is some initial ontological information specified during the System Specification phase, as one identifies the information needed within scenarios. This can be brought into the Social Design and provides the basis for more thorough refinement and development. In our example the types of data that have been identified are Hotel Info, Flight Info and Booking. We determine that Booking really needs to be specialized into Flight Booking and Hotel Booking, so these are added to the ontology.

As messages are developed in a scene, this typically results in further additions to the ontology. For example when defining the messages in the Hotel Info scene we recognize the need for a Hotel Info data type and add this into the ontology.

Step 6: Define the Information Model. Having defined the details of scenes, we also need to specify what information needs to be maintained within the system, for use either by the institution, or by the agents filling the roles. All information that will be referenced within constraints or norms, needs to be part of the information model. Actions then need to be defined for the roles which modify and access this information model. For each property in the information model it must be considered whether the information should be defined per role, or per institution.

One particular type of information that needs to be maintained in our example is the bookings that a customer has, and the payments which are due for those bookings. This is clearly information which is required for each Customer role. Consequently we create Payment Due, as a list of Payment Details, within the Customer role. We then add actions that update this. For example an accept in the Booking scene causes the action to add the payment to the list of payments due for that Customer. In the Payment scene when a payment is successful (i.e. confirmed by the Bank) this results in an action to remove that payment from the list.

Constraints are also added at this stage. An example constraint in our model is that a Customer can only request to make a Payment that is in its Payments Due list.

Step 7: Identify and Specify Norms. Norms are conditions that should be ensured by the infrastructure of the institution. They are specified in Islander, in terms of an antecedent utterance which triggers the commitments associated with the norm, a consequent which captures the commitment or obligation, and an utterance (called the defeasible antecedent) which specifies when the commitment is regarded as being fulfilled. The norms are usually defined towards the end of the Social Design process when the infrastructure is fully defined. An example norm from our travel institution is that if a Booking is made, the agent cannot leave the institution until the corresponding payment is made.

Step 8: Check all Social Goals are Achieved. Finally we check through all of the social goals to ensure that some aspect of the institution does ensure that these are met. In our example one of the social goals that was identified was ensuring that service providers were reliable. This is not something that can be specified by a norm or constraint based on the current specification. One solution may be to introduce a scene where customers can make complaints which will be maintained by the institution, and any provider having too many complaints could then be banned from entering the institution, thus providing some level of realization of this social goal.

Iteration through the Islander Models: The steps described should ensure a thorough design of the electronic institution within Islander. They cover each of the Islander models: the Dialogical Framework with the roles and ontology, the Performative Structure that captures the scenes and transitions between them, the Interaction Model which specifies the allowable communication patterns within each scene, and the Norms and Commitments.

3.3 Architectural Design

The main tasks of the Architectural Design in Prometheus are to determine the agent types, to specify various details regarding these, and to develop protocol specifications, including messages. This results in a system overview diagram which gives an overview of the agents, the interactions between them, and the interface to the environment (in terms of percepts and actions); as well as *interaction protocols* specified in AUML[5], which are developed by refining scenarios to give interaction diagrams, which in turn are generalized to provide protocol specifications. As part of developing the protocols, the messages between agents are also specified.

---

[5] http://www.auml.org

The decision as to which roles to combine into agents is based on standard software engineering concepts of cohesion, coupling and modularity. The agent goals, along with the percepts they receive and the actions they execute, are then propagated from the system specification. In addition the developer is prompted to consider a range of questions regarding initialization, cardinality, and other aspects of the agent.

This step, of deciding how to group roles into agents, remains essentially unchanged, except that the Social Design phase may well influence this. We do add a field in the agent descriptor to allow specification of norms that apply to an agent. This information will then be passed to the detailed design where agent behaviour should be developed to respect these norms.

The introduction of the Social Design phase means that a large part of the message and interaction specification has already been done. We note though that there is some difference in that the interactions of the Social Design phase are between roles, whereas standard Prometheus design specifies interactions between agent types. If the choice is made to implement an agent type for each role in the Social Design there is no difference. However, if some roles are combined into a single agent type, then some adjustments may be needed.

For example in our travel institution we may decide to combine the Flight Provider and the Hotel Provider into a single Travel Agent agent type. This combination is straightforward in that none of the specified interactions are between Flight Provider and Hotel Provider. Consequently we can just replace Flight Provider and Hotel Provider by Travel Agent as we convert the interaction specified in the scene, to an AUML protocol.[6] In cases where there are potential interactions between roles that have been incorporated into the same agent type, we must ensure that we do still specify the interactions that may happen as a result of two agent instances of this type, playing different roles.

The ontology of the Social Design phase can be incorporated directly into the Architectural Design, and once the mapping between roles and agents is clear, it is obvious which agents deal with which data.

It may be the case that not all agents in the system being developed participate in the electronic institution. If this is the case standard Prometheus process needs to be followed to develop the interaction protocols involving these agents. In some cases there may be a situation where an agent is interacting with another agent outside the EI, within the same protocol that it is interacting within the EI. From the point of view of the EI, these additional interactions are part of the agent internals. But from the point of view of the entire system they are part of a larger interaction protocol. For example if our system included an agent, outside of the EI, whose job it was to continually search the Internet for good flight deals within Europe, then our flight provider may well interact with this agent to get up to date information, between the request and the inform within the Islander flight info scene.

Consequently, although a substantial amount of information can be incorporated from the Social Design into the Architectural Design, it is still necessary to consider all the Prometheus steps, in the case that there are some parts of the system that do not participate in the electronic Institution.

---

[6] This can likely be automated, but we have not yet done this, nor investigated it fully.

4 Related Work

Engineering multi agent systems (MAS) is an intricate task that sits on top of disciplines like distributed and normative systems, and that frequently uses metaphors from the social sciences (e.g. sociology, economy, or psychology). It would therefore be lengthy to try and make a complete summary of the state of the art that covers all the sources of influence. We will therefore concentrate on work that is more directly related to MAS organizations and software development methodologies.

The organization of a MAS consists of the roles, relationships, and power and authority relationships among the roles that structure the behaviour of the agents. For any agent, the access permissions, actions allowed, and interactions permitted depend to a large extent on what roles the agent might incarnate within an organization. For instance, the organization associated to an electronic institution is called its *social model* and is specified as a set or roles, a role hierarchy, and user-defined relationships. The actions permitted are determined by some system-defined relationships (static and dynamic separation of duties), by the role flow policy in the performative structure, and by the protocols within scenes.

All MAS have an organization of some sort underpinning them, and in the literature of agents there is a large corpus of work devoted to studying the algorithmics and the problem solving capabilities that different organizations may show. Some of the most-studied organizational structures are *hierarchies, coalitions* and *teams*.

Hierarchies [14] are the most primitive, where the tree of the hierarchy determines the interactions that might happen (between parents and children only) and thus how the information flows (up and down), and the authority relationship (top-down). Electronic institutions could be embedded with hierarchical organizations if care is taken in the performative structure to only allow the type of interactions that the hierarchy establishes. The authority relationship is mapped easily by the hierarchy defined in the social model.

Coalitions [15] are organizations that are much more dynamic in the sense that the structure is not fixed at specification time but it is an 'agreement' that agents commit to in order to act in a co-ordinated way. Coalitions need therefore to be formed at run time upon a certain common goal. Algorithms to determine the optimal coalition structure for a problem have been studied [16].

Teams [17], like coalitions, are dynamically organized groups of agents that have different individual goals but that co-operate to attain a certain global goal that requires the concourse of all of the members of the team. In both cases, coalitions and teams, the institutional perspective is that of laying down the infrastructure that would permit the dialogues and commitments among the agents (together perhaps with norms that would punish the violation of agreements).

A large number of MAS software development methodologies have been proposed recently (e.g. see [18,19]). Although they are based on strong agent-oriented foundations and offer original contributions at the design level, they are unsatisfactory for developing EIs: most MAS methodologies, although they necessarily deal with structures of agents and interations between agents, do not explicitly represent community or social concepts. More generally, the formal definition of organization-centered patterns and social structures in general (e.g. [5,20,21]), and their computational realization remain open issues (as noted in [22]).

This work provides a detailed methodology for developing an explicit institutional structure, and embeds this into an existing MAS methodology. The integration within the Prometheus methodology means that Prometheus (and PDT) can then be used to design and develop the agents that will participate in the specified Electronic Institution.

Our approach shares some similarities with the OperA methodology [5]. OperA builds upon the idea of an organizational model, consisting of roles and their relationships, similar to those we use, and an interaction model inspired by the electronic institution concept, that determines the activities agents get engaged in. Norms are non-operational concepts in OperA that describe the behaviour of agents in an abstract way. In our approach we opt for a more grounded approach that permits certain verifications of agent behaviour. Finally, OperA defines the initial part of the interaction network (start scene) as the setting of a social model where agents agree on social contracts that later on they will freely respect in their interactions.

Although some agent infrastructures such as DARPA COABS[7] and FIPA compliant platforms such as JADE [23] deal with many issues that are essential for open agent interactions — communication, identification, synchronization, matchmaking — they are arguably too distant from organization-centered patterns or social structures. Also, although some infrastructure work, perhaps most notably the work on TuCSoN [24], has investigated linking lower-level infrastructure with social laws (e.g. [25]), clear methodological guidance for a designer has not been well addressed.

Among the few other proposals we can mention the proposal by Hanachi [26] that allows for specifications of interaction protocols that need to be subsequently compiled into a sort of executable protocol brokers called moderators. Also, in Tropos, the specifications are transformed into agent skeletons that must be extended with code. However, at execution time there is no mechanism to ensure that agents follow the specification of the system.

A promising line of work is the one adopted by Omicini and Castelfranchi (e.g. [27]). It postulates some significant similarities with the EI approach: focus on the social aspects of the interactions, a unified metaphor that prevails along the development cycle, and the construction of tools to implement methodological ideas. However, the actual development of the methodology and the associated tools appears to be still rather tentative.

5   Conclusion

We have presented a methodology for designing e-institutions that extends the Prometheus methodology with a social design phase, where Islander is used to design an institution.

It appears to be relatively straightforward to actually integrate the two tools (PDT and Islander) by means of XML specifications of entities that are passed between them. This work is currently in progress. We are also investigating developing skeleton code from the Prometheus Detailed Design, which can be integrated into Ameli at runtime.

---

[7] http://coabs.globalinfotek.com/

References

1. Horling, B., Lesser, V.: A survey of multi-agent organizational paradigms. The Knowledge Engineering Review **19** (2005) 281–316
2. Esteva, M.: Electronic Institutions: from specification to development. IIIA PhD Monography. Vol. 19 (2003)
3. Rodríguez-Aguilar, J.A.: On the Design and Construction of Agent-mediated Electronic Institutions. IIIA Phd Monography. Vol. 14 (2001)
4. Noriega, P.: Agent-Mediated Auctions: The Fishmarket Metaphor. IIIA Phd Monography. Vol. 8 (1997)
5. Dignum, V.: A Model for Organizational Interaction. PhD thesis, Dutch Research School for Information and Knowledge Systems (2004) ISBN 90-393-3568-0.
6. Esteva, M., de la Cruz, D., Sierra, C.: Islander: an electronic institutions editor. In: Proceedings of the First International Joint Conference on Autonomous Agents and Multi-agent Systems (AAMAS 2002), Bologna, Italy (2002) 1045–1052
7. Arcos, J.L., Esteva, M., Noriega, P., Rodríguez, J.A., Sierra, C.: Engineering open environments with electronic institutions. Journal on Engineering Applications of Artificial Intelligence **18** (2005) 191204
8. Padgham, L., Winikoff, M.: Developing Intelligent Agent Systems: A Practical Guide. John Wiley and Sons (2004) ISBN 0-470-86120-7.
9. Padgham, L., Thangarajah, J., Winikoff, M.: Tool Support for Agent Development using the Prometheus Methodology. In: First international workshop on Integration of Software Engineering and Agent Technology (ISEAT 2005), Melbourne, Australia (2005)
10. Esteva, M., Rodríguez-Aguilar, J.A., Sierra, C., Arcos, J.L., Garcia, P.: On the formal specification of electronic institutions. In Sierra, C., Dignum, F., eds.: Agent-mediated Electronic Commerce: The European AgentLink Perspective. Number 1991 in Lecture Notes in Artificial Intelligence. Springer-Verlag (2001) 126–147
11. Rodríguez-Aguilar, J.A., Noriega, P., Sierra, C., Padget, J.: Fm96.5 a Java-based Electronic Auction House. In: Second International Conference on The Practical Application of Intelligent Agents and Multi-Agent Technology(PAAM'97). (1997) 207–224
12. Cuní, G., Esteva, M., Garcia, P., Puertas, E., Sierra, C., Solchaga, T.: MASFIT: Multi-agent Systems for Fish Trading. In: 16th European Conference on Artificial Intelligence (ECAI 2004), Valencia, Spain (2004) 710–714
13. van Lamsweerde, A.: Goal-oriented requirements engineering: A guided tour. In: Proceedings of the 5th IEEE International Symposium on Requirements Engineering (RE'01), Toronto (2001) 249–263
14. Fox, M.S.: Organization structuring: Designing large complex software. Technical Report CMU-CS-79-155, Carnegie-Mellon University (1979)
15. Shehory, O., Kraus, S.: Methods for task allocation via agent coalition formation. Artificial Intelligence **101** (1998) 165–200
16. Chvatal, V.: A greedy heuristic for the set covering problem. Mathematics of Operations Research **4** (1979)
17. Tambe, M.: Towards flexible teamwork. Journal of Artificial Intelligence Research **7** (1997) 83–124
18. Henderson-Sellers, B., Giorgini, P., eds.: Agent-Oriented Methodologies. Idea Group Publishing (2005)
19. Bergenti, F., Gleizes, M.P., Zambonelli, F., eds.: Methodologies and Software Engineering for Agent Systems. The Agent-Oriented Software Engineering Handbook. Kluwer Publishing (2004) ISBN 1-4020-8057-3.

20. Parunak, H., Odell, J.: Representing social structures in UML. In: Agent-Oriented Software Engineering II. LNCS 2222. Springer-Verlag (2002) 1–16
21. Vazquez, J., Dignum, F.: Modelling electronic organizations. In: Multi-Agent Systems and Applications III. Volume 2691 of LNAI. Springer-Verlag (2003) 584–593
22. Zambonelli, F., Jennings, N., Wooldridge, M.: Developing multiagent systems: The gaia methodology. ACM Transactions on Software Engineering and Methodology **12** (2003) 317–370
23. Bellifemine, F., Poggi, A., Rimassa, G.: Developing Multi-Agent Systems with JADE. In Castelfranchi, C., Lesperance, Y., eds.: Intelligent Agents VII. Number 1571 in Lecture Notes in Artificial Intelligence. Springer-Verlag (2001) 89–103
24. Cremonini, M., Omicini, A., Zambonelli, F.: Multi-agent systems on the Internet: Extending the scope of coordination towards security and topology. In Garijo, F.J., Boman, M., eds.: Multi-Agent Systems Engineering. Volume 1647 of LNAI., Springer-Verlag (1999) 77–88 9th European Workshop on Modelling Autonomous Agents in a Multi-Agent World (MAA-MAW'99), Valencia, Spain, 30 June – 2 July 1999. Proceedings.
25. Ciancarini, P., Omicini, A., Zambonelli, F.: Multiagent system engineering: The coordination viewpoint. In Jennings, N.R., Lespérance, Y., eds.: Intelligent Agents VI. Agent Theories, Architectures, and Languages. Volume 1757 of LNAI., Springer-Verlag (2000) 250–259 6th International Workshop (ATAL'99), Orlando, FL, USA, 15–17 July 1999. Proceedings.
26. Hanachi, C., Sibertin-Blanc, C.: Protocol Moderators as Active Middle-Agents in Multi-Agent Systems. Journal of Autonomous Agents and Multiagent Systems **8** (2004)
27. Omicini, A., Ricci, A., Viroli, M., Castelfranchi, C., Tummolini, L.: Coordination artifacts: Environment-based coordination for intelligent agents. In: Third International Joint Conference on Autonomous Agents and Multi-agent Systems (AAMAS'04), New York, USA (2004) 286–293

Modeling Mental States in the Analysis of Multiagent Systems Requirements

Alexei Lapouchnian[1] and Yves Lespérance[2]

[1] Department of Computer Science, University of Toronto, Toronto, ON, M5S 3G4, Canada
alexei@cs.toronto.edu
[2] Department of Computer Science and Engineering, York University, Toronto,
ON, M3J 1P3, Canada
lesperan@cs.yorku.ca

Abstract. This paper describes an agent-oriented requirements engineering approach that combines informal i^* models with formal specifications in the multiagent system specification formalism CASL. This allows the requirements engineer to exploit the complementary features of the frameworks. i^* can be used to model social dependencies between agents and how process design choices affect the agents' goals. CASL can be used to model complex processes formally. We introduce an intermediate notation to support the mapping between i^* models and CASL specifications. In the combined i^*-CASL framework, agents' goals and knowledge are represented as their mental states, which allows for the formal analysis and verification of, among other things, complex agent interactions where agents may have different goals and different (incomplete) knowledge. Our models can also serve as high-level specifications for multiagent systems.

1 Introduction

Modern software systems are becoming increasingly complex, with lots of intricate interactions. The recent popularity of electronic commerce, web services, etc. confirms the need for software engineering methods for constructing applications that are open, distributed, and adaptable to change. This is why many researchers and practitioners are looking at agent technology as a basis for distributed applications.

Agents are active, social, and adaptable software system entities situated in some environment and capable of autonomous execution of actions in order to achieve their set objectives [25]. Furthermore, most problems are too complex to be solved by just one agent; one must create a multiagent system (MAS) with several agents having to work together to achieve their objectives and ultimately deliver the desired application. Therefore, adopting the agent-oriented approach to software engineering means that the problem is decomposed into multiple, autonomous, interacting agents, each with their own objectives (goals). Agents in MAS frequently represent individuals, companies, etc. This means that there is an "underlying organizational context" [7] in MAS. Like humans, agents need to coordinate their activities, cooperate, request help from others, etc., often through negotiation. Unlike in object-oriented or component-based systems, interactions in multiagent systems occur through high-level agent communication

L. Padgham and F. Zambonelli (Eds.): AOSE 2006, LNCS 4405, pp. 104–121, 2007.

languages, so these interactions are mostly viewed not at the syntactic level, but "at the knowledge level, in terms of goal delegation, etc." [7].

In requirements engineering (RE), *goal-oriented approaches* (e.g, KAOS [3]) have become prominent. In Goal-Oriented Requirements Engineering (GORE), high-level stakeholder objectives are identified as goals and later refined into fine-grained requirements assignable to agents/components in the system-to-be or in its environment. Reliance on goals makes goal-oriented requirements engineering methods and agent-oriented software engineering a great match. Moreover, agent-oriented analysis is central to requirements engineering since the assignment of responsibilities for goals and constraints among the components in the system-to-be and the agents in the environment is the main result of the RE process. Therefore, it is natural to use a goal-oriented requirements engineering approach when developing MAS. With GORE, it is easy to make the transition from the requirements to the high-level MAS specifications. For example, strategic relationships among agents will become high-level patterns of inter-agent communication. Thus, it would be desirable to devise an *agent-oriented RE approach with a formal component that supports rigorous formal analysis, including reasoning about agents' goals and knowledge*.

In the above context, while it is possible to informally analyze small systems, formal analysis is needed for any realistically-sized system to determine whether such distributed requirements imposed on each agent in a MAS are correctly decomposed from the stakeholder goals, consistent and, if properly met, achieve the system's overall objectives. Thus, the aim of this work is to devise an agent-oriented requirements engineering approach with a formal component that supports reasoning about agents' goals (and knowledge), thereby allowing for rigorous formal analysis of the requirements expressed as the objectives of the agents in a MAS.

In our approach, we integrate the i^* modeling framework [27] with CASL [19, 18], a formal agent-oriented specification language that supports the modeling of agent mental states. This gives the modeler the flexibility and intuitiveness of the i^* notation as well as the powerful formal analysis capability of CASL. To bridge the gap between informal i^* diagrams and formal CASL specifications we propose an intermediate notation that can be easily obtained from i^* models and then mapped into CASL. With our i^*-CASL-based approach, a CASL model can be used both as a requirements analysis tool and as a formal high-level specification for a multiagent system that satisfies the requirements. This model can be formally analyzed using the CASLve [20, 18] tool or other tools and the results can be fed back into the requirements model.

One of the main features of this approach is that goals (and knowledge) are assigned to particular agents thus becoming their subjective attributes as opposed to being objective system properties as in many other approaches (e.g., Tropos [1] and KAOS [3]). This allows for the modeling of conflicting goals, agent negotiation, information exchange, complex agent interaction protocols, etc.

The rest of the paper is organized as follows: Section 2 briefly describes the concepts of i^* and CASL, Section 3 discusses our approach in detail, and Section 4 concludes the paper.

2   Background

2.1   The i^* Framework

i^* [27] is an agent-oriented modeling framework that is mostly used for requirements engineering. i^* centers on the notion of *intentional actor* and *intentional dependency*. Actors are described in their organizational setting and have attributes such as goals, abilities, beliefs, etc. In i^*, an actor can use opportunities to depend on other actors in achieving its objectives, at the same time becoming vulnerable if those actors do not deliver. Dependencies in i^* are *intentional* since they appear as a result of actors pursuing their goals.

To illustrate the approach, we use a variant of the meeting scheduling problem, which has become a popular exemplar in Requirements Engineering. In the context of the i^* modeling framework a meeting scheduling process was first analyzed in [27]. We modified the meeting scheduling process to make our models easier to understand. For instance, we take the length of meetings to be the whole day. We also introduced a legacy software system called the Meeting Room Booking System (MRBS) that handles the booking of meeting rooms. The complete case study is presented in [8].

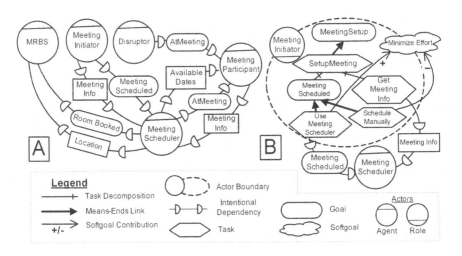

Fig. 1. SD (A) and SR (B) models for the meeting scheduler process

The i^* framework has two main components: the *Strategic Dependency (SD) model* and the *Strategic Rationale (SR) model*. The former describes the external relationships among actors, while the latter focuses on exploring the rationale behind the processes in organizations from the point of view of participating actors. SD models are networks of actors (which can be agents, positions, and roles) and dependencies. Depending actors are called *dependers* and depended-upon actors are called *dependees*. There can be four types of dependencies based on what is being delegated — a goal, a task, a resource, and a softgoal. Softgoals are related to the notion of non-functional requirements [2] and model quality constraints on the system.

Fig. 1A is the SD diagram showing the computerized Meeting Scheduler (MS) agent in its environment. Here, the role Meeting Initiator (MI) depends on the MS for scheduling meetings and for being informed about the meeting details. The MS, in turn, depends on the MP (Meeting Participant) role for attending meetings and for providing his/her available dates to it. The MS uses the booking system to book rooms for meetings. The Disruptor actor represents outside actors that cause changes in participants' schedules, thus modeling the environment dynamics.

SR models enable the analyst to assess alternatives in the definition of actor processes to better address their concerns. Four types of nodes are used in SR models — goals, tasks, softgoals, and resources — and three types of links — means-ends links, task decompositions links, and softgoal contribution links. Means-ends links specify alternative ways to achieve goals; task decomposition links connect tasks with components needed for their execution. For example, Fig. 1B is a simple SR model showing some details of the MI process. To schedule meetings, the MI can either do it manually, or delegate it to the scheduler. Quality requirements (softgoals), such as `MinimizeEffort` in Fig. 1B, are used to evaluate these alternatives. Contribution links specify how alternatives contribute to quality constraints.

2.2   The Formal Foundations: CASL

The Cognitive Agents Specification Language (CASL) [19, 18] is a formal specification language that combines theories of action [15, 16] and mental states [17] expressed in the situation calculus [10] with ConGolog [4], a concurrent, non-deterministic agent-oriented programming language with a formal semantics. In CASL, agents' goals and knowledge are modeled formally; communication actions are provided to update these mental states and ConGolog is then used to specify the behaviour of agents. This combination produces a very expressive language that supports high-level reasoning about the agents' mental states. The logical foundations of CASL allow it to be used to specify and analyze a wide variety of MAS including non-deterministic systems and systems with an incompletely specified initial state.

CASL specifications consist of two parts: the model of the domain and its dynamics (the declarative part) and the specification of the agents' behaviour (the procedural part). The domain is modeled in terms of the following entities: 1) *primitive actions* — all changes in the domain are due to primitive actions being executed by agents; 2) *situations*, which are states of the domain that result from the execution of sequences of actions (there is a set of initial situations, with no predecessor, corresponding to the ways agents think the world might be like initially); 3) *fluents*, which are predicates and functions that may change value from situation to situation. The fluent `Room(meetingID,date,room,s)`, where s is a situation parameter, models the fact that a room has been booked on some day for some meeting in a situation s.

To specify the dynamics of an application domain, we use the following types of axioms: 1) *action precondition axioms* that describe under what conditions actions can be performed; 2) *successor state axioms* (SSA), which were introduced in [15] as a solution to the frame problem and specify how primitive actions affect fluents; 3) *initial state axioms*, which describe the initial state of the domain and the initial mental states of the agents; 4) *other axioms* that include unique name axioms for actions and domain independent foundational axioms.

Agents' behaviour is specified using a rich high-level programming language with recursive procedures, loops, conditionals, non-determinism, concurrency, and interrupts [4]. The following table lists most of the available constructs:

α,	primitive action
ϕ?,	wait for a condition (test)
$\delta_1 \; ; \; \delta_2$,	sequence
$\delta_1 \mid \delta_2$,	nondeterministic branch
$\pi \, v. \, \delta$,	nondeterministic choice of argument
δ^*,	nondeterministic iteration
if ϕ **then** δ_1 **else** δ_2 **endIf**,	conditional
while ϕ **do** δ **endWhile**,	while loop
for $v : \phi$ **do** δ **endFor**,	for loop
$\delta_1 \parallel \delta_2$,	concurrency with equal priority
$\delta_1 \rangle\!\rangle \delta_2$,	concurrency with δ_1 at a higher priority
guard ϕ **do** δ **endGuard**,	guard
$\langle \, v : \phi \rightarrow \delta \, \textbf{until} \, \alpha \, \rangle$,	interrupt
$p(\boldsymbol{\theta})$,	procedure call

The guard operator (defined in [8]) blocks execution of the program δ until its condition ϕ holds. For an interrupt operator, when its condition ϕ holds for some value of v, the interrupt triggers and the body δ is executed. Afterwards, the interrupt may trigger again provided that the cancellation condition α does not hold. The "for loop" construct is defined in [18].

Also, CASL supports formal modeling of agents' goals and knowledge. The representation for both goals and knowledge is based on a *possible worlds semantics* incorporated into the situation calculus, where situations are viewed as possible worlds [11, 17]. CASL uses accessibility relations K and W to model what an agent knows and what it wants respectively. K(agt,s',s) holds if the situation s' is compatible with what the agent agt knows in situation s, i.e., in situation s, the agent thinks that it might be in the situation s'. In this case, the situation s' is called K-*accessible*. When an agent does not know the value of some formula ϕ, it considers possible (formally, K-accessible) some situations where ϕ is true and some where it is false. An agent knows some formula ϕ if ϕ is true in all its K-accessible situations: **Know**(agt,ϕ,s) = $\forall$ s'(K(agt,s',s) $\supset$ ϕ[s']). Constraints on the K relation ensure that agents have positive and negative introspection (i.e., agents know whether they know/don't know something) and guarantee that what is known is true. Communication actions such as inform are used for exchanging information among agents. The preconditions for the inform action ensure that no false information is transmitted. The changes to agents' knowledge due to communication and other actions are specified by the SSA for the K relation. The axiom ensures that agents are aware of the execution of all actions. This formal framework is quite simple and idealized. More complex versions of the SSA can be specified, for example, to handle encrypted messages [19] or to provide belief revision [21]. For convenience, abbreviations **KWhether**(agt,ϕ,s), which means that the agent knows either ϕ or its negation, and **KRef**(agt,θ,s), which indicates that the agent knows the value of θ, are used.

The accessibility relation W(agt,s',s) holds if in situation s an agent considers that everything that it wants to be true actually holds in s', which is called W-accessible. **Goal**(agt,ψ,s) indicates that in situation s the agent agt has the goal that ψ holds. The definition of **Goal** says that ψ must be true in all W-accessible situations that have a K-accessible situation in their past. This way, while agents may want something they know is impossible to obtain, the goals of agents must be consistent with what they currently know. In our approach, we mostly use achievement goals that specify the desired states of the world. We use the formula **Goal**(agt,**Eventually**(ψ),s) to state that agt has the goal that ψ is eventually true. The request and cancelRequest actions are used to request services and cancel these requests. Requests are used to establish intentional dependencies among agents. The dynamics of the W relation, which is affected by request, etc., are specified by a SSA. There are constraints on the W and K relations, which ensure that agents' goals are consistent and that agents introspect their goals. See [18, 19] for more details about CASL, as well as [8] for details about how we have adapted it for use with i^* for requirements engineering.

3   The i^*-CASL Process

3.1   Increasing Precision with iASR Models

Our aim in this approach is to tightly associate SR models with formal specifications in CASL. The standard SR diagrams are geared to informal analysis and can be very ambiguous. For instance, they lack details on whether the subtasks in task decompositions are supposed to be executed sequentially, concurrently, under certain conditions, etc. CASL, on the other hand, is a precise language. To handle this precision mismatch we use Intentional Annotated SR (iASR) models that help in bridging the gap between SR models and CASL specifications. Our goal is to make iASR models precise graphical representation for the procedural component of CASL specifications. The starting point for developing an iASR diagram for an actor is the regular SR diagram for that actor (e.g., see Fig. 1B). It can then be appropriately transformed into an iASR model through the steps described below.

Annotations. The main tool that we use for disambiguating SR models is *annotations*. Annotations allow analysts to model the domain more precisely and to capture data/control dependencies among goals and other details. Annotations, proposed in [24] for use with SR models and ConGolog, are textual constraints on iASR models and can be of several types: composition and link annotations, and applicability conditions. Composition annotations (specified by σ in Fig. 2A) are applied to task and means-ends decompositions and specify how the subtasks/subgoals are to be combined to execute/achieve the supertask/supergoal. Four types of compositions are allowed: sequence (";"), which is default for task decompositions, concurrency ("∥"), prioritized concurrency ("⟫"), and alternative ("|"), which is the default for means-ends decompositions. These annotations are applied to subtasks/subgoals from left to right. The choice of composition annotations is based on the ways actions and procedures can be composed together in CASL. In some approaches, for example, the Trust-Confidence-Distrust method of [6] that also uses i^*, sequencing among subtasks/subgoals is captured using precedence links. We believe that the arrangement of nodes from left to right based on their sequence/priority/etc. simplifies the understanding of models.

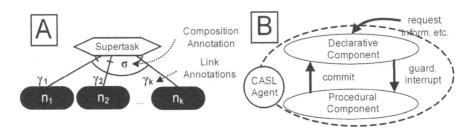

Fig. 2. Specifying annotations (A) and using them to synchronize procedural and declarative components (B) in CASL specifications

Link annotations (γ_i in Fig. 2A) are applied to subtasks/subgoals (n_i) and specify how/under what conditions they are supposed to be achieved/executed. There are six types of link annotations (corresponding to CASL operators): *while* and *for* loops, the *if* condition, the pick, the interrupt, and the guard. The pick (`pick(variableList, condition)`) non-deterministically picks values for variables in the subtask that satisfy the condition. The interrupt (`whenever(variableList, condition, cancelCondition)`) fires whenever there is a binding for the variables that satisfies the condition unless the cancellation condition becomes true. Guards (`guard(condition)`) block the subtask's execution until the condition becomes true. The absence of a link annotation on a particular decomposition link indicates the absence of any conditions on the subgoal/subtask.

The third annotation type is the *applicability condition* (`ac(condition)`). It applies to means-ends links used with goal achievement alternatives and specifies that the alternative is only applicable when the condition holds.

Agent Goals in iASR Models. A CASL agent has procedural and declarative components. iASR diagrams only model agent processes and therefore can only be used to represent the procedural component of CASL agents. The presence of a goal node in an iASR diagram indicates that the agent knows that the goal is in its mental state and is prepared to deliberate about whether and how to achieve it. For the agent to modify its behaviour in response to the changes to its mental state, it must detect that change and synchronize its procedural and declarative components (see Fig. 2B). To do this we use interrupts or guards with their conditions being the presence of certain goals or knowledge in the mental state of the agent. Procedurally a goal node is interpreted as invoking the means to achieve it.

In CASL, as described in [19], only communication actions have effects on the mental state of the agents. We, on the other hand, would like to let agents change their mental state on their own by executing the action `commit(agent, φ)`, where ϕ is a formula that the agent/modeler wants to hold. Thus, in iASR diagrams all agent goals must be acquired either from intentional dependencies or by using the `commit` action. By introducing goals into the models of agent processes, the modeler captures the fact that multiple alternatives exist in these processes. Moreover, the presence of goal nodes suggests that the designer envisions new possibilities for achieving these goals. By making the agent acquire the goals, the modeler makes sure that the agent's mental state reflects the above intention. By using the `commit` action, the modeler is able to "load" the goal decomposition hierarchy into the agents' mental states. This way the agents would be able to reason about various alternatives available to them or come up with new ways to achieve their goals at runtime. This is unlike the approach in [24] where agent goals had to be operationalized before being formally analyzed.

Softgoals. Softgoals (quality requirements) are imprecise and thus are difficult to handle in a formal specifications language. Therefore, we use softgoals to help in choosing the best process alternatives (e.g., by selecting the ones with the best overall contribution to all softgoals in the model) and then remove them before iASR models are produced. Alternatively, softgoals can be operationalized or metricized, thus becoming hard goals. Since in this approach softgoals are removed from iASR models, applicability conditions can be used to capture in a formal way the fitness of the alternatives with respect to softgoals (this fitness is normally encoded by the softgoal contribution links in SR diagrams). For example, one can specify that phoning participants to notify them of the meeting details is applicable only in cases with few participants (see Fig. 5), while the email option is applicable for any number of participants. This may be due to the softgoal "Minimize Effort" that has been removed from the model before the iASR model was produced.

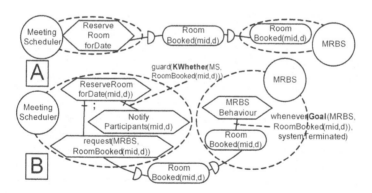

Fig. 3. Adding iASR-level agent interaction details

Providing Agent Interaction Details. i^* usually abstracts from modeling any details of agent interactions. CASL, on the other hand, models high-level aspects of inter-agent communication. Because of the importance of agent interactions in MAS, in order to formally verify MAS specifications in CASL, all high-level aspects of agent interaction must be provided in the iASR models. This includes the tasks that request services or information from agents in the system, the tasks that supply the information or inform about success or failure in providing the service, etc. We assume that the communication links are reliable.

For example, the SR model with the goal dependency RoomBooked (see Fig. 1A) in Fig. 3A is refined into the iASR model in Fig. 3B showing the details of the requests, the interrupts with their trigger conditions referring to mental states of the agents, etc. Here, the parameter mid ("meeting ID") is a unique meeting identifier. Since achieved goals remain in the mental state of an agent, all interrupts dealing with the acquisition of goals through dependencies must be triggered only for new instances of these goals. We usually leave these details out in iASR models. For instance, we have left out the part of the interrupt condition that makes sure that only unachieved instances of the goal RoomBooked trigger the interrupt in Fig. 3B. We present an example of the fully specified interrupt in the next section.

3.2   Mapping iASR Diagrams into CASL

Once all the necessary details have been introduced into an iASR diagram, it can be mapped into the corresponding formal CASL model, thus making the iASR model amenable to formal analysis.

The modeler defines a mapping **m** that maps every element (except for intentional dependencies) of an iASR model into CASL. Specifically, agents are mapped into constants that serve as their names as well as into CASL procedures that specify their behaviour; roles and positions are mapped into similar procedures with an agent parameter so that they can be instantiated by individual agents. For concrete agents playing a number of roles, the procedures corresponding to these roles will be combined to specify the overall behaviour of the agent. These procedures are normally executed in parallel. However, one may also use prioritized concurrency, which is available in CASL, to combine agent's roles. Leaf-level task nodes are mapped into CASL procedures or primitive actions; composition and link annotations are mapped into the corresponding CASL operators, while the conditions present in the annotations map into CASL formulas.

Mapping Task Nodes. A task decomposition is automatically mapped into a CASL procedure that reflects the structure of the decomposition and all the annotations.

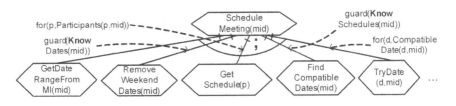

Fig. 4. Example iASR task decomposition

Fig. 4 shows how a portion of the Meeting Scheduler's task for scheduling meetings can be decomposed. This task will be mapped into a CASL procedure with the following body (it contains portions still to be recursively mapped into CASL; they are the parameters of the mapping **m**):

```
proc ScheduleMeeting(mid)
   m(GetDateRangeFromMI(mid));
   guard m(KnowDates(mid)) do
      m(RemoveWeekendDates(mid))
   endGuard;
   for p: m(Ptcp(mid)) do m(GetSchedule(p)) endFor;
   guard m(KnowSchedules(mid)) do
      m(FindCompatibleDates(mid))
   endGuard;
   for d: m(CompatibleDate(d,mid)) do
      m(TryDate(d,mid))
   endFor;
   ...
endProc
```

Note how the body of the procedure associated with the ScheduleMeeting task is composed of the results of the mapping of its subtasks with the annotations providing the composition details. This procedure can be mechanically generated given the mapping for leaf-level tasks and conditions.

Leaf-level tasks in our approach can be mapped either into primitive actions or CASL procedures. While mapping leaf-level tasks into CASL procedures may reduce model size and increase the level of abstraction (since in this way further details of agent processes will be hidden inside these procedures), restricting the mapping of the leaf-level tasks to primitive actions with the same name allows the CASL procedures to be automatically constructed from these actions based on iASR annotations.

Mapping Goal Nodes. In our approach, an iASR goal node is mapped into a CASL formula, which is the formal definition for the goal, and an achievement procedure, which encodes how the goal can be achieved and is based on the means-ends decomposition for the goal in the iASR diagram. For example, a formal definition for MeetingScheduled(mid,s) could be: $\exists$d [AgreeableDate(mid,date,s) $\land$ AllAccepted(mid, date,s) $\land$ RoomBooked(mid,date,s)]. This says that there must be a date agreeable for everybody on which a room is booked and all participants agree to meet. This definition is too ideal since it is not always possible to schedule a meeting. One can *deidealize* [22] MeetingScheduled to allow for the possibility of no common available dates or no available meeting rooms. To weaken the goal appropriately, one needs to know when the goal cannot be achieved. Modeling an achievement process for a goal using an iASR diagram allows us to understand how that goal can fail and thus iASR models can be used to come up with a correct formal definition for the goal. The following is one possibility for deidealizing the goal MeetingScheduled:

```
MeetingScheduledIfPossible(mid,s)=
```
//1. The meeting has been successfully scheduled
```
SuccessfullyScheduled(mid,s) ∨
```
//2. No agreeable (suitable for everybody) dates
```
∀d[IsDate(d) ⊃ ¬ AgreeableDate(mid,d,s)] ∨
```
//3. For every agreeable date at least one participant declined
```
∀d[AgreeableDate(mid,d,s) ⊃ SomeoneDeclined(mid,d,s)] ∨
```
//4. No rooms available
```
∀d[SuggestedDate(mid,d,s) ∧ AllAccepted(mid,d,s)] ⊃
   RoomBookingFailed(mid,date,s)]
```

The ability of CASL agents to reason about their goals gives us an opportunity to avoid maintaining agents' schedules explicitly in the meeting scheduler example. Instead, we rely on the presence of goals AtMeeting(participant,mid,date,s) in the agents' mental states as indications of the participants' willingness and intention to attend meetings on specific dates (the absence of meeting commitments indicates an available time slot). Then, we can use the initial state axiom below (which can be shown to persist in all situations) to make the agents know that they can only attend one meeting per time slot (day):

```
∀agt[Know(agt,∀p,mid1,mid2,date[
   AtMeeting(p,mid1,date,now) ∧ AtMeeting(p,mid2,date,now)
   ⊃ mid1=mid2],S₀)]
```

Since CASL prevents agents from acquiring conflicting goals, requests from the Meeting Scheduler that conflict with already acquired AtMeeting goals will not be accommodated.

Generating Goal Achievement Procedures. The achievement procedures for goals are automatically constructed based on the means for achieving them and the associated annotations (see Fig. 5). By default, the alternative composition annotation is used, which means that some applicable alternative will be non-deterministically selected (other approaches are also possible). Note that the applicability condition (ac) maps into a guard operator to prevent the execution of an unwanted alternative.

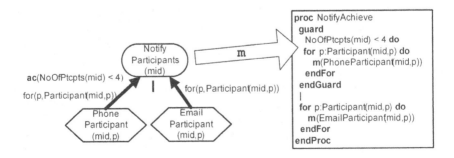

Fig. 5. Generating achievement procedures

Generally, an agent's means to achieve its goals typically work, but it is rare that they will always work. Thus, we cannot guarantee that the means for achieving the goal that are represented in the achievement procedure for that goal are always capable of achieving it. We therefore state that the achievement procedure will sometimes achieve the goal, instead of saying that it will, in fact, always achieve the goal. This semantic constraint is expressed in the following formula. It says that there exist situations s and s' such that the achievement procedure starts executing in s, terminates successfully in s', and the CASL formula representing the agent's goal holds in s':

$$\exists s, s'.\textbf{Do}(\texttt{AchievementProcedure}, s, s') \wedge \texttt{GoalFormula}[s']$$

However, if one needs more assurance that the goal will, in fact, be achieved, then one must use agent *capabilities* in place of the regular procedures. There has been a lot of work on capabilities in the agent community (e.g., [13]). Here, we view goal capabilities as goal achievement procedures that are guaranteed to succeed under certain circumstances. Goal capabilities (task capabilities are also discussed in [8]) are represented in iASR models by special nodes (see Fig. 6) that are mapped into a CASL formula that represents the goal of the capability, the achievement procedure that is constructed similarly to a goal achievement procedure, a context condition that must hold when the capability is invoked, and the specification of the behaviour of the other agents in the environment that is compatible with the capability. The following formula describes the constraints on goal capabilities:

$$\forall s.\texttt{ContextCond}(s) \supset$$
$$\textbf{AllDo}((\texttt{AchieveProc}; \texttt{GoalFormula}?) \parallel \texttt{EnvProcessesSpec}, s)$$

The formula states that if we start the execution in a situation where the context condition of the capability holds, then all possible executions of the goal achievement procedure in parallel with the allowable environment behaviours terminate successfully and achieve the goal. The designer needs to determine what restrictions must be placed on the processes executing concurrently with the capability. One extreme case is when no concurrent behaviour is allowed (EnvProcessesSpec = nil). The other extreme is to allow the execution of any action. Of course, the specification for most capabilities will identify concrete behaviours for the agents in the environment, which assure the successful execution of the achievement procedure. For example, suppose an agent has a goal capability to fill a tank with water. It is guaranteed to succeed unless the tank's valve is opened. Here is the corresponding specification for the outside processes compatible with the capability (pick an action; if the action is not openValve, execute it; iterate):

$$\texttt{EnvProcessesSpec} =$$
$$(\pi\,\texttt{action}.(\texttt{action} \neq \texttt{openValve})? \;;\; \texttt{action})^{\leq k}$$

Here, $\delta^{\leq k}$ represents a bounded form of nondeterministic iteration where δ can be executed up to k times (k is a large constant). We must bound the number of environment actions, otherwise the process will have nonterminating executions.

Fig. 6 shows the graphical notation for capabilities. Here, T1Cap is a task capability that executes Task_1, while G1Cap is a goal capability that achieves the goal G1.

Note that G1Cap shows the internals of the capability, while T1Cap is an abbreviated form that hides all the details of the capability. Detailed discussion of capabilities in this approach is presented in [8].

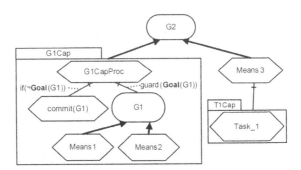

Fig. 6. Using goal and task capability nodes in iASR models

Modeling Dependencies. Intentional dependencies are not mapped into CASL per se — they are established by agent interactions. iASR tasks requesting help from agents will generally be mapped into actions of the type request(FromAgt,ToAgt, **Eventually**(ϕ)) for an achievement goal ϕ. We add a special abbreviation **DoAL**(δ,s,s') (Do At Least) to be used when establishing task dependencies. It stands for **Do**($\delta \parallel (\pi a.a)^*$,s,s'), which means that the program δ must be executed, but that other actions may occur. Thus, to ask an agent to execute a certain known procedure, the depender must request it with: request(FromAgt,ToAgt, **DoAL**(SomeProcedure)).

In order for an intentional dependency to be established we also need a commitment from a dependee agent to act on the request from the depender. Thus, the dependee must monitor its mental state for newly acquired goals. Here is an interrupt that is used by the MP to check for a request for the list of its available dates:

⟨mid:
Goal(mp, **DoAL**(InformAvailableDates(mid,MS),now,then)) ∧
Know(mp, ¬∃s,s'(s ⪯ s' ⪯ now ∧
    DoAL(InformAvailDates(mid,MS),s,s'))) →
InformAvailDates(mid,MS)
until SystemTerminated⟩

Here, if the MP has the goal to execute the procedure InformAvailDates and knows that it has not yet executed it, the agent sends the available dates. The cancellation condition SystemTerminated indicates that the MP always monitors for this goal. Requesting agents use similar interrupt/guard mechanism to monitor for requested information or confirmations. Cancellation conditions in interrupts allow the agents to monitor for certain requests/informs only in particular contexts (e.g., while some interaction protocol is being enacted).

The i^* notation, even if modified as presented in this paper, may not be the most appropriate graphical notation for representing agent interaction protocols since it usually concentrates on strategic dependencies and does not have facilities for modeling low-level agent interaction details. A notation like AgentUML [12] may be more suitable for this task. However, iASR models still can be used for modeling agent interactions. To illustrate this, we present a simplified version of an interaction protocol called Net-Bill [26]. The protocol describes the interactions between a customer and a merchant. In NetBill, once a customer accepts a product quote, the merchant sends the encrypted goods (e.g., software) and waits for payment from the customer. Once the payment is received, the merchant sends the receipt with the decryption key (see Fig. 7).

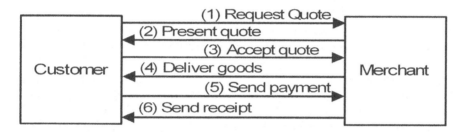

Fig. 7. The NetBill interaction protocol

Fig. 8 shows a fragment of a high-level iASR representation of the NetBill protocol (note that we omit goal/task parameters for brevity) centered on the customer side. Here, we specify a particular context for the use of the protocol by including the actor Customer that has the goal `PurchaseProduct`, which can be achieved by using the NetBill interaction protocol. Since, i^* allows for creation of modular diagrams where agents can exhibit certain behaviour by playing appropriate roles, we make use of the protocol by delegating the task `PurchaseProduct` to a role NetBill Customer, which in turn interacts with another role NetBill Merchant. While Customer and Netbill Customer are two separate roles in Fig. 8, they will most likely be played by the same agent (by concurrently executing the procedures for the two roles).

Inside the NetBill Customer role, the task `PurchaseProduct` is decomposed into two tasks, `request(KnowPrice)` and `EvaluateQuote`, and the goal `SendPayment`. These tasks and goal represent the important chunks of the customer's behaviour in the NetBill protocol: the request of a product quote, the evaluation and possible acceptance of the quote, and the payment for the product. We use guard annotations to make sure that these sub-behaviours are only executed when appropriate. Note that the conditions in the guards refer to the mental state of the agent. Thus, the request for product quote is executed only when the agent does not know the quote's value ($\neg$**KRef**(`Quote`))), while the evaluation of the quote only takes place once the agent knows it. Similarly, a payment is made only after the agent knows that it has received the desired product. The parallel decomposition (note the concurrency annotation) together with the use of the guard annotations allow for the possibility of agents executing their protocols flexibly. For example, in case of NetBill, if the agent already

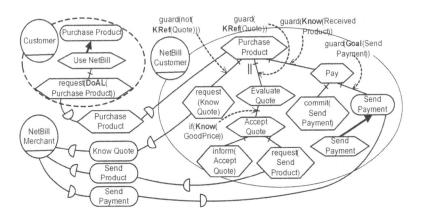

Fig. 8. iASR model for NetBill

knows the price for a product, the quote request step will be skipped. Similarly, if the customer agent knows that some particular merchant always has the best price for certain products, it can request the delivery of the product right away. We now show how the customer part of the NetBill protocol modeled in Fig. 8 is represented in CASL:

```
procPurchaseProduct(cust,merch,product)
  KRef(cust,Quote(product)) do
    request(cust,merch,Eventually(
      KRef(cust,Quote(product))))
  endGuard
  ‖
  guard KRef(cust,Quote(product)) do
    if Know(cust,GoodPrice(Quote(product))) then
      AcceptQuote(cust,merch,product)
    endIf
  endGuard
  ‖
  guard Know(cust,ReceivedProduct(merch,product)) do
    Pay(cust,merch,product)
  endGuard
endProc,
```

where the procedure Pay is defined as follows:

```
procPay(cust,merch,product)
  commit(cust,Eventually(SendPayment(merch,product)));
  guard Goal(cust,Eventually(SendPayment(merch,product))) do
    SendPayment(merch,product)
  endGuard
endProc
```

3.3 Formal Verification

Once an iASR model is mapped into the procedural component of the CASL specification and after its declarative component (e.g., precondition axioms, SSAs, etc.) has been specified, it is ready to be formally analyzed. One tool that can be used for that is CASLve [20, 18], a theorem prover-based verification environment for CASL. CASLve provides a library of theories for representing CASL specifications and lemmas that facilitate various types of verification proofs. [18] shows a proof that there is a terminating run for a simplified meeting scheduler system as well as example proofs of a safety property and consistency of specifications. In addition to physical executability of agent programs, one can also check for the *epistemic feasibility* [9] of agent plans, i.e., whether agents have enough knowledge to successfully execute their processes.

Other approaches could be used as well (e.g., simulation or model checking). However, tools based on these techniques work with much less expressive languages than CASL. Thus, CASL specifications must be simplified before these methods can be used on them. For example, most simulation tools cannot handle mental state specifications; these would then have to be operationalized before simulation is performed. The Con-Golog interpreter can be used to directly execute such simplified specifications, as in [24]. Model checking methods (e.g. [5]) are restricted to finite state specifications, and work has only begun on applying these methods to theories involving mental states (e.g., [23]).

If expected properties of the system are not entailed by the CASL model, it means that the model is incorrect and needs to be fixed. The source of an error found during verification can usually be traced to a portion of the CASL code and to a part of its iASR model since our systematic mapping supports traceability.

3.4 Discussion

Our choice of CASL as the formal language is based on the fact that compared to other formalisms (e.g., [14]), it provides a richer language for specifying agent behaviour (with support for concurrency), so it makes it easier to specify complex MAS. We use a version of CASL where the precondition for the `inform` action requires that the information being sent by an agent be known to it. This prevents agents from transmitting false information. The removal of this restriction allows the modeling of systems where agents are not always truthful. This can be useful when dealing with security and privacy requirements. However, dealing with false information may require belief revision (see [21]). Similarly, the precondition for `request` makes sure that when requesting services from other agents, the sender does not itself have goals that conflict with the request. Relaxing this constraint also allows for the possibility of modeling malicious agents. Other extensions to CASL to accommodate various characteristics of application domains are possible (e.g., a simple way of modeling trust is discussed in [8]). We also note that in CASL all agents are aware of all actions being executed in the system. Often, it is useful to lift this restriction, but dealing with the resulting lack of knowledge about agents' mental states can be challenging.

4 Conclusion

In the approach presented in this paper and in [8], we produce CASL specifications from i^* models for formal analysis and verification. The approach is related to the Tropos framework in that it is agent-oriented and is rooted in the RE concepts. Our method is not the first attempt to provide formal semantics for i^* models. For example, Formal Tropos (FT) [5], supports formal verification of i^* models through model checking. Also, in the i^*-ConGolog approach [24], on which our method is based, SR models are associated with formal ConGolog programs for simulation and verification. The problem with these methods is that goals of the agents are abstracted out and made into objective properties of the system in the formal specifications. This is because the formal components of these approaches (the model checker input language for FT and ConGolog for the i^*-ConGolog approach) do not support reasoning about agent goals (and knowledge). However, most agent interactions involve knowledge exchange and goal delegation since MAS are developed as social structures, so formal analysis of goals and knowledge is important in the design of these systems. We propose a framework where goals are not removed from the agent specifications, but are modeled formally and can be updated following requests. This allows agents to reason about their objectives. Information exchanges among agents are also formalized as changes in their knowledge state. In our approach, goals are not system-wide properties, but belong to concrete agents. The same applies to knowledge. This subjective point of view provides support for new types of formal analysis. Our method is more agent-oriented and allows for precise modeling of stakeholder goals. Modeling of conflicting stakeholder goals, a common task in RE, and agent negotiations is also possible. In future work, we plan to develop a toolkit to support requirements engineering using our approach, to look into handling quality constraints (softgoals) in our approach, as well as to test the method on more realistic case studies.

References

[1] Castro J., Kolp M., Mylopoulos, J.: Towards Requirements-Driven Information Systems Engineering: The Tropos Project. Information Systems, 27(6) (2002) 365–389

[2] Chung, L.K., Nixon, B.A., Yu, E., Mylopoulos, J.: Non-Functional Requirements in Software Engineering. Kluwer (2000)

[3] Dardenne, A., van Lamsweerde, A., Fickas, S.: Goal-Directed Requirements Acquisitions. Science of Computer Programming, 20 (1993) 3–50

[4] De Giacomo, G., Lespérance, Y., Levesque, H.: ConGolog, A Concurrent Programming Language Based on the Situation Calculus. Artificial Intelligence, 121 (2000) 109–169

[5] Fuxman, A., Liu, L., Mylopoulos, J., Pistore, M., Roveri, M., Traverso, P.: Specifying and Analyzing Early Requirements in Tropos. RE Journal, 9(2) (2004) 132–150

[6] Gans, G., Jarke, M., Kethers, S., Lakemeyer, G., Ellrich, L., Funken, C., Meister, M.: Requirements Modeling for Organization Networks: A (Dis-)Trust-Based Approach. In Proc. RE'01 (2001) 154–163

[7] Jennings, N.R.: Agent-Oriented Software Engineering. In Proc. MAAMAW-99 (1999) 1–7

[8] Lapouchnian, A.: Modeling Mental States in Requirements Engineering — An Agent-Oriented Framework Based on i^* and CASL. M.Sc. Thesis. Department of Computer Science, York University, Toronto (2004)

[9] Lespérance, Y.: On the Epistemic Feasibility of Plans in Multiagent Systems Specifications. In Proc. ATAL-2001, Revised papers, LNAI 2333, Springer, Berlin (2002) 69–85

[10] McCarthy, J., Hayes, P.: Some Philosophical Problems From the Standpoint of Artificial Intelligence, Machine Intelligence, Vol. 4, Edinburgh University Press (1969) 463–502

[11] Moore, R.C.: A Formal Theory of Knowledge and Action. Formal Theories of the Common Sense World, J.R. Hobbs, R.C. Moore (eds.). Ablex Publishing (1985) 319–358

[12] Odell, J., Van Dyke Parunak, H. and Bauer, B.: Extending UML for Agents. In Proc. AOIS-2000, Austin, TX, USA (2000) 3–17

[13] Padgham, L., Lambrix, P.: Agent Capabilities: Extending BDI Theory. In Proc. AAAI-2000, Austin, TX, USA (2000) 68–73

[14] Rao, A.S., Georgeff, M.P.: Modeling Rational Agents within a BDI Architecture. In Proc. KR'91 (1991) 473–484

[15] Reiter, R.: The Frame Problem in the Situation Calculus: A Simple Solution (Sometimes) and a Completeness Result for Goal Regression. Artificial Intelligence and Mathematical Theory of Computation: Papers in Honor of John McCarthy, V. Lifschitz (ed.), Academic Press (1991) 359–380

[16] Reiter, R.: Knowledge in Action: Logical Foundations for Specifying and Implementing Dynamical Systems. MIT Press, Cambridge MA (2001)

[17] Scherl, R.B., Levesque, H.: Knowledge, Action, and the Frame Problem. Artificial Intelligence, 144(1–2) (2003) 1–39

[18] Shapiro, S.: Specifying and Verifying Multiagent Systems Using CASL. Ph.D. Thesis. Department of Computer Science, University of Toronto (2004)

[19] Shapiro, S., Lespérance, Y.: Modeling Multiagent Systems with the Cognitive Agents Specification Language — A Feature Interaction Resolution Application. In Proc. ATAL-2000, LNAI 1986, Springer, Berlin (2001) 244–259

[20] Shapiro, S., Lespérance, Y., Levesque, H.: The Cognitive Agents Specification Language and Verification Environment for Multiagent Systems. In Proc. AAMAS'02, Bologna, Italy, ACM Press (2002) 19–26

[21] Shapiro, S., Pagnucco, M., Lespérance, Y., Levesque, H.: Iterated Belief Change in the Situation Calculus. In Proc. KR-2000 (2000) 527–538

[22] van Lamsweerde, A., Darimont, R., Massonet, P.: Goal-Directed Elaboration of Requirements for a Meeting Scheduler: Problems and Lessons Learnt. Proc. RE'95, York, UK, (1995) 194–203

[23] van Otterloo, S., van der Hoek, W., Wooldrige, M.: Model Checking a Knowledge Exchange Scenario. Applied Artificial Intelligence, 18:9-10 (2004) 937–952

[24] Wang, X., Lespérance, Y.: Agent-Oriented Requirements Engineering Using ConGolog and i^*. In Proc. AOIS-01 (2001) 59–78

[25] Wooldridge, M.: Agent-Based Software Engineering. IEE Proceedings on Software Engineering, 144(1) (1997) 26–37

[26] Yolum, P., Singh, M.P.: Commitment Machines. In Proc. ATAL-2001, Revised Papers, LNAI 2333, Springer, Berlin (2002) 235–247

[27] E. Yu. Towards modeling and reasoning support for early requirements engineering. In Proc. RE'97, Annapolis, USA (1997) 226–235

Observed-MAS: An Ontology-Based Method for Analyzing Multi-Agent Systems Design Models

Anarosa A.F. Brandão[1], Viviane Torres da Silva[2], and Carlos J.P. de Lucena[3]

[1] Laboratório de Técnicas Inteligentes - PCS-POLI-USP,
Av. Prof. Luciano Gualberto, trav. 3, 158, sala C2-50
São Paulo - Brazil - 05508-900
anarosabrandao@gmail.com
[2] Departamento de Sistemas Informáticos y Programación, UCM
C/ Profesor José García Santesmases, s/n,
Ciudad Universitaria, 28040 Madrid
viviane@fdi.ucm.es
[3] Computer Science Department, PUC-Rio
R. Marquês de São Vicente, 225,
Rio de Janeiro - Brazil - 22453-900
lucena@inf.puc-rio.br

Abstract. Agents are becoming a popular technology for the development of distributed, heterogeneous and always available systems. The application of agent technologies requires extensions to the existing object-oriented modeling languages to accommodate agent-related abstractions such as roles, organizations and environments. If it is difficult to analyze and establish the well-formedness of a set of diagrams of a UML-like object-oriented modeling language, it gets far more complex when the language is extended to add a set of agency related abstractions. In order to tame such complexity, we propose an ontology-based method for analyzing MAS specifications described using a modeling language that extends UML to accommodate the agency characteristics. The method proposes a two-phase approach that covers different sets of MAS design properties. These properties are the ones related to each individual diagram and the ones associated with pairs of diagrams. The later take into consideration the interdependencies between diagrams. The method also provides features that allow the suggestion of some design guidelines which may improve the MAS design quality.

1 Introduction

Object-orientation (OO) proved to be a powerful computational model for the development of real scale software systems. In order to help the design of such systems, several modeling languages for large OO applications have been consolidated. The UML standard [27] is an example that consists of a set of diagrams that capture different views of an OO software system. These views cover aspects such as how the system is to be used, how it is structured and how it will behave. The models that represent real size OO applications using UML usually

L. Padgham and F. Zambonelli (Eds.): AOSE 2006, LNCS 4405, pp. 122–139, 2007.
© Springer-Verlag Berlin Heidelberg 2007

lead to very complex sets of diagrams whose well-formedness is very difficult to check, even independently of the applications. Until recently, the analysis of UML models to check the proper use of its many design artifacts and their allowed interrelationships has mostly been done in an ad hoc manner in successive versions of UML support tools such as [26]. Only recently, more systematic approaches to UML design checking have been developed [3][11][15][17][30]. They will be discussed in the related work section of this paper.

The nature of nowadays distributed, heterogeneous, always available systems composed by autonomous components popularized the software agent and related abstractions (eg.: roles, organizations, environments) [28][32]. Since agents co-exist with objects for the solution of large scale distributed and heterogeneous systems, extensions of UML that incorporate the abstractions of the agent world have been proposed [2][29][31].

If the establishment of the well-formedness of a set of UML diagrams used to design a particular OO application is itself a difficult problem, it gets far more complex when UML is extended by adding the set of agency abstractions required by the new computational paradigm. The analysis of MAS designs represented by modeling languages that extend UML is indeed very complex and may compromise the adoption of the agent technology. Therefore, there is a need for an approach that facilitates the analysis of such designs by helping the designers to automatically detect inconsistencies in them.

The paper presents Observed-MAS, an ontology-based method for analyzing MAS design models. The goal of the method is to facilitate the design activity by providing automatic detection of design inconsistencies and improvements. The design models are translated to formal specifications based on *ontologies* which describe the MAS domain and the specification of the modeling language being used to design the MAS. Therefore, each generated specification is composed by an ontology [5][12] that specifies a set of domain and modeling language *properties* and also by sets of previously defined *queries* used to analyze the designs, which are represented by ontology instances.

This paper is organized as follows: Section 2 presents an overview of the proposed method; Sections 3 and 4 explain the first and the second phases of the method, respectively; Section 5 describes some related work and, finally, in Section 6 we present our conclusions and future work.

2   The Method Overview

The proposed method provides support for the analysis of MAS designs represented by MAS modeling languages. The method is based on the specification of MAS and on the specification of the modeling language being used to design the MAS. By analyzing the designs according to both specifications, it is possible to check both the MAS properties (independently of the modeling language) and the modeling language properties themselves.

The specification of the MAS domain is described by the TAO metamodel [28]. The main role of the TAO (Taming Agents and Objects) metamodel is to provide a conceptual framework to understand the distinct abstractions that compose a MAS and the relationships that occur between them in order to support the development of large-scale MAS. The proposed framework elicits an ontology that connects consolidated abstractions, such as objects and classes, and other abstractions, such as agents, roles and organizations, which are the foundations for object and agent-based software engineering. The framework defines the core abstractions found in MAS and also their properties, relationships and the way these entities execute and interact. TAO metamodel was defined based on the analysis of several methods, methodologies and modeling languages.

In TAO, a MAS comprises classes and instances of agents, objects and organizations. TAO entities are *agent*, *object*, *organization*, *role* (agent and object role), *environment* and *event*. Agents, organizations, and objects inhabit environments [13]. While objects represent passive elements, such as resources, agents represent autonomous elements that manipulate objects. Agents have beliefs and goals, they know how to execute some actions and plans, and they are always playing a role in an organization. An organization describes a set of roles [4] that might limit the behavior of its agents, objects and sub-organizations [32]. Furthermore, organizations have axioms that guide the behavior of agents that play roles in it. Agents and objects can be members of different organizations and play different roles in each of them [21]. Agents may interact with each other and cooperate either to achieve a common goal, or to achieve their own goals [33]. TAO defines several relationships such as *Inhabit*, *Play*, *Ownership*, *Control*, *Dependency*, *Association*, and *Aggregation* that are used to characterize the interaction kinds between the linked entities. Fig. 1. illustrates the entities and the relationships defined in TAO. In general, the specification of a modeling

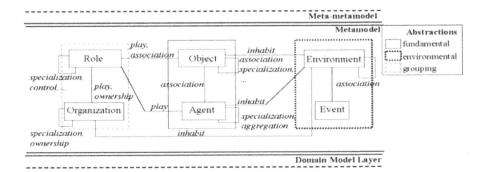

Fig. 1. The abstractions and relationships of the TAO conceptual framework

language is based on a metamodel that describes the properties and characteristics of the language. In order to illustrate our approach, the modeling language being used in this paper is MAS-ML (Multi-Agent System Modeling Language) [28]. MAS-ML extends UML by including the agent-related abstractions identified in TAO. The MAS-ML metamodel describes the artifacts (or diagrams) that are used to express both the structural and the behavioral aspects of MAS. MAS-ML defines three structural diagrams (the extended UML class diagram, the organization diagram and the role diagram) and two dynamic diagrams (the extended UML sequence and activity diagrams).

Both specifications - MAS domain and modeling language specifications - are represented by using ontologies and related queries. Ontologies are composed by concepts, properties and axioms, where properties represent the relations between the concepts and axioms represent the constraints over the concepts and relations. Therefore, the use of ontologies to formalize the MASs domain and the modeling language is justified through the direct translation from design models into ontology instances and, consequently, the creation of knowledge-bases (KBs) that can be manipulated by using the reasoning services (or queries answers) that are available for this kind of data. The general idea of the Observed-MAS applied to the MAS-ML modeling language is presented on Fig. 2. From

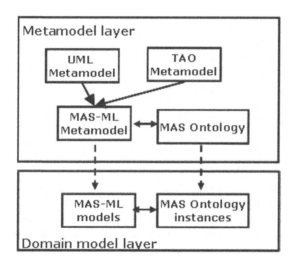

Fig. 2. Observed-MAS applied to MAS-ML: general idea

the general idea presented in Fig. 2, the method definition was based in two principles: flexibility and consistency analysis. The first is related to the desired flexibility during the modeling activity, when the existence of some design inconsistencies is natural and even expected. The second is related to the analysis of the modeling, when the diagrams that compose it are analyzed individually and parwise. Therefore, the method was divided in two phases whose schema is briefly described on Fig. 3. Both phases present an ontology to formally support the design analysis and two sets of queries: one related to the MAS design or domain properties violations and the other related to guidelines for designers to improve or facilitate the building of their design models. During phase one (F1), the design is analyzed according to the MAS domain properties and to the

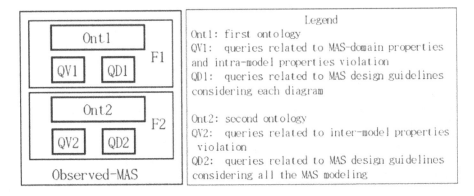

Fig. 3. The Observed-MAS schema

modeling language intra-model properties by using queries. The MAS domain properties focus on the characteristics of MAS, independently of the modeling language used to describe it. Intra-model properties are related to the internal specification of a diagram defined by the MAS modeling language metamodel. The *ontology* used in phase one (Ont1) identifies the MAS domain entities and relationships as well as the modeling language diagrams, by stating what are the entities and relationships that are commonly used in MAS and specified in the modeling language diagrams. The *ontology properties* are also defined in order to relate the identified entities and relationships. These properties are specially important for the definition of the sets of *queries* (QV1 and QD1) which analyze *ontology instances* (the design of MAS) to: (i) find out violations of the MAS domain properties and of intra-model properties (QV1), and (ii) offer the designer some guidelines to improve the design of each MAS-ML diagram according to the MAS domain properties (QD1). Moreover, Ont1 doesn't describe the axioms which restrict both the internal specification of the MAS entities and the structure of the modeling language diagrams. These characteristics are responsible for the desired flexibility during the building of design models.

In phase two (F2), the design is analyzed according to the modeling language inter-model properties by using queries (QV2 and QD2). A MAS inter-model property is related to the interdependence defined by the MAS modeling language metamodel concerning pairs of different diagrams. The analysis of these properties begins when the analysis of the first phase has been completed and the design has been updated according to the inconsistencies detected during the first phase by the QV1 *queries*. The *ontology* of phase two (Ont2) is an extension of Ont1 with the addition of axioms which describe the MAS domain and modeling language intra-model properties. These characteristics of Ont2 assure that each MAS entity and each diagram of the modeling is individually consistent with their specification. The *queries* QV2 are used to reason about ontology instances (that represent design models) in order to find out parts of the design that violate the modeling language inter-model properties. In addition, the QD2 queries are also used to reason about the design and to provide guidelines related to MAS-ML inter-model properties helping designers to improve their models according to the MAS domains properties. Nevertheless, phase two contemplates the principle of consistency analysis.

To formalize the specification of the MAS domain and the modeling language, we adopted Description Logics (DL) [1] because it is a decidable subset of first order logic and there is a recommendation from OMG [17] of using a DL-based language (OWL [19]) as a standard for ontologies description. Therefore, the ontologies that support the proposed method are described using a state-of-the-art DL reasoning system, which implements the DL $ALCHIQr+(D)$- [23]. Note that the user of the method can choose any ontology language to describe the ontologies and the queries proposed in phase one and two. The user does not need to be an expert in DL to use the method itself. However, to use the MAS domain properties and the first ontology as they are described in this paper there is a need to understand DL characteristics.

To validate the results of the method applied to the MAS-ML modeling language, a case study was developed considering the domain of conference management [8], where authors can submit papers and a chair distributes these papers among the reviewers for evaluation. The Expert Committee is an application solution developed as an example of MAS for the conference management domain. In the Expert Committee system, agents play different roles to achieve their goals. The system supports the following activities: paper submission, reviewer assignment, review submission, and acceptance or rejection notification. The case study will be partially illustrated during the method phases description.

3   Phase One: Analyzing MAS and Intra-model Properties

The specification produced by using Ont1 represents a MAS design, since it uses MAS abstractions defined in the ontology. However, such design may be not consistent with MAS domain properties and with the modeling language properties since Ont1 does not describe axioms that guarantee such consistence. For that reason, queries (QV1) are described and associated with the ontology to analyze the design and detect MAS domain or MAS-ML intra-model inconsistencies. The detection is automatically provided by the reasoning services from the DL-based system and the query answers inform the designer where the inconsistencies are.

3.1   Ont1: The First Ontology

Ont1 partially formalizes the MAS domain by identifying the MAS entities' classes and properties, and the relationships that can be used between them. The ontology does not fully formalize the MAS domain since it does not state axioms that are associated with the entities' properties and relationships. For instance, although Ont1 identifies the MAS entities, it does not describe their internal properties. Moreover, Ont1 does not completely specify the modeling

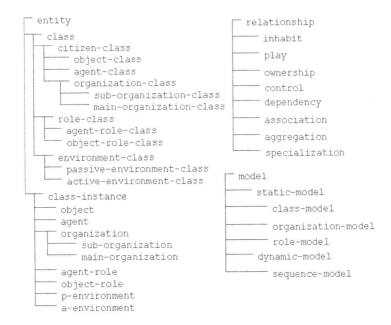

Fig. 4. Part of Ont1 concepts hierarchy

```
(signature
   :atomic-concepts (...
           static-model class-model organization-model
           role-model)
   :roles ((has-class :domain static-model
                   :range class
                   :inverse is-in-static-model)
           (has-relationship :domain static-model
                   :range relationship
                   :inverse is-relationship-of)
   ...) ...) ...
```

Fig. 5. Example of some ontology properties

language because it does not describe rules related to intra and inter-model properties. Fig. 4 illustrates part of the Ont1 concepts hierarchy.

An important issue during the description of Ont1 is the specification of the ontology properties, which are used during the queries definition. Fig. 5 illustrates part of the ontology code showing the definition of two ontology properties (has-class and has-relationship), which are used to define queries that analyze intra-model properties of MAS-ML static diagrams. During the modeling of the Expert Committee MAS an organization model was designed to describe the relations between the organization who was responsible for managing the reviewing

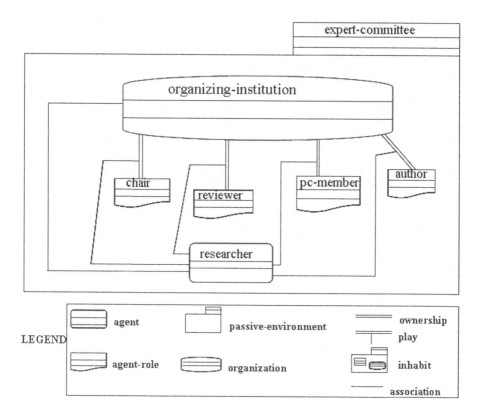

Fig. 6. The organization-model of the Expert Committee case study

process of scientific papers (`organizing-institution`) and the other participants of the process. Therefore, an `agent-class` was defined (`researcher`) related to role classes (`author`, `reviewer`, `pc-member`···) in order to provide means for the agent to play those roles. Fig. 6 briefly presents the referred diagram, whose associated ontology instance code in the KB is partially showed in Fig. 7.

3.2   QV1: The Intra-model Queries

While describing Ont1, the MAS entities were not completely specified. The ontology only states the available entities but does not describe its internal properties to provide   the desired flexibility during early stages of the design activity. For instance, the organization model presented on Fig. 6. is incomplete according to the MAS domain properties. In fact, TAO states that each `agent-class` must have at least one assigned goal. Fig. 8 illustrates *Query I* that detects the agent classes that have not assigned goals, i.e., the agent classes that are not being used according to such specification. It is clear in Fig.6 that the researcher agent hasn't any goal assigned. Therefore, after applying *Query I* to the KB associated with our case study (Fig. 7), we obtain the answer presented on Fig. 9. Fig. 8 and

```
(instance researcher agent-class)
   (instance organizing-institution main-organization-class)
   (instance expert-committee passive-environment-class)
   (instance chair agent-role-class)
   (instance pc-member agent-role-class)
   (instance the-organizing-model organization-model)
   (instance play-1 play)
   (instance assoc-1 association)
   ...
   (related the-organizing-model assoc-1 has-relationship)
   (related the-organizing-model play-1 has-relationship)
   ...
   (related the-organizing-model researcher has-class)
   (related the-organizing-model organizing-institution has-class)
   (related the-organizing-model pc-member has-class)
   ...
   (related play-1 researcher has-end1)
   (related play-1 pc-member has-end2)
   (related assoc-1 researcher has-end1)
   (related assoc-1 organizing-institution has-end2)...
```

Fig. 7. Expert Committee entities and relationships represented in the KB

```
(retrieve (?agentwithoutgoal)
          (and (?agentwithoutgoal agent-class)
               (?agentwithoutgoal NIL has-goal)))
```

Fig. 8. (Query I) Agent classes without assigned goals

```
-- >((?AGENTWITHOUTGOAL RESEARCHER))
```

Fig. 9. Query I result for the Expert Committee design

```
(retrieve (?orgmd ?relation)
      (and (?orgmd organization-model)
           (?relation relationship)
           (?orgmd ?relation has-relationship)
           (not (?relation (or ownership play inhabit)))))
```

Fig. 10. (Query II) Finding bad structured organization diagram

```
-- >(((?ORGMD THE-ORGANIZING-MODEL) (?RELATION ASSOC-1)))
```

Fig. 11. Query II result for the Expert Committee design

```
(retrieve (?role-1 ?role-2 ?prtcl)
      (and (?role-1 agent-role-class)
           (?role-2 agent-role-class)
           (?prtcl protocol)
           (?role-1 ?prtcl has-protocol)
           (?role-2 ?prtcl has-protocol)))
```

Fig. 12. (Query III) Suggesting agent role classes that define common protocols

```
(instance chair agent-role-class)
(instance pc-member agent-role-class)...
(related pc-member solve-conflict-prtcl has-protocol)
(related chair solve-conflict-prtcl has-protocol)
```

Fig. 13. Agent role classes that have same protocols

Fig. 9 show how queries can be used to analyze the design according to the MAS domain properties. But they are also used to analyze the design according to the modeling language intra-model properties. In fact, the MAS-ML metamodel specifies that only the relationships *ownership*, *play* and *inhabit* can be modeled in organization diagrams. The organization diagram presented on Fig. 6 has a violation to the aforementioned property, since there is an *association* relationship between the researcher agent and the organizing-institutionorganization. Fig. 10 depicts *Query II* that analyzes the design to detect if there is an organization diagram that has not allowed relationships. This is one of the queries that compose QV1. Applying *Query II* to this diagram specification, the result will contain the pairs (organization-model, relationship) which are detected by *Query II* (Fig. 11).

3.3   QD1: MAS-ML Intra-model Design Queries

The definition of some MAS-ML design guidelines rules is based on MAS properties, such as interaction. It is an agreement in the MAS community that agents interact through the use of *protocols*. Therefore, it is interesting to suggest the designers how one can represent its use. The MAS-ML metamodel specifies that protocols are defined in the context of agent role classes and the interaction between agents is made while they play roles. The objective of Query III (Fig. 12) is to inform the designer about agent role classes that have at least one common

```
--> (((?ROLE-1 PC-MEMBER) (?ROLE-2 CHAIR) (?PRTCL
SOLVE-CONFLICT-PRTCL))... )
```

Fig. 14. Query III result for the Expert Committee design

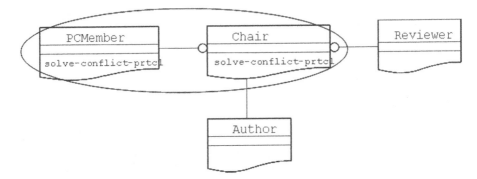

Fig. 15. Example of a role model for the Expert Committee case study

```
(implies agent-class (some has-goal goal))
```

Fig. 16. Formalization of an agent internal property: having at least one goal

protocol, meaning that agent classes related to the agents that play those agent roles can interact. Fig. 13 illustrates the `solve-conflict-prtcl`protocol being defined by two agent role classes, `chair`and `pc-member`, represented in our case study KB. By applying Query III to the KB, the result is the tuple (`pc-member, chair, solve-conflict-with-pc-prtcl`) shown in Fig. 14. This means that two agents playing the roles `pc-member`and `chair`may interact since they have common protocols. This answer will guide the designer during the construction of a role model which describes a relationship between the roles `chair`and `pc-member`, as shown in Fig. 15.

4   Phase Two: Analyzing Inter-model Properties

Phase two should begin only after all inconsistencies detected at phase one have been solved. In this context, the ontology instance that represents the design has no MAS domain or intra-model inconsistencies remaining. However, it is possible that some inter-model inconsistencies remain since inter-model properties have not been analyzed yet. In order to guarantee that the ontology instance being used in this phase has no MAS domain or intra-model inconsistencies, the rules described by the queries QV1 were transformed into axioms of the ontology used in phase two. The ontology used in this phase (Ont2) fully formalizes the

```
(implies organization-model (and (some has-class class))
        (all has-relationship (or ownership play inhabit)))
```

Fig. 17. Formalization of an organization diagram

MAS domain and the intra-model properties of the modeling language. Queries (QV2) are used in this phase to analyze the design according to the inter-model properties that have not been checked yet.

4.1   Ont-2: The Second Ontology

Ont2 is an extension of Ont1 through the addition of new axioms defined based on the MAS domain and intra-model queries from phase one. In order to exemplify the Ont2 axioms, consider *queries I* and *II* described in Section 3. These queries were transformed into axioms to formalize the agent internal property of having goals (Fig. 16) and the organization diagram structure (Fig. 17).

4.2   QV2: The MAS-ML Inter-model Queries

Since the MAS domain and intra-model properties are already described in the ontology axioms, it is now necessary to analyze the design according to the modeling language inter-model properties. Such properties state restrictions between the modeling diagrams. Fig. 18 illustrates a query related to one of the inter-model properties that relates two static diagrams - the role and the organization diagrams. In fact, the MAS-ML metamodel states that every role class must be defined in an organization diagram since every role is defined in the context of an organization. *Query IV* (Fig. 18) analyzes the design to find out if there is an agent role class defined in a role diagram and not defined in any organization diagram of the modeling. Unfortunately, *Query IV* is computationally complex and the RACER system doesn't answer it for large KBs. Therefore, we combine the results (*Query IV*) from the two queries described in Fig. 19 and get the desired answers. Considering our case study, suppose that the designer hasn't modeled the `pc-member`agent role only in the organization diagram but do it in the role diagram. According to the MAS-ML metamodel all the agent role classes modeled in a role model must be modeled in some organization model as well. In the considered example, as we had only one of each MAS-ML static diagrams, the results of *Query IV-A*, illustrated in Fig. 20, indicate that the agent role class `reviewer`, which is modeled in the role diagram called `the-role-model`, must be modeled in the organization diagram called `the-organizing-model`, as well.

4.3   QD2: MAS-ML Inter-model Design Queries

Query VI (Fig. 21) is an example of an inter-model guideline query related to the interaction of agents in MAS. As stated before, agents interact through protocols and the MAS-ML metamodel defines protocols in the context of agent role classes. Agent role classes are specified in organization diagrams and the relations among them are specified in role diagrams. If there is an agent role class modeled in an organization diagram and isn't modeled in any role diagram, it means that the agent playing that role cannot interact with any other agent. Since agents are interactive entities, its interesting to inform the designer about

```
(retrieve (?agrl ?rlmd)
  (and (?agrl agent-role-class)
      (?rlmd role-model)
      (?rlmd ?agrl has-class)
      (not (?agrl (some is-in-static-model
                        organization-model)))))
```

Fig. 18. (Query IV) Interdependence between role and organization diagrams

```
(retrieve (?agrl ?rlmd)
  (and (?agrl agent-role-class)
      (?rlmd role-model)
      (?orgmd organization-model)
      (?rlmd ?agrl has-class)
      (not (?orgmd ?agrl has-class))))

(retrieve (?orgmd) (?orgmd organization-model))
```

Fig. 19. (Query IV-A) Combining queries to find the interdependence between role and organization diagrams

such situation. Query VI finds out the agent role classes that were modeled in an organization diagram but were not modeled in a role diagram. Observe that *Query VI* is similar to *Query IV* (Fig. 18) and again, due to computational limitations for large KBs, we combine the results of the queries described in *Query VI-A* (Fig. 22) to get the desired results.

5   Related Work

Dong and colleagues [9] used Z and the theorem proving Z/EVES to verify domain ontologies coded in DAML+OIL [7]. They defined the Z semantics for the DAML+OIL language primitives and their associated constraints to check if the ontology definition is according to them. In this sense, they check the static (or structural) part of the ontology which means class (concept) inconsistency, subsumption and instantiation testing. They also show that it is possible to check other ontology properties by defining theorems that relate ontology classes and roles. Our work is related to theirs in the sense that we define the semantics for a MAS modeling language metamodel with its associated diagrams and constraints using a DL-based language to check if the design models coded in that

```
--> (((?AGRL REVIEWER) (?RLMD THE-ROLE-MODEL)))
--> (((?ORGMD THE-ORGANIZING-MODEL)))
```

Fig. 20. Inter-model query result

```
(retrieve (?agrl ?orgmd)
    (and (?agrl agent-role-class)
         (?orgmd organization-model)
         (?orgmd ?agrl has-class)
         (not (?agrl (some is-in-static-model role-model)))))
```

Fig. 21. (Query VI) Agent roles in organization and role diagrams

```
(retrieve (?agrl ?orgmd)
    (and (?agrl agent-role-class)
         (?rlmd role-model)
         (?orgmd organization-model)
         (?orgmd ?agrl has-class)
         (not (?rolemd ?agrl has-class))))

(retrieve (?rolemd) (?rolemd role-model))
```

Fig. 22. (Query VI-A) Combining queries to help designers to use good practices during MAS design

modeling language and translated to DL are consistent with their metamodel. Our approach allows not only the checking of structural properties of the models, but some dynamic properties as well.

Kalfoglou and Robertson [14] used ontologies to reason about domain specifications correctness. They considered the correctness of an application specification relatively to the application domain. In this sense, they propose the use of an ontology that describes the application domain to guide the specification engineer. Therefore, as they are considering a formal specification for the application which is based on an ontology which describes the application domain, they can automatically check the existence of ontological inconsistencies in the application specification. Considering the four layer cake of the metadata architecture from OMG-MOF [19], their work navigates between the domain model layer (M1) and the instance layer (M0) while ours navigates between the metamodel layer (M2) and the domain model layer (M1), which means that we are considering the overall class of MAS applications, independently of the considered application domain.

Since modeling languages do not have a precise semantics yet, several works address the problem of design models verification [3][11][15][17][30]. Kim and Carrington [15] give a translation from a UML class model to an Object-Z specification, but they don't provide means to verify the model. Our work defines an ontology-based method that provides a formal description of MAS design models and uses knowledge-based reasoning techniques to verify these models consistency.

Ekenberg and Johannesson [11] define a logic framework for determining design correctness. Their framework is described in FOL (first order logic) and it provides guidelines to translate UML models and to detect some inconsistencies in the models. Their framework is general and the use of the translation rules depend on the designer skills in FOL, since there is not an automatic support for this activity yet. We define an ontology-based method that uses an ontology description language based on DL, which is a decidable subset of FOL. The translation of MAS design models to the ontology description language can be done automatically by using systems such as RICE [25] or ProtÂ©gÂ© [23] with RACER, among others. Also, the verification of consistency is automated by applying the reasoning and inference services to the generated KB.

Mens, Straeten and Simmonds [17][30] use DL to detect inconsistencies and to maintain consistency between UML models in a context of software evolution. Due to the context of their work, they only consider consistency checking between different models. They define the Classless instance conflict [30] as the conflict that arises when an object in a sequence diagram is the instance of a class that doesn't exist in any class diagram. Their work is related to ours in the way they check consistency between models. Our work considers a MAS context and extends the idea of classless instance when, for example, we verify the absence, in any organization diagram, of classes that were predefined in role diagrams or class diagrams.

Berardi [3] uses DL to formally describe a UML class diagram and the CORBA-FaCT [10] and the RACER system to reason about them in order to classify the models concerning their consistency. Such approach is very similar to ours since the diagram description using DL could be considered an ontology for the UML class diagrams. However, while they provide support for verification of a class of models according to an object-oriented metamodel we do the same for all possible models according to a multi-agent-oriented metamodel.

Perini et al [22] combine formal and informal specification to model agent systems using the TROPOS methodology and the Formal Tropos specification. A Formal Tropos specification extends a Tropos specification by adding annotations and constraints that characterize valids behaviors of the model. Their work is concerned about the specification of functional requirements. Our method also combines formal and informal specification of MAS, since we translate an informal specification to a formal one, but we are concerned about a specification that allows the analysis of the design structure and properties. Although our method is focused on non-functional requirements analysis, functional requirements specified through the use of sequence diagrams can be verified using it.

6   Conclusions and Future Work

This paper presents an ontology-based method for analyzing MAS design models based on ontologies that describe the MAS domain and the metamodel of a MAS UML-like modeling language. The proposed method is composed of two phases that support the desired flexibility during the design activity. Such flexibility allows syntactical incorrectness during the creation of design models. The models themselves are checked in phase 1 (by analyzing the intra-model properties) while the interdependencies between the models are checked in phase 2 (by analyzing the inter-model properties). Finally, the method also provides features that allow the suggestion of some design guidelines which may improve the design quality. Such guidelines are good practices rules of design using the modeling language.

The proposed method provides a back-end for graphical tools that support the modeling activity of MAS described in MAS modeling languages. We implemented a tool called MAS-DCheck [6] that can be integrated to a graphical tool such as the ones previously described. We are integrating MAS-DCheck to a MAS-ML graphical tool for editing MAS-ML models [16] in order to allow the analysis of the models during their building. Thus, the inconsistencies that arise during design construction will be automatically detected and informed to the designer. This will help designer not even to decrease the time of building but to improve quality of MAS designs, as well.

An issue that we are considering is the computational cost associated with the models analysis. In this sense, we are classifying the properties that are analyzed in this version of the method in order to select the ones that must be analyzed and the ones that may be analyzed. After such a classification we'll intend to generate an optimized version of the method.

References

1. Baader, F., Calvanese, D. McGuiness, D., Nardi, D. and Patel-Schneider, P. *The description Logic Handbook - Theory, Implementation and Applications*, Cambridge Univ. Press, (2003)
2. Bauer, B. MÃ¼ller, J.P. and Odell, J. Agent UML: A Formalism for Specifying Multiagent Software Systems In: Ciancarini and Wooldridge (Eds) *Agent-Oriented Software Engineering*, Springer-Verlag, LNCS vol 1957, (2001).
3. Berardi,D. Using DLs to reason on UML class diagrams, in *Proceedings of th KI-2002 Workshop on Applications of Description Logics*, (2002).
4. Biddle, J; Thomas, E. *Role Theory: Concepts and Research*, John Wiley and Sons, New York, (1966).
5. Borst, W.N. *Construction of Engineering Ontologies*, University of Twente, Enschede, NL, Center for Telematica and Information Technology, (1997).
6. Brandão, A.A.F. *An ontology-based method for structuring and analyzing multiagent systems models* PhD Thesis, Pontifical Catholic University of Rio de Janeiro - PUC-Rio, Brazil, (2005) (in Portuguese)
7. DAML+OIL - DARPA Agent Markup Language http://www.daml.org/
8. DeLoach, S. A. Analysis and Design of Multiagent Systems Using Hybrid Coordination Media. In: *Proceedings of the 6th World Multi-Conference on Systemic, Cybernetics and Informatics (SCI 2002)* , Florida - USA, (2002), pp. 14–18.
9. Dong,J.S., Lee,C.H., Li, Y.F. and Wang, H. Verifying DAML+OIL and Beyond in Z/EVES, In *Proceedings of the 26th International Conference on Software Engineering (ICSE'04)*, (2004), pp. 201–210.
10. FaCT - Fast Classification of Terminologies, available at: http://www.cs.man.ac.uk/~horrocks/FaCT

11. Ekenberg L. and Johannesson,P. A framework for determining design correctness, *Knowledge Based Systems*, Elsevier, **17** (5-6), (2004), pp. 249–262.

12. Gruber,T.R. A Translation Approach to Portable Ontology Specification, *Knowledge Acquisition*, **5**, (1993), pp. 199–220.

13. Jennings, N. Agent-Oriented Software Engineering. In: *Proceedings of the 20th Intl. Conf. on Industrial and Engineering Applications of Artificial Intelligence*, (1999), pp 4–10.

14. Kalfoglou, Y. and Robertson, D. A case study in applying ontologies to augment and reason about the correctness of specifications, in *Proceedings of the 11th International Conference on Software Engineering and Knowledge Engineering (SEKE99)*, Kaiserlautern, Germany, (1999), available at http://www.ecs.soton.ac.uk/people/yk1/ (04/19/2005).

15. Kim,S and Carrington,D. A Formal Mapping Between UML Models and Object-Z Specifications, in *Proceedings of the ZB'2000, International Conference of B and Z Users*, York, UK, (2000).

16. de Maria, B.A.; Silva, V.T.; Lucena, C.J.P., Choren, R. VisualAgent: A Software Development Environment for Multi-Agent Systems, In *Proceedings of the 19th Brazilian Symposiun on Software Engeneering (SBES 2005)*, Tool Track, Uberlândia, MG, Brazil, October 3-7, (2005).

17. Mens,T., Straeten,R. and Simmonds,J. Maintaining Consistency between UML Models with Description Logic Tools, in *Proceedings of the Workshop on Object-Oriented Reengineering at ECOOP 2003*, (2003).

18. Object Management Group - OMG http://www.omg.org/

19. Object Managment Group: OMG - Meta Object Facility (MOF) Specification, version 1.4, available at http://www.omg.org/cgi-bin/doc?formal/2002-04-03 (last visited 04/25/2005).

20. OWL -Ontology Web Language, available at http://www.w3c.org/TR/owl-features/

21. Parunak, H. and Odell, J. Representing Social Structures in UML. In: *Proceedings of Agent Oriented Software Engineering*,(2001), pp 1–16.

22. Perini, A. Pistore, M. Roveri, M. and Susi, A. Agent-oriented modeling by interleaving formal and informal specification, in Giorgini, P., Muller, J. and Odell, J. (Eds) *Modeling Agents and Multi-Agent Systems*, **LNCS 2935**, Springer-Verlag, (2003), pp 36–52.

23. Protégé 2000 Ontology Editor - available at http://protege.stanford.edu/

24. RACER, Renamed Abox and Concept Expression Reasoner, a vailable at: http://www.sts.tu-harburg.de/ r.f.moeller/racer

25. RICE, Racer Interactive Client Environment
http://www.cs.concordia.ca/ haarslev/racer/rice.jar

26. Rational Rose. http://www-306.ibm.com/software/rational/

27. Rumbaugh,J., Jacobson,I. and Booch,G. *The Unified Modeling Language Reference Manual.* Addison-Wesley, (1999).

28. Silva, V., Garcia, A., Brandão, A., Chavez, C., Lucena, C., Alencar, P. Taming Agents and Objects in Software, in Garcia, Lucena, et al (Eds) *Software Engineering for Large-Scale Multi-agent Systems- Research Issues and Practical Applications*, Lecture Notes in Computer Science, **2603**, (2003), 1–16.

29. Silva, V. and Lucena, C. From a Conceptual Framework for Agents and Objects to a Multi-Agent System Modeling Language, In: Sycara, K., Wooldridge, M. (Eds.), *Journal of Autonomous Agents and Multi-Agent Systems*, **9**, (2004), 145–189.

30. Straeten,R. and Simmonds,J. Detecting Inconsistencies between UML Models Using Description Logic, in *Proceedings of the 2003 International Workshop on Description Logics*, available at http://CEUR-WS.org

31. Wagner, G. The Agent-Object-Relationship Metamodel: Towards a Unified View of State and Behavior, *Information Systems*, **28**, 5, (2003), 475–504.

32. Wooldridge, M. and Ciancarini, P. Agent-Oriented Software Engineering: The State of the Art, In: Ciancarini and Wooldridge (Eds) *Agent-Oriented Software Engineering*, Springer-Verlag, LNCS, **1957**, (2001).

33. Zambonelli, F., Jennings, N. and Wooldridge, M. Organizational Abstractions for the Analysis and Design of Multi-Agent Systems, In: Ciancarini and Wooldridge (Eds) *Agent-Oriented Software Engineering*, Springer-Verlag, LNCS, **1957**, (2001).

Using Risk Analysis to Evaluate Design Alternatives

Yudistira Asnar, Volha Bryl, and Paolo Giorgini

Department of Information and Communication Technology
University of Trento, Italy
{yudis.asnar,volha.bryl,paolo.giorgini}@dit.unitn.it

Abstract. Recently, multi-agent systems have proved to be a suitable approach to the development of real-life information systems. In particular, they are used in the domain of safety critical systems where availability and reliability are crucial. For these systems, the ability to mitigate risk (e.g., failures, exceptional events) is very important. In this paper, we propose to incorporate risk concerns into the process of a multi-agent system design and describe the process of exploring and evaluating design alternatives based on risk-related metrics. We illustrate the proposed approach using an Air Traffic Management case study.

1 Introduction

Multi-Agent Systems (MAS) have recently proved to be a suitable approach for the development of real-life information systems. The characteristics they exhibit (e.g., autonomy and ability to coordinate their activities), are indeed useful for safety critical and responsive systems [1]. This is because their subsystems can work independently and respond to events (e.g., failure, exceptional situation, unexpected traffic, etc.) as quick and correct as possible. For instance, a disaster management involves several stakeholders that work autonomously, cooperatively and responsively in unpredictable environments. In this scenario, agents can be used, for example, to assist stakeholders in managing traffic during the rescue period and then reduce the probability of chaotic situations [2].

In a safety critical system, human lives heavily depend on the availability and reliability of the system [3]. For this reason, countermeasures are introduced to mitigate as much as possible the effects of occurring failures. For instance, OASIS Air Traffic Management system [4], which exploits autonomous and responsive agents, is used to manage airspace and schedule air traffic flow. In this case, a designer ensures that agents perform their tasks properly and do not endanger the aircrafts. OASIS implements monitor components/agents that compare the prediction of aircraft locations (i.e., the results of predictor agents) and the actual aircraft position. In case of a significant discrepancy, the monitor agent notifies the scheduler agent to re-schedule the landing time of related aircraft. The introduction of a monitor agent corresponds to a countermeasure to prevent the risk of a collision. However, since designers can not have a complete knowledge about future events/situations, they are not able to elicit all the necessary countermeasures.

A different approach is adopted in the Autonomous Nano Technology Swarm (ANTS) project [1], where three different types of agents (ruler, messenger and worker)

L. Padgham and F. Zambonelli (Eds.): AOSE 2006, LNCS 4405, pp. 140–155, 2007.

cooperate one another in order to explore asteroids. An important feature of ANTS is that, since agents can be damaged or even destroyed by the asteroid, rulers have the ability to re-organize the remaining messenger and worker agents. Basically, this run-time re-organization corresponds to a countermeasure that is adopted to compensate the loss of damaged agents. This introduces at design-time the problem of enabling agents with automatic adaptation capabilities [5] to deal with the effect of failures occurring at run-time.

In [6,7], we have proposed an approach to support the design of secure and coopera-tive systems. The main idea was to use planning techniques to find and evaluate possible design alternatives. The objective of this paper is to extend the approach to MAS design and introducing a suitable risk-based metric for evaluating alternatives. We introduce a process based on the following steps:

- system actors, their goals and capabilities, goal decompositions, and possible de-pendency relationships among actors are identified;
- the above information are passed as input to a planner that search for a possible plan able to satisfy all actors' goals;
- the plan is evaluated w.r.t. risk, that is it is checked whether the risk associated to goals is under a predefined threshold;
- if the evaluation reveals that changes are still necessary, the problem is refined, a new plan is generated and then evaluated.

In safety critical systems, it is important to have a responsible for any decision taken. This requires that the human designer being part of the decisional process and, par-ticularly, being the responsible of the approval of the final solution. Our framework is meant to be a Computer-Aided Software Engineering (CASE) tool that helps a designer in defining and evaluating each design alternative with respect to the associate risk level. The approach can also be used to assist the designer in performing the runtime design of a MAS.

The paper is structured as follows. We start by introducing a case study which then will be used to illustrate our approach. The approach itself is detailed in Section 3, where we explain how the problem of selecting a suitable MAS design can be framed as a planning one, and then in Section 4, where the process of the risk-based evaluation of the obtained alternative design is explained. The application of our approach to the case study is presented in Section 5, which is followed by a short overview of the related work and some conclusive remarks in Sections 6 and 7, respectively.

2   Case Study

In this paper, we use the Air Traffic Management (ATM) case study that is used in the SERENITY Project[1] to validate security and dependability patterns. An ATM is categorized as a safety-critical system because it is closely related to the safety of human lives. Therefore, an ATM system is required to be available and reliable all the time of its operation. However, having a 100% available and reliable system is hardly possible,

---

[1] http://www.serenity-project.org

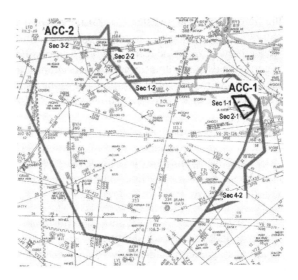

Fig. 1. Airspace Division between ACC-1 and ACC-2

because there are many events that can obstruct the system which can not be known in advance (i.e., during the system development phase). For example, in a specific sector, aircraft traffic can exceed the safety threshold which was not anticipated during the design of the ATM. These events can compromise the availability and reliability of sub-components of the ATM system (e.g., radar processor, CWP[2]).

An Air traffic Control Center (ACC) is a body authorized to provide air traffic control (ATC) services in certain airspace. These services comprise controlling aircraft, managing airspace, managing flight data of controlled aircraft, and providing information about the situation of the air. Suppose there are two adjacent ACCs, namely ACC-1 and ACC-2 (Fig. 1), where the airspace of ACC-1 is surrounded by the airspace of ACC-2. The airspace is organized into several adjacent volumes, called sectors. For instance, the airspace of ACC-1 is divided into sectors (Sec 1-1 and Sec 2-1), and ACC-2 has its airspace divided into 4 sectors (Sec 1-2, 2-2, 3-2, and 4-2). Each sector is operated by a team, consisting of a controller (e.g., Sec 1-1 has C1-1 as a controller), and a planner (e.g., P1-1 is a planner for Sec 1-1). For the sake of communication, several adjacent sectors in an ACC are supervised by a supervisor (e.g., SU1-1 supervises Sec 1-1 and 2-1 and SU1-2 supervises Sec 1-2 and 2-2). In this scenario, the supervisor role is assigned to a human agent, while software agents cover the role of controller and planner. To simplify, we simple call actor, both human agent and software agent. The supervisor also acts as a designer and so, responsibly, approve/decline the new plans. The scenario starts from the normal operation of ATM in which SU1-1 delegates the control of sector 1-1 to team 1 formed by controller C1-1 and planner P1-1.

C1-1 and P1-1 work together providing ATC services to the aircraft in sector 1-1. C1-1 controls aircraft to guarantee the safe vertical and horizontal separation of each

---

[2] Controller Working Position (CWP) is a set of resources allocated to support a controller to perform his/her tasks.

aircraft, while P1-1 manages the flight data of the controlled aircraft and the airspace of sector 1-1.

One day during summer holidays, a flight bulletin reports that there will be an increase of the en-route traffic in sector 1-1. According to the analysis made by P1-1, this goes beyond the capacity of a single controller (C1-1). Thus, SU1-1 needs to re-design his sectors in a way that the en-route traffic can be handled safely. He can

- divide the airspace into smaller sectors s.t. each controller covers a smaller area and consequently, the number of sectors that are supervised by SU1-1 is increased; or
- delegate a part of the airspace to the adjacent supervisor (it could be from the same or different ACC).

Each alternative introduces different requirements. For instance, when dividing the airspace, SU1-1 needs to ensure the **availability of a controlling team** (G_{14}, G_{21} in Table 1) and the **availability of a set of CWP** (G_{15}, G_{22} in Table 1). Conversely, if SU1-1 decides to delegate a part of his airspace to another supervisor, then SU1-1 needs to **define delegation schema** (G_{10} in Table 1) and to have sufficient level of "trust" towards the target supervisor and his team to manage the delegated airspace. Moreover, SU1-1 needs to be sure that the target supervisor has sufficient infrastructure (e.g., radar, radio communication coverage) to provide ATC services in the delegated airspace.

The details of the ATM case study are presented in Section 5, including organizational setting and capabilities of each actor. In the following sections, we explain how to encode the case study as a planning problem, and then how to evaluate and refine the candidate plan so to maintain the level of risk below a predefined threshold.

3 Planning Domain

Generating design alternatives can be framed as a planning problem: generating a design alternative means constructing a plan that satisfies the system's goals. The basic idea behind the planning approach is to automatically determine the course of actions (i.e. a plan) needed to achieve a certain goal, where an action is a transition rule from one state of the system to another [8,9]. Actions are described in terms of preconditions and effects: if a precondition is true in the current state of the system, then the action is performed. As a consequence of an action, the system will be in a new state where the effect of the action is true.

Thus, to define the planning problem, we need to formalize

- the initial and the desired states of the system;
- the actions of the planning domain;
- the planning domain axioms.

In order to represent the initial state of the system (i.e. actor and goal properties, and social relations among actors), first order logic is used with conjunctions of predicates and their negations, specifying the states of the system. To describe our domain we use the following predicates.

- For the goal properties:
  - satisfied(G – goal), which becomes true when the goal G is fulfilled. The predicate is used to define the goal of the planning problem (i.e., to specify, which goals should be satisfied in the final state of the system);
  - and/or_subgoal$_n$(G, G$_1$, G$_2$, ..., G$_n$ – goal) represents the predefined way of goal refinement, namely, it states that G can be and/or-decomposed into n and/or-subgoals;
  - type(G – goal, GT – goal_type) is used to typify goals;
  - criticality_h/m/l(G – goal) represents the criticality of the goal, one of high, medium, or low. The criticality level implies the minimum needed level of trust between the actors when the goal is delegated. For instance, if the criticality of the goal G is high, then it could be delegated from the actor A$_1$ to the actor A$_2$ only if A$_1$ can depend on A$_2$ for the type of goals which G belongs to with the high level of trust.
- For the actor properties:
  - wants(A – actor, G – goal) represents the initial actor's desires;
  - can_satisfy(A – actor, G – goal) and can_satisfy_gt(A – actor, GT – goal_type) are used to represent the capabilities of an actor to satisfy a goal, or a specific type of goal, respectively.
- For the actor dependencies:
  - can_depend_on_gt_h/m/l(A$_1$, A$_2$ – actor, GT – goal_type) means that actor A$_1$ can delegate the fulfillment of the goal of type GT to actor A$_2$, and the trust level of the dependency between these actors for this specific goal type is high, medium, or low, respectively.

A plan, constructed to fulfill the goals, can contain the following actions, defined in terms of preconditions and effects, expressed with the help of the above predicates.

- *Goal satisfaction.* An actor satisfies a goal if it is among its desires (either initially, or after the delegation from another actor), and it has the capability to satisfy it.
- *Goal decomposition.* A goal could be decomposed either into the and-subgoals, meaning that all of them should be satisfied to satisfy the initial goal, or into the or-subgoals, which represent alternative ways of achieving the goal.
- *Goal delegation.* An actor might not have enough capabilities to achieve its goals by itself and therefore, it has to delegate the responsibility of their satisfaction to other actors. As was mentioned before, the delegation can only take place if the level of trust between the actors is not lower than the criticality level required for the goal to be delegated.
- *Goal relaxation.* If there is no way to find a dependency relation which satisfies the required level of trust, then the goal criticality might be relaxed (i.e., lowered). This can be a risky action, as in many cases it is not safe to lower the level of criticality. Therefore, to minimize the risk, as soon as the delegation has been performed, the goal criticality is restored to the original value.

To complete the planning domain, we use axioms which hold in every state of the system and are used to complete the description of the current state. For example, to propagate goal properties through goal refinement, the following axiom is used: a goal is satisfied if all its and-subgoals or at least one of the or-subgoals are satisfied.

We have chosen LPG-td [10], a fully automated system for solving planning problems, for implementing our planning domain. LPG-td supports the PDDL (Planning Domain Definition Language) 2.2 specification, which was used to formalize system states, actions and axioms described above. The details on how and why this planner has been chosen have been addressed in [6]. We also refer the reader to [6] and [7] for the details on how the actions and axioms of the planning domain were implemented in PDDL 2.2.

4   Evaluation Process

After a design alternative, called a candidate plan, is generated by the planner, it should also be evaluated and modified based on a number of criteria, and finally approved by a designer. By modifying the candidate plan we mean refining the problem definition by identifying the actions that should be avoided to get the less risky design alternative. The refinement of the problem definition is followed by replanning.

Previously, we proposed a way of evaluating a candidate plan, which is based on the load distribution concerns [7]. It is assumed that the actors want to keep the number and complexity of actions they are involved in, below the predefined thresholds. In this work, we propose another form of evaluation, namely adopting a risk evaluation metric. The goal of the iterative planning-and-evaluation procedure is to select a plan among the available alternatives that has an acceptable level of risk. In this framework, we consider two types of risk. The first type is the risk about the satisfaction of a goal, called satisfaction risk (sat-risk). Sat-risk represents the risk of a goal being denied/failed when an actor attempts to fulfill it. The value of this risk is represented in terms of the following predicates: *FD* (Fully Denied), *PD* (Partially Denied), and *ND* (Not Denied). These predicates are taken from [11], and represent the high, medium, and low level of sat-risk, respectively. The second type of risk is related to the risk of goal delegation. It is based on the requirement that the level of trust between two actors should match the criticality of the delegated goal. For instance, if a link between two agents is highly trusted, than it can be used for delegating goals of any criticality level, but if the level of trust of a delegation link is medium then only goals with low and medium criticality can be delegated through this link, and the risk is introduced when the criticality of a goal should be lowered before it could be delegated.

The process of selecting a suitable design alternative is illustrated in Algorithm 1, which should be run twice. In the first execution, the algorithm constructs a plan without any relaxation actions (i.e., *relax*=false). If there is no solution then the second execution is preformed allowing relaxation actions. Some steps in the algorithm are fully automated (e.g., *run_planner* line 3), while some still need a human involvement (e.g., adding the allowed actions to the *whitelist* in line 7). The algorithm is iterative and comprises the following phases: planning, evaluation, and, finally, plan refinement. There are two evaluation steps in the algorithm: STEP-1 evaluates the risks of goal satisfactions (line 4), and STEP-2 evaluates relaxation actions (line 6). The first execution does only STEP-1, and if the second execution is necessary, both STEP-1 and

---

Algorithm 1. Planning and Evaluation Process

Require: domain {domain description in PDDL}
     problem {goal and initial state of the problem in PDDL}
     whitelist {a list of allowed action}
     relax{allow/not relaxation}
1: boolean finish←false
2: **while not** finish **do**
3:    plan ←$run\_planner(domain, problem, relax)$
4:    **if not** $evaluate\_sat(plan)$ **then**
5:       $refine\_sat(plan, problem)$
6:    **else if** relax **and not** $evaluate\_act(plan)$ **then**
7:       $refine\_act(plan, problem, whitelist)$
8:    **else**
9:       finish ←true
10:   **end if**
11: **end while**
12: **return** plan

STEP-2 are executed. Each evaluation step is followed by a refinement action (line 5 or 7), which aims at changing the planner input s.t. during the next iteration it will produce the better (i.e. less risky) candidate plan. In the following we give details on the two evaluation steps of the algorithm.

STEP 1: Goal Satisfaction Evaluation

After a candidate plan is elicited (line 3), it should be evaluated and refined, s.t. it meets the requirements imposed on it (i.e., the level of risk associated with the plan is below the predefined threshold). The aim of the first evaluation step (line 4 of the Algorithm) is to assure that **sat-risk** values of the candidate plan, i.e. the likelihood of each system goal being denied/failed, are at most equal to the accepted ones, specified by a designer.

By examining the candidate plan, the goal model of each top goal can be constructed, as the one in Fig. 3. A goal model shows how a top goal is refined into atomic tangible leaf goals, i.e. for each leaf goal there is an actor that can fulfill it. Starting from the **sat-risk** values of leaf goals, the risk values are propagated up to the top goals with the help of so called forward reasoning. Forward reasoning is an automatic reasoning technique introduced in [11], which takes a set of **sat-risk** of leaf goals as an input. Notice that **sat-risk** value depends on which actor satisfies the leaf goal according to the candidate plan. The algorithm propagates the qualitative values assigned to the leaf goals along the goal tree up to the top goal, and thus the corresponding value for the top goal is calculated.

If **sat-risk** of one top goal is higher than the specified threshold, then the refinement process needs to be performed. The refinement (line 5) identifies those assignments of the leaf goals to actors that should be avoided in order to have the **sat-risk** values of the top goals within the specified thresholds. The refinement process starts by generating a possible set of assignment (i.e., **sat-risk** values of the leaf goals) that results in the top goals having the **sat-risks** below the specified thresholds. This set of assignments is called a reference model. Basically, the reference model is a set of maximum sat-risk values of leaf goals that results in the top goals, which sat-risks do not violate the thresholds. If the sat-risk values of leaf goals in the goal model are below the maximum specified in the reference model, then the sat-risk of the top goals are acceptable. The reference model can be obtained automatically using backward reasoning [12], which aims at constructing the assignments of leaf goals to actors s.t. the specified sat-risk value for the top goals are achieved. According to [12], a goal model is encoded as a satisfiability (SAT) problem, and a SAT solver is used to find the possible assignments that satisfy the SAT formula.

By comparing the sat-risk values of leaf goals in the goal model with the corresponding values in the reference model, the riskier goal satisfaction actions are detected (i.e., the leaf goal in the goal model that has higher sat-risk than the corresponding value in the reference model). For instance, in Fig. 3 the risk-sat of goal capable managing airspace (G_{19}) that is satisfied by actor P1-1 is FD (Fully Denied), while according to the reference model, the value of G_{19} should be at most PD (partially denied). Therefore, the problem definition needs to be refined s.t. P1-1 does not satisfy G_{19}. However, we can not refine the problem by simply specifying G_{19} must not be satisfied by P1-1, because in Fig. 3 the goal model states that the satisfaction of G_{19} by P1-1 is too risky. Ideally, we specify "the path of actions" from the top goal that lead to the goal G_{19} being satisfied by P1-1. To simplify the refinement process, we only consider one action involving G_{19}, performed just before P1-1 satisfies it. In case of Fig. 2(b), such an action (called *previous related action*) is *and_decompose* G_3 into G_{18} and G_{19}, which is performed by P1-1. Thus, the refinement predicate that should be introduced in the problem definition is the following.

$$\neg(satisfy(P_{1-1}, G_{19}) \land and\_decompose_2(P_{1-1}, G_3, G_{18}, G_{19}))$$

After the problem definition is refined, the planner is run again to elicit a new candidate plan using the refined problem definition. All the above described steps can be done automatically, without any interference a designer.

STEP 2: Action Evaluation

The second evaluation step (line 6 of the Algorithm) is performed to guarantee that the relaxation actions in a candidate plan are acceptable/not risky. In our framework, we assume that relaxing the criticality of a goal from high to medium, or from medium to low, can be performed safely only by the owner of a goal. We say that goal G is owned by A if G was initially wanted by A (i.e., in the initial state A wants G to be satisfied). In this case all the subgoals of G are also said to be owned by A. We use the term *further relaxation* to refer to the situation when the relaxation is done by another actor (i.e., not the owner). *Further relaxation* is assumed to be a risky action, but sometimes it is impossible to find a plan without it. This action could be allowed by the interference of a designer adding it to the *whitelist*.

For instance, in the ATM case study SU1-1 intends to increase his airspace capacity in response to the traffic increase by delegating his airspace(G_{11})to SU1-2. As the fulfillment of G_{11} is critical (the criticality level is high), SU1-1 needs to have high trust level towards SU1-2 for delegating G_{11} (i.e., $can\_depend\_on\_gt\_h(SU_{1-1}, SU_{1-2}, G_{11})$

should be true). Later, SU1-2 refines G_{11} into the subgoals control the aircraft (G_2) and manage the airspace (G_3). For satisfying these goals, SU1-2 needs to depend on the controller C1-2 for G_2, and on the planner P1-2 for G_3, because they are the ones that have the capabilities to satisfy the corresponding goals. Let us assume the trust level of the dependency of SU1-2 towards C1-2 for G_2 is medium. Thus, SU1-2 needs to *further relax* the criticality of G_2 s.t. it can be delegated to C1-2.

Basically, the evaluation aims to guarantee that there is no relaxation action taken by an actor which is not the owner of the goal. Otherwise, the designer needs to explicitly allow the actor to do this action (i.e., add it to the *whitelist*). Notice that relaxation actions are introduced only in the second run of algorithm. During the refinement phase (line 7) the problem definition is changed to meet this requirement, which is followed by replanning.

5   Experimental Results

In this section, we illustrate the application of our approach to the ATM case study. The following subsections detail the case study formalization, and the planning-and-evaluation process, performed in accordance with Algorithm 1. The aim of the process is to elicit an appropriate plan for SU1-1's sector, taking into account the constraints and the risk of each alternative. The scenario starts with the intention of SU1-1 to increase the capacity of airspace (G_6) as a response to the air traffic increase in sector 1-1. SU1-1 faces a problem that C1-1 is not available to control (G_{14}) more traffic. Therefore, SU1-1 needs to modify sector 1-1 without involving C1-1 s.t. the increase of air traffic can be handled.

5.1   Case Study Formalization

The following inputs should be provided for Algorithm 1:

- A formalized problem definition, which contains all the properties of the actors of the ATM system, and their goals. The complete list of properties can be found in Table 2.
- Goals of the planning problem (e.g., satisfy G_6 without involving C1-1 in satisfying G_{14}).
- A list of authorized further relaxation actions (*whitelist*).
- Risk values of goal satisfaction actions. Table 1 shows all sat-risk values of the satisfaction actions.
- Accepted risk values (e.g., risk value of G_6 is at most PD).

In Table 1, the goal criticality values are presented in column Crit. Goal criticality (high, medium, or low) denotes a minimum level of trust between two actors that is needed if one actor decides to delegate the goal to another actor. For instance, goal manage airspace (G_3) is categorized as a *highly critical* goal, and goal analyze air traffic (G_8) has *low* criticality. Thus, these goals require different level of trust for being delegated to another actor.

Moreover, Table 1 shows the risk levels of satisfying a goal when an actor tries to achieve it. Note that, the sat-risk level of a goal depends on which actor satisfies the

Table 1. Goals Criticality and Satisfaction Risk (Criticality = H: High, M: Medium, L: Low and sat-risk = Full Denied, Partial Denied, and Not Denied)

Id.	Description	Crit.	C1-1	C2-1	P1-1	P2-1	SU1-1	C1-2	P1-2	SU1-2
G1	Manage Aircraft within ACC									
G2	Control Aircraft	H								
G3	Manage Airspace	H								
G4	Manage Flight Data	M						PD		
G5	Maintain Air Traffic Flow in Peak-Time									
G6	Increase Airspace Capacity									
G7	Analyze Air Traffic	L								
G8	Re-sectorize within ACC									
G9	Delegate Part of Sector									
G10	Define Schema Delegation	M			ND					PD
G11	Delegate Airspace	H								
G12	Have Controlling Resources									
G13	Have Capability to Control the Aircraft		ND	PD				PD		
G14	Avail to Control		FD	ND						
G15	Have Control Working Position for Controller	H					ND			PD
G16	Have Authorization for FD Modification	M	ND	ND						
G17	Have Capability to Manage FD				ND	PD				
G18	Have Resources for Planning	M					ND			
G19	Have Capability to Manage Airspace				FD	PD			PD	
G20	Have Capability to Analyze Air Traffic				PD					
G21	Avail to Plan				ND	ND			ND	
G22	Have Control Working Position for Planner	H					ND			ND

goal. sat-risk takes one of the tree values: *FD* (Fully Denied), *PD* (Partially Denied), or *ND* (Not Denied). For instance, the table states G_{19} can be satisfied either by actor P1-1, P2-1, or P1-2, and each actor has different level of risk (sat-risk) – *full*, *partial*, and *partial*, respectively. The empty cells in Table 1 imply the actor does not have capabilities to fulfill the corresponding goal.

Table 2 shows properties of actors and their goals in ATM case study. Namely, it represents actor capabilities (can_satisfy), possible ways of goal refinements (decompose), and possible dependencies among actors (can_depend_on) together with the level of trust for each dependency. For instance, actor SU1-1 can_satisfy goals G_{15}, G_{18}, and G_{22}, and the actor has knowledge to decompose G_1, G_5, G_6, G_8, and G_9. And SU1-1 has *high* level of trust to delegate G_2 to C1-1 or C2-2. The same intuition is applied for the other cells.

5.2 Planning and Evaluation Process

STEP 0: Planning. After specifying the inputs, the planner is executed to elicit a candidate plan to fulfill the predefined goals, which is shown in Fig. 2(a). These goals state that the plan should satisfy G_6, and the solution should not involve C1-1 to satisfy G_{14} because C1-1 is already overloaded controlling the current traffic. Moreover, the planner should not involve the other ACC (i.e., SU1-2) by avoiding the delegation of G_{11} to SU1-2 even it is possible in Table 2. Before adopting the candidate plan (Fig. 2(b)), two evaluation steps explained in previous section should be performed to ensure the risk of the candidate plan is acceptable.

Table 2. List of Actors and Goal Properties for the ATM Case Study. (Level of trust: H: High, M: Medium, L: Low).

Actor	can_satisfy	decompose			can_depend_on		
		type	top-goal	sub-goals	level	dependum	dependee
SU1-1	G15	And	G1	G2, G3	H	G2	C1-1, C2-1
	G18	And	G5	G6, G7	H	G3	P1-1, P2-1
	G22	Or	G6	G8, G9	H	G4	P1-1, P2-1
		And	G8	G2, G3, G4	M	G7	P1-1
		And	G9	G10, G11	M	G10	P1-1
					L	G10	SU1-2
					H	G11	SU1-2
P1-1, P2-1	G17	And	G3	G18, G19	H	G22	SU1-1
	G19	And	G4	G16, G17, G18			
	G21	And	G7	G18, G20			
P1-1	G10				L	G16	C1-1
	G20						
P1-2					L	G16	C2-1
C1-1, C2-1	G13	And	G2	G4, G12, G13	H	G15	SU1-1
	G14	And	G12	G14, G15			
	G16						
C1-1					M	G4	P1-1
C2-1					M	G4	P2-1
					M	G4	P1-1
SU1-2	G10	And	G11	G2, G3	M	G2	C1-2
	G15				M	G3	P1-2
	G22						
P1-2	G19	And	G3	G19, G21, G22	M	G22	SU1-2
	G21						
C1-2	G4	And	G2	G4, G13, G15	M	G15	SU1-2
	G13						

STEP 1: Goal Satisfaction Evaluation assesses the satisfaction risk of a candidate plan. The goal model of goal G_6 (in Fig. 3) is constructed on the basis of the candidate plan (in Fig. 2(b)). The goal model shows which actors are responsible for satisfying the leaf goals. For instance, G_{19} must be satisfied by P1-1 and, moreover, in this scenario, G_9 is left unsatisfied because the other or-subgoal, G_8, was selected to satisfy G_6.

In this scenario, we assume that the acceptable sat-risk value for G_6 is PD. To calculate the sat-risk value of goal G_6, forward reasoning is performed (i.e., the sat-risk values of leaf goals in Table 1 are propagated up to the top goal). This reasoning mechanism is a part of the functionality of the GR-Tool[3], a supporting tool for goal analysis. By means of the forward reasoning, we obtain that the sat-risk of G_6 is FD, which is higher than the acceptable risk (i.e., PD). Thus, the refinement is needed to adjust the problem definition, so that a less risky plan is constructed during the next replanning. The refinement starts with the elicitation of a reference model using backward reasoning. The reference model specifies that all leaf goals must have at most PD sat-risk value in order the sat-risk of top goal G_6 not to be higher than PD.

By comparing the sat-risks of leaf goals in the goal model with the reference model, G_{19} (satisfied by P1-1) is detected to be a risky goal; its sat-risk (in Table 1) is FD which is higher than the one in the reference model. Therefore, the problem definition is refined to avoid P1-1 satisfying G_{19}. As G_{19} is a subgoal of G_3, the decomposition action is also negated, as the previous related action, according to the procedure

---

[3] http://sesa.dit.unitn.it/goaleditor

```
(satisfied G6)
(not(satisfy C1-1 G14))
(not(delegate SU1-1 SU1-2 G11))
```
(a) Goal of Problem Definition

```
0:  (OR_DECOMPOSES2 SU1-1 G6 G8 G9)
1:  (AND_DECOMPOSES3 SU1-1 G8 G2 G3 G4)
2:  (DELEGATES SU1-1 C2-1 G2)
3:  (AND_DECOMPOSES3 C2-1 G2 G4 G12 G13)
4:  (SATISFIES C2-1 G13)
5:  (AND_DECOMPOSES2 C2-1 G12 G14 G15)
6:  (SATISFIES C2-1 G14)
7:  (DELEGATES C2-1 SU1-1 G15)
8:  (SATISFIES SU1-1 G15)
9:  (DELEGATES C2-1 P2-1 G4)
10: (DELEGATES SU1-1 P2-1 G4)
11: (AND_DECOMPOSES3 P2-1 G4 G16 G17 G18)
12: (SATISFIES P2-1 G17)
13: (DELEGATES P2-1 SU1-1 G18)
14: (SATISFIES SU1-1 G18)
15: (RELAX2L P2-1 G16)
16: (DELEGATES P2-1 C2-1 G16)
17: (SATISFIES C2-1 G16)
18: (DELEGATES SU1-1 P1-1 G3)
19: (AND_DECOMPOSES2 P1-1 G3 G18 G19)
20: (SATISFIES P1-1 G19)
```
(b) The Candidate Plan after STEP 0

Fig. 2. Plan for Increasing Air Space Capacity

explained in the previous section. Thus, the problem definition is refined, and the goal of the planning problem is now of the form shown in Fig. 4(a). Afterwards, the planner is run to elicit a new candidate plan. Basically, the new candidate plan is almost the same with the previous plan (Fig. 2(b)), the only difference is in lines 18-20 (see Fig. 4(b)). Later, this candidate plan is evaluated by going through the next step to ensure all the actions (especially, further relaxations) are acceptable in terms of risks.

STEP 2: Action Evaluation filters the malicious relaxation actions. The scenario starts from the goal G_6 which is wanted by SU1-1. As all the other goals of the candidate plan are the result of the refinement of G_6, the owner of all of them is again SU1-1. Thus, relaxing the criticality of any goals that is performed by any actors except SU1-1 is seen as a risky action.

For instance, P2-1 relaxes the criticality of G_{16} (line 15 in Fig. 2(b)) to low instead of medium. By default this action is a risky one and should be avoided, unless the designer states explicitly that this action is not risky by adding it to the *whitelist*. Once it is considered unacceptable, the goal of the planning problem should be extended with the negation of the relaxation action (i.e., (not (relax2l P2-1 G1))).

Moreover, the designer can also introduce rules to avoid certain actions. For instance, the designer may prevent C2-1 from delegating G_4 to P2-1 (line 9 in Fig. 2(b)) by adding a new predicate to the goal of the planning problem (namely, (not (delegate C2-1 P2-1 G4))). For the sake of simplicity all the possible relaxation actions in the candidate plan are put to the *whitelist*, so we do not refine the problem definition any further.

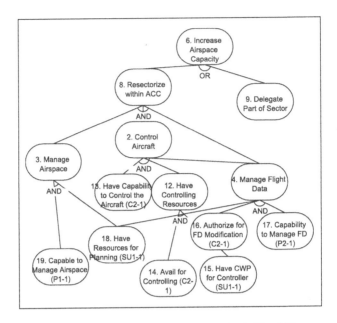

Fig. 3. The Goal Model of Candidate Plan in Fig. 2(b)

```
(satisfied G6)
(not (satisfy C1-1 G14))
(not (delegate SU1-1 SU1-2 G11))
(not (and (satisfy P1-1 G19)(and_decompose2 P1-1 G3 G18 G19)))
```
(a) Problem Definition Refinement after STEP 1

```
...........
18: (DELEGATES SU1-1 P2-1 G3)
19: (AND_DECOMPOSES2 P2-1 G3 G18 G19)
20: (SATISFIES P2-1 G19)
```
(b) Final Plan for Satisfying G_6

Fig. 4. Final Problem Definition and Plan for **increase the airspace capacity** (G_6)

Thus, the last candidate plan to redesign SU1-1's sector is approved s.t. the traffic increase can be handled. Moreover, the plan is guaranteed to have risk values less/equal than the predefined thresholds (i.e., **sat-risk** of G_6 is less or equal than PD).

6   Related Work

Several approaches have been proposed in literature to use risk analysis in the design of a software system. CORAS [13] has been developed as a framework for risk analysis of security critical systems. Basically, CORAS consists of context identification, risk identification, risk analysis, risk evaluation, and risk treatment. CORAS can be integrated with other risk modeling frameworks, such as Failure Mode, Effects, and Criticality

Analysis (FMECA) [14], Fault Tree Analysis (FTA) [15], Hazard and Operability (HA-ZOP) [16]. This methodology has been tested with security systems, especially in the E-Commerce and Telemedicine area. In reliability engineering community, Defect Detection and Prevention (DDP) [17] has been proposed to assess the impact of risk and related mitigation to the system. The DDP framework deals with three types of data: Objective, Risk, and Mitigation. The objective is defined as the goal the system has to achieve. The risk is defined as the thing that, once it occurs, leads to the failure of the objective. Finally, the mitigation is a course of actions that can be applied to reduce the risk. With the help of DDP the designer can assess how the introduction of a mitigation impacts to the objectives. In this approach, a designer must construct the system design before assessing the risk. Our approach, on the other hand, is aimed to automate both the design and its evaluation.

The field of AI planning has been intensively developing during the last decades, and has found a number of interesting applications (e.g., robotics, process planning, autonomous agents, etc.). There are two basic approaches to the solution of planning problems [8]. One is graph-based planning algorithms in which a compact structure, called Planning Graph, is constructed and analyzed. In the other approach the planning problem is transformed into a SAT problem and a SAT solver is used. There exist several ways to represent the elements of a classical planning problem (i.e. the initial state of the world, the system goal, or the desired state of the world, and the possible actions system actors can perform). The most widely used, and to a certain extent standard representation is PDDL (Planning Domain Definition Language), the problem specification language proposed in [18]. Current PDDL version, PDDL 2.2 [19] used during the last International Planning Competition [20], supports many useful features (e.g., derived predicates and timed initial literals).

A few works can be found which relate planning techniques with information system design. In [21] a program called ASAP (Automated Specifier And Planner) is described, which automates a part of the domain-specific software specification process. ASAP assists the designer in selecting methods for achieving user goals, discovering plans that result in undesirable outcomes, and finding methods for preventing such outcomes. The disadvantage of the approach is that the designer still performs a lot of work manually while determining the combination of goals and prohibited situations appropriate for the given application, defining possible start-up conditions and providing many other domain-specific expert knowledge. Some works present a planning application to assist an expert in designing control programs in the field of Automated Manufacturing [22]. The system they have built integrates POCL (Partial Order Causal Link), hierarchical and conditional planning techniques [22,9]. The authors consider standard planning approaches to be not appropriate with no ready-to-use tools for the real world, while in our paper the opposite point of view is advocated, and the off-the-shelf planner is used.

7   Conclusion

In this paper, we have proposed an approach to incorporate risk analysis into the process of MASs design. The approach is based on the use of planning to explore the space of alternative designs and risk-based evaluation metrics to evaluate the resulting solutions.

We argue that the approach is particularly suitable for the design of critical and responsive systems, such as air traffic management, health-care systems, disaster management (e.g., post-disaster urban planning), traffic management, etc.

The proposed framework is meant to support a designer in generating, exploring, and evaluating design alternatives either during the initial, classical design, or during runtime redesign of a MAS. We consider runtime redesign of high importance for modern information systems, which operates in continuously changing environment and then require highly adaptable characteristics. Among the limitations of our approach, we would like to mention that it only supports a centralized viewpoint (i.e., the designers viewpoint), while the different actors of a system may have different priorities and criticalities. We consider this issue being an interesting direction for future work.

Acknowledgments

We would like to thank to Gabriel Kuper, Sameh Abdel-Naby, Hamza Hydri Syed, and anonymous reviewers for all the useful comments. This work has been partially funded by EU Commission, through the SENSORIA and SERENITY projects, by the FIRB program of MIUR under the ASTRO project, and also by the Provincial Authority of Trentino, through the MOSTRO project.

References

1. Truszkowski, W., Rash, J., Rouff, C., Hinchey, M.: Asteroid exploration with autonomic systems. In: Engineering of Computer-Based Systems, 2004. Proceedings. 11th IEEE International Conference and Workshop on the. (May 2004) 484–489
2. Matsui, H., Izumi, K., Noda, I.: Soft-restriction approach for traffic management under disaster rescue situations. In: ATDM'06: 1st Workshop on Agent Technology for Disaster Management. (2006)
3. Avizienis, A., Laprie, J.C., Randell, B., Landwehr, C.E.: Basic Concepts and Taxonomy of Dependable and Secure Computing. IEEE Trans. Dependable Sec. Comput. 1(1) (2004) 11–33
4. Ljungberg, M., Lucas, A.: The OASIS Air-Traffic Management System. In: PRICAI'92: In Proceedings of the Second Pacific Rim International Conference on Artificial Intelligence. (1992)
5. Truszkowski, W., Hinchey, M., Rash, J., Rouff, C.: Autonomous and autonomic systems: a paradigm for future space exploration missions. Systems, Man and Cybernetics, Part C, IEEE Transactions on 36(3) (2006) 279–291
6. Bryl, V., Massacci, F., Mylopoulos, J., Zannone, N.: Designing security requirements models through planning. In: CAiSE'06, Springer (2006) 33–47
7. Bryl, V., Giorgini, P., Mylopoulos, J.: Designing cooperative IS: Exploring and evaluating alternatives. In: CoopIS'06. (2006) 533–550
8. Weld, D.S.: Recent Advances in AI Planning. AI Magazine 20(2) (1999) 93–123
9. Peer, J.: Web Service Composition as AI Planning – a Survey. Technical report, University of St. Gallen (2005)
10. LPG Homepage: LPG-td Planner. http://zeus.ing.unibs.it/lpg/
11. Giorgini, P., Mylopoulos, J., Nicchiarelli, E., Sebastiani, R.: Formal Reasoning Techniques for Goal Models. Journal of Data Semantics (October 2003)

12. Sebastiani, R., Giorgini, P., Mylopoulos, J.: Simple and Minimum-Cost Satisfiability for Goal Models. In: CAISE '04: In Proceedings International Conference on Advanced Information Systems Engineering. Volume 3084., Springer (June 2004) 20–33

13. Fredriksen, R., Kristiansen, M., Gran, B.A., Stolen, K., Opperud, T.A., Dimitrakos, T.: The CORAS framework for a model-based risk management process. In: Safecomp '02: In Proceedings Computer Safety, Reliability and Security. Volume LNCS 2434., Springer (2002) 94–105

14. DoD: Military Standard, Procedures for Performing a Failure Mode, Effects, and Critical Analysis (MIL-STD-1692A). U.S. Department of Defense (1980)

15. Vesely, W., Goldberg, F., Roberts, N., Haasl, D.: Fault Tree Handbook. U.S Nuclear Regulatory Commission (1981)

16. USCG: Risk Based Decision Making Guidelines. http://www.uscg.mil/hq/g-m/risk/e-guidelines/RBDMGuide.htm (November 2005)

17. Feather, M.S.: Towards a Unified Approach to the Representation of, and Reasoning with, Probabilistic Risk Information about Software and its System Interface. In: 15th IEEE International Symposium on Software Reliability Engineering, IEEE Computer Society (November 2004) 391–402

18. Ghallab, M., Howe, A., Knoblock, C., McDermott, D., Ram, A., Veloso, M., Weld, D., Wilkins, D.: PDDL – The Planning Domain Definition Language. In: Proceedings of the Fourth International Conference on Artificial Intelligence Planning Systems. (1998)

19. Edelkamp, S., Hoffmann, J.: PDDL2.2: The language for the classical part of the 4th international planning competition. Technical Report 195, University of Freiburg (2004)

20. IPC-4 Homepage: International Planning Competition 2004. http://ls5-www.cs.uni-dortmund.de/ edelkamp/ipc-4/

21. Anderson, J.S., Fickas, S.: A proposed perspective shift: viewing specification design as a planning problem. In: IWSSD '89: 5th Int. workshop on Software specification and design. (1989) 177–184

22. Castillo, L., Fdez-Olivares, J., Gonzlez, A.: Integrating hierarchical and conditional planning techniques into a software design process for automated manufacturing. In: ICAPS 2003, Workshop on Planning under Uncertainty and Incomplete Information. (2003) 28–39

SUNIT: A Unit Testing Framework for Test Driven Development of Multi-Agent Systems

Ali Murat Tiryaki, Sibel Öztuna, Oguz Dikenelli, and Riza Cenk Erdur

Ege University, Department of Computer Engineering,
35100 Bornova, Izmir, Turkey
ali.murat.tiryaki@ege.edu.tr, sibel.tamer@gmail.com,
oguz.dikenelli@ege.edu.tr, cenk.erdur@ege.edu.tr

Abstract. Complex and distributed nature of multi-agent systems (MASs) makes it almost impossible to identify of all requirements at the beginning of the development. Hence, development of such systems needs an iterative and incremental process to handle complexity and the continuously changing na-ture of the requirements. In this paper, a test driven multi-agent system devel-opment approach that naturally supports iterative and incremental MAS con-struction is proposed. Also a testing framework called as SUnit which supports the proposed approach by extending JUnit framework is introduced. This framework allows writing automated tests for agent behaviors and interactions between agents. The framework also includes the necessary mock agents to model the organizational aspects of the MAS.

1 Introduction

Agent oriented software engineering (AOSE) [1] aims to build complex and distrib-uted software systems based on agent abstraction. To build such systems, developers need agent-specific methodologies. As a result, definition of such methodologies is one of the most explored topics in AOSE area.

Lots of agent-specific methodologies which use a waterfall like process, such as Gaia [2,3], SODA [4] and Prometheus [5] and which use an incremental process but do not provide any implementation level support to handle this iterative process, such as INGENIAS [6] and Tropos [7] have been proposed in the literature. But, it's clear that it is almost impossible to collect all the requirements in the beginning of the development of such complex systems. Moreover, MASs may operate as open organizations that further complicate, to comprehend all functional and nonfunctional requirements at the early phases of the development. Therefore, we need an iterative and incremental development approach and its implementation level support to handle the complexity and continuously changing nature of the requirements.

Software engineering researchers and practitioners have also realized that they need a different development process rather than the traditional ones to model the complex systems in dynamically changing domains [8]. So, agile processes have been proposed to tackle these complexities. All of these agile processes

L. Padgham and F. Zambonelli (Eds.): AOSE 2006, LNCS 4405, pp. 156–173, 2007.

basically introduce some light-weight practices to execute iterative and incremental development in a controllable way. It is natural to think that these practices can be transferred to AOSE, since the basic problems have similar characteristics [9,10].

In the literature, there are some pioneering works which try to apply agile practices to MAS development. For example, Knublauch [11,12] used practices of extreme programming (XP) [8], which is the one of the most known agile development processes for MAS development. Although this work proves the effectiveness of XP practices in terms of MAS development, the agent development framework and process meta model, which are used during development, are very simple. Based on the selection of a very simple framework infrastructure, test driven practice of XP looks like object based test driven development. So the scalability of these practices is questionable when they are applied using a realistic development framework and meta models.

Another important work has been introduced by Chella et. all [13] to transform well known Passi methodology to Agile Passi. This group also developed a testing framework to provide automated testing approach for testing multi-agent systems [14,15]. Although this framework allows testing an agent's internal behaviors, they didn't introduce an approach to develop MASs with the iterative and evolutionary style and dependently their testing framework does not support such an approach.

In this paper, first of all, we propose a test driven approach to develop MASs iteratively and incrementally. For each MAS scenario, proposed approach identifies agent task(s), interactions and organizational responsibilities in an iterative and evolutionary way during test driven implementation. Agent oriented test driven de-velopment (AOTDD) is an approach to develop MASs in an incremental and iterative way with a testing framework support. This approach is used in the implementation level of MAS development. So, other well-known MAS development methodologies can use AOTDD after the design artifacts are identified, to support iterative development. To support the proposed approach, a testing framework, called as SUnit, was implemented on the top of the Seagent multi-agent system development framework [16]. This testing framework allows developers to write automated tests for agent behaviors, agent to agent and agent to organization interactions to verify the functionality of the scenario at hand.

This document is organized as follows; in the following section, we define a conceptual framework to present our test driven approach. In section 3, we mention Seagent framework briefly. Section 4 presents software architecture of the testing framework implemented. Each subtitle in this section deals with one of the modules of this framework. During the representation of SUnit framework an example plan structure is used to show usage and effectiveness of AOTDD approach and SUnit testing framework. Section 5 evaluates SUnit frame-work on an experimental case study.

2   Conceptual Framework for Test Driven Development of MASs

Test driven development (TDD) [17] is a style of software development in which development is driven by automated tests. The development cycle of TDD is very simple; developer defines functional tests for a unit/task, then implements the code that passes these written tests and finally, the code is refactored [18] to improve the design. Although this cycle seems very simple, it implicitly supports the iterative and incremental construction of task at hand such as; the cycle begins with writing the test(s) for a single unit. During the implementation of the unit, interactions of the unit with other units are defined simply by using mock and/or dummy objects. Then the process flows iteratively and incrementally by developing real units to replace the mock/dummy ones. Of course, initial design decisions such as specified interactions and unit functionalities can be improved through out the process with refactoring practice.

In XP, TDD can only be applied successfully, if developer has an implicit knowl-edge about the general system metaphor [8]. System metaphor is a story that everyone -customers, programmers and managers- can tell about how the system works. The metaphor in XP replaces of what other software researchers call "software architecture". Implicit knowledge of the metaphor allows developers to identify architectural units and their dependencies with the functional units during the execution of the TDD process.

To transfer the TDD style to the agent oriented development, we first have to define the necessary concepts for agent oriented test driven development (AOTDD) to replace the traditional ones. First concept is scenario. Each scenario defines an elementary process within MASs, which produce a net value for the initiator of the scenario. In AOTDD, scenarios are conceptually different than traditional ones in a way that they can be initiated by autonomous agents themselves. Another concept is the agent itself which replaces the traditional objects/units.

Beyond the basic AOTDD concepts, agents form an organization and live within an environment. So, we have to define a metaphor for the target MAS model to apply AOTDD. Our metaphor which is shown in figure 1 is the synthesis of Gaia [2,3] and Passi [13] meta-models.

Now, it is time to define AOTDD process based on the concepts and metaphor defined so far. Figure 2 shows the visual description of AOTDD cycle. In the following paragraphs, each step will be explained in detail.

At first, we take a role that will be played by an agent. At the beginning of the scenario development, developer identifies the initiator role of the scenario to start the AOTDD cycle.

In the second step, developer selects an agent that executes the role and identifies one of its tasks to satisfy the responsibility of selected role in terms of scenario at hand. At this stage, developer simply draws and/or thinks about the initial plan structure that will execute the developed tasks at hand.

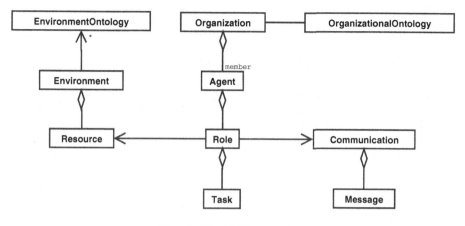

Fig. 1. The MAS metaphor

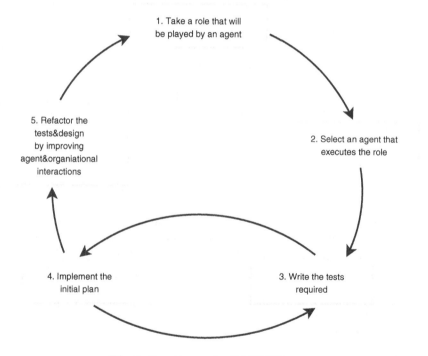

Fig. 2. Iterative cycle of AOTDD

In the third step, developer writes tests that will validate the task(s) being developed. Writing the automatic tests for autonomous agents is not simple as in the object oriented development case. MASs have different levels for testing. We specified three testing level for MAS development. These levels are;

- **Structural Test Level**: Agent tasks are implemented using a planning paradigm such as Hierarchical Task Network (HTN) [19] formalism. These plan structures can be in very complex forms. Hence, developer has to validate correctness of the plan structure at the first test level.
- **Action Test Level**: Each plan may have more than one executable action. At this level, developer has to test functionality of these actions separately.
- **Flow Test Level**: Each agent interacts with other agents and organizational units -such as directory facilitator- to satisfy the requirements of the developed plan. Hence, some tests must be written to verify the correctness of the specified interactions.

Of course, a testing framework is required to manage this process. In section 4, we will introduce SUnit framework that is developed to manage the AOTDD cycle.

In step four, developer implements the task at hand based on the defined plan structure in step 2 and the tests written in step 3. To execute this step, testing framework must provide mock agent(s) and an infrastructure to develop dummy agent(s) based on the metaphor defined. SUnit framework provides a mock agent to simulate FIPA's directory facilitator structure[1]. Developer simply implements the plan which runs the written tests, using the provided mock agents and the real agents developed at the earlier cycles if necessary.

Agent tasks can be very complex to identify all tests and to construct the overall structure in a single step. During the implementation of the plan structure, develop-ers can identify additional requirements that expand the plan structure. At this point, they write required test by backing the previous step and then continue to implement the plan structure. So, there is an internal iteration between step three and step four.

In the final step, developer may refactor the initial design decisions. For example, previous plan structure can be transferred to a better structure by identifying reusable task(s) within the task and/or the new agent(s) or organizational interactions can be identified to improve modularity or robustness of the system.

At the end of the cycle, HTN plan of the target task is completed by validating all written tests using the mock agents. Then, this cycle is repeated for each of these mock agents to transform them to the real agent that plays a specific role within the scenario. Consequently, the scenario is implemented in an iterative and incremental style following the cycle defined.

3   Seagent MAS Development Framework

SUnit testing framework was implemented on the top of the Seagent multi agent system development framework and it has some dependences to this framework. Therefore, we mention Seagent framework briefly in this section. This framework was implemented by Seagent research group that includes authors of this paper.

---

[1] http://www.fipa.org/specs/fipa00023/

Seagent is specialized for semantic web based multi agent system development and includes some new built-in features for this purpose. It uses semantic web ontology standards in each layer of its software architecture. For example, an OWL based content language is used within the FIPA communication protocols and Seagent agent internal architecture can interpret this language. Moreover, its internal architecture has necessary infrastructure to handle OWL and RDF models within its internal memory and has a pluggable architecture to connect different knowledge bases like Jena[2].

Seagent's layered software architecture is shown in figure 3. Each layer and packages of the layers have been specially designed to provide build-in support for se-mantic web based multi agent system (MAS) development. In the following, we briefly mention each layer with an emphasis on the semantic support given by that layer.

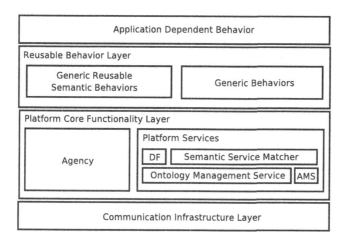

Fig. 3. Seagent Platform Overall Architecture

The bottom layer is responSeagent framework brieflysible of abstracting platform's communication infrastructure implementation. Seagent implements FIPA's Agent Communication and Agent Message Transport specifications to handle agent messaging. Although Communication Infrastructure Layer can transfer any content using FIPA ACL and transport infrastructure, Seagent platform only supports FIPA RDF content language since it is very suitable to transfer semantic web enabled content.

The second layer includes packages, which provide the core functionality of the platform. The first package, called as Agency, handles the internal functionality of an agent. Agency package provides a built-in 'agent operating system' that matches the goal(s) to defined plan(s), which are defined using HTN planning formalism [19]. It then schedules, executes and monitors the plan(s).

---

[2] http://jena.sourceforge.net

From semantic web based devel-opment perspective, an agent's internal architecture must support semantic web on-tology standards for messaging and internal knowledge handling to simplify seman-tic based development. For this purpose, Agency package provides a build-in support to parse and interpret FIPA RDF content language to handle semantic web based messaging.

The second package of the Core Functionality Layer includes service sub-packages, one for each service of the platform. These services follow the FIPA standards but they are implemented differently using the capabilities of a semantic web infrastructure. In the Seagent implementation, DF uses an OWL ontology to hold agent capabilities and includes a semantic matching engine to be able to return agent(s) with semantically similar capabilities to the requested ones. Similarly, AMS stores agents' descriptions in OWL using FIPA Agent Management Ontology and can be queried semantically to learn descriptions of any agent that is currently resi-dent on the platform.

Besides implementing standard services in a semantic way, Seagent platform provides two new services to simplify semantic web based MAS development. The first one is called as Semantic Service Matcher (SSM). SSM is responsible for connecting the platform to the semantic web services hosted in the outside of the platform. SSM uses 'service profile' construct of the Web Ontology Language for Semantic Web Services (OWL-S) standard for service advertisement and this knowledge is also used by the internal semantic matching engine for discovery of the service(s) upon a request. The second unique service is the Ontology Manager Service (OMS). The most critical support of the OMS is its translation support between the ontologies. Through the usage of the ontology translation support, any agent of the platform may communicate with MAS and/or services outside the platform even if they use different ontologies.

Third layer of the overall architecture includes pre-prepared generic agent plans. We have divided these generic plans into two packages. Generic Behavior package collects domain independent reusable behaviors that may be used by any MAS such as well known auction protocols (English, Dutch etc.). On the other hand, Generic Semantic Behaviors package includes only the semantic web related behaviors. In the current version, the most important generic semantic behavior is the one that executes dynamic discovery and invocation of the external services. This plan is defined as a pre-prepared HTN structure and during its execution, it uses SSM ser-vice to discover the desired service and then using OWL-S 'service grounding' construct it dynamically invokes the found atomic web service(s). Hence, developers may include dynamic external service discovery and invocation capability to their plan(s) by simply inserting this reusable behavior as an ordinary complex task to their HTN based plan definition(s).

4   The SUnit Testing Framework

In this section basic functionalities and software architecture of the SUnit testing framework are defined. SUnit introduces a test environment that supports the developer to create and execute tests in a uniform and automatic way during

MAS development. It lets developers to build the tests and to collect these tests in a test suite effortlessly in an incremental way. It also supports test creation on the plan structure being developed, confirmation of internal behavior of the plans, and validation of plan execution at run time.

SUnit framework is built on top of the Seagent [16] MAS development environment. As mentioned section 3, Seagent support HTN approach as the planning paradigm like well-known RETSINA [20] and DECAF [21] architectures. Therefore, SUnit has a slight dependency to HTN approach. However, we think that our test driven approach can be used for other planning paradigms with the help of test environments that would be developed for these paradigms specially. In addition to the dependency described above, there is another dependency between SUnit and Seagent framework. Flow test module uses events sent by the Seagent planner to check the plan flow. This module can also be used for other environments that send similar events with the simple modifications.

The SUnit which is implemented in the Java programming language extends the JUnit unit testing framework[3]. In JUnit, unit tests are written by using *TestCase* class that extends *Assert* class. Hence, written test cases directly use the assertion method of *Assert* class. *Assert* class is the focal point of the JUnit. This class includes static methods that help the user to create private test cases. Each of these assertion methods asserts that a condition is true, and if it isn't, it throws an *AssertionFailedError* with the given message. *AssertionFailedError* is caught by the *TestRunner* and it reports a test failure - in case the user is using the graphical version of *TestRunner*, the famous red bar appears. So, every assertion method in JUnit Framework have return type void. JUnit's class diagram and its relationships with SUnit's main classes are shown in figure 4.

Agent plan structures, tasks in these structures and interactions between these tasks have different characteristics from traditional class structures and relationships among them. Hence, specialized assertion methods are required for testing agent plan structures. SUnit is built on JUnit to provide these assertion methods for agent level verification. All SUnit methods use JUnit methods inside for object level verification and are specialized for testing agent plans and interactions.

Each SUnit method throws *AssertionFailedError* exception through the use of JUnit. *AssertionFailedError* is caught by the *SeagentTestRunner* that extends the *TestRunner* of JUnit framework. Thus, every assertion method in SUnit framework have return type void like JUnit methods. Besides the availability of the standard JUnit interface, an extended interface is also appended to view the specialized messages about the relevant errors. This paves the way for eliminating the errors. The SUnit interface is shown in figure 5.

At run time, HTN structure is expanded to a graph structure whose leaf nodes include executable actions. So, agent functionality can be verified by writing test cases for each executable action and correctness of the plan structure. MAS organization functionality can be verified using methods of flowTest module since they can check the correctness of the messages coming from other agents and organizational entities (like directory service).

---

[3] http://www.junit.org

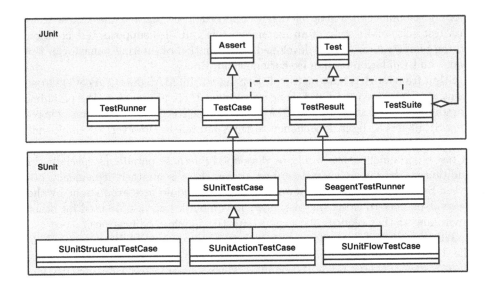

Fig. 4. JUnit and SUnit classes

The test environment consists of three submodules that handle three testing levels discussed in section two. These sub modules are Structural Test Module for structural test level, the Action Test Module for action test level and the Flow Test Mod-ule for flow test level. Each of these modules has an abstract class which is extended from *SunitTestCase* as shown in figure 4. *SunitTestCase* class extends the *TestCase* class of JUnit framework whose functionalities can be inherited through this extension.

In the following subsections, we discuss the design and usage of each module of SUnit using a HTN diagram from an implemented case study. This case study is an experimental work on the tourism domain and HTN example given in figure 6 is the plan of "Traveler" agent that is used to find and book a proper room for the human traveler.

In HTN formalism, a complex task is the task that includes one or more tasks. "Find and book a room" is a complex task in our plan structure. The directly executable tasks are called as primitive tasks. "Get reservation informa-tion" task in the plan above is an example of primitive task. Provisions represent the information needs of a task and can be thought as a generalization of both parameters and runtime variables. In our plan, "Hotel info" is a provision of the task "Get reservation information". An outcome is a state which shows how a task is finished and returns the result(s) of this task. In the plan structure shown in figure 6, OK is the outcome of task "Find hotels". Information flow relationships between the tasks are represented by the provision-outcome links. In the plan structure mentioned above, there is a provision-outcome link be-tween the outcome OK of the task "Find hotels" and "hotel info" provision of

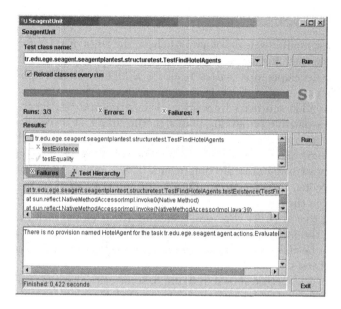

Fig. 5. SUnit interface

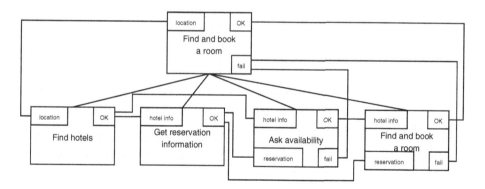

Fig. 6. Initial HTN diagram of the "arrange holiday" plan

the task "Get reservation information". The meaning of this link is that if the execution of "Find hotels" raises the outcome OK, its result is supplied to "hotel info" provision of the task "Get reservation information". The outcome and provision transmissions between subtasks and parent tasks are represented by inheritance and disinheritance links. In our sample plan structure, there is an inheritance between provision "location" of "Find and book a room" task and provision "location" of "find hotels" task.

4.1 Structural Test Module

Structural test module was developed to check the rules of HTN formalism and assist the developer for developing structurally correct plan structures. Using this module, developer first writes tests for a high level HTN plan and then develops this plan while validating its structural correctness using written tests. Later, he/she adds sub-tasks by writing their structural test firstly. Thus, this module makes possible to develop plan structure in a test driven way.

Methods that are used for structural testing are situated in an abstract class called as *SunitStructuralTestCase*. The methods of this class deal with the facts like, accuracy of some critical components of a complex task, consistency of provision-outcome links between subtasks or integrity of plan task. For each complex task in the plan, at least one structural test case should be implemented by extending this abstract class and assigning the complex task that would be tested, using the *setBehaviourClass()* method of this class. Then, these written test cases can be collected in a *junit.framework.TestSuite* to take the advantage of automated tests.

For the HTN structure shown in figure 6, some critical structural tests which were defined during the "writing tests" step of AOTDD cycle, are shown in figure 7.

First assert method named "assertProvisionSender" checks whether provision "reservation" of the "askAvailability" task is supplied by an outcome of the task "getReservationInformation". If not; asserts false with an explanatory message.

Second assert method named "assertDisinheritanceSender" checks whether disinheritance named "disinheritOK" is sent by the "bookingARoom" sub-task and received by "findAndBookingARoom" complex task. This method also checks whether the "findAndBookingARoom" complex task has a proper provision to send. If not; asserts false with a suitable message.

By writing tests iteratively and then developing the structure to pass these tests, a high level accurate task structure is obtained. Afterwards, it is time to jump to the lower levels of the plan structure.

For each sublevel of the plan, structural test steps mentioned before are applied again and an accurate structure that passes all structural tests, developed. This process is pursued until all complex task structures in the original plan are implemented. At the end of this process, whole structure of "Find and book a room" task was fully defined.

With this top-down development approach, whole HTN structure is developed iteratively beginning from the higher level tasks. This strategy also enabled designing more realistic HTN structures by specifying the detailed structure at the implementation phase.

4.2 Action Test Module

In the Hierarchical Task Network manner, complex tasks are reduced to primitive tasks (sometimes called as actions) to operate. In this sense, primitive tasks are executable components of a complex task. So, one has to define consistent and accurate primitive tasks to develop an efficient plan.

```
public void testLevelOne(){
    assertProvisionSender(askAvailability , reservation ,
                            getReservationInformation);
    assertDisinheritanceSender (disinheritOK , bookingARoom);
}
```

Fig. 7. A sample structural test case

A primitive task operates according to the provided provisions and may generate an outcome and/or some messages to another agent in the platform. Considering the distributed and dynamic nature of multi agent systems, provision values are unstable in these systems. This makes handling extreme provision values mandatory. Action Test Module was designed to examine outcomes or messages in respect to user defined provision sets for primitive tasks.

Methods that are used for action testing are situated in an abstract class called as *SunitActionTestCase*. To write an action test for a task, one has to extend this abstract class by passing the task name as parameter. So, action tests know its task. Also, *assignActionClass()* method knows the return value since it can access the task's original outcome value(s). Methods of this class check the results of primitive task(s) such as outcomes and/or generated messages.

For every primitive task in a plan, a set of action test cases should be implemented. These test cases can be generated for a set of ordinary provision values or possible extreme provision values. All implemented test cases could then be collected in a *junit.framework.TestSuite* to take the advantage of the automated tests.

In our example plan, test cases for each primitive task such as "get reservation in-formation" and "evaluate hotel information" must be defined. Such a test case for "evaluate hotel information" action is shown in figure 8.

The first assert method named "assertActionOutcome" checks whether task "evaluate hotel information" generates an outcome named "outcome1" when the user defined provision value for the "hotelInfo" provision is provided. If not; asserts false with a message.

The second assert method named "assertOutcomeType" checks whether "evaluate hotel information" task generates an outcome named "outcome1" which return the value of the type "hotel.class" when the user defined provision value for "hotelInfo" provision is provided. If not; asserts false with a message.

During the implementation of primitive tasks, it may be observed that some of the tests do not cover some extreme provision values. For example; if none of the hotels is selected as the proper hotel after execution of the "evaluate hotel information" task, an empty list is generated as the value of the "OK" outcome. This fault probably would cause problems in the dependent subtasks. To solve this problem, an outcome named "FAIL" is added to the "evaluate hotel information" task and the task code is changed to produce "FAIL" outcome when "hotel list" provision is empty. By applying this adjustment, "find and book a proper room" task is run without producing any error for these extreme values.

```
public void test1 () {
   Outcome outcome1 = new Outcome ("EvaluateAvailibility",
                                   "OK", "availability");
   outcome1.setValue(hotel2);
   assertActionOutcome(outcome1);
   assertActionOutcomeType(outcome1, hotel.class);
}
```

Fig. 8. A sample action test case

This adjustment naturally required rearrangement of some structural and action test cases.

At the end of the action test phase, well-defined primitive tasks which executed as expected and could handle extreme provision values are implemented. Besides this, with the guidance of action tests, plan structure is improved as mentioned above.

4.3   Flow Test Module

To execute a plan, an agent has to interact with other agents on the platform via messages. These messages affect operation of the plan. Hence, run time behavior against various messages has to be tested to build reliable plans.

Flow Test Module of SUnit was designed to evaluate outcomes or outgoing messages of the tasks in respect to the incoming messages or predefined message sets. Execution order and status of tasks are also examined. Test environment provides an infrastructure to validate the values and the types of the returned result. Infrastructure is dependent on the communication standards of Seagent platform. Seagent uses FIPA RDF content language and OWL[4] to transfer knowledge within the message content. SUnit gets the returned value and/or type of the OWL concept from the Seagent framework and can check the correctness of this concept's type with the expected type. Developers are capable to assess these criteria by extending the SunittFlowTestCase via particular assert methods. SunitFlowTestCase class includes assert methods which operate through interacting the *PlanHandler* component of SUnit. It handles the *PlanListenerObject* that listens to the generated plan events by the concerned agent. The test class which is extended from the SunitFlowTestCase is responsible to launch the agent in to the platform. As implied, all concerned events are kept in the *PlanHandler* component to be reasoned after the plan execution. The class diagram of the Flow Test Module of the SUnit is shown in figure 9.

As mentioned above, an agent has to interact with other agents and organizational units such as FIPA's Directory Facilitator via messages to execute a plan. Even when the agents being communicated with are not on the platform, the plan being developed has to be tested at runtime. Abnormal messages that influence the plan execution should also be managed. On the other hand,

[4] http://www.w3.org/2004/OWL/

it may not be possible to find the provider of the exceptional messages at the desired time.

For these reasons, a mock agent called as *MessageSet* was included to the Flow Test Module. This agent has a mechanism to hold some or all of the incoming message requirements of the plan and provides the required message to the concerned agent and/or organizational units during execution. The message need is deduced from the plan events generated by the agent under interest.

In the case of not to find the required message in the message set, the agent has to wait for a real message which is provided from the other agents on the platform. This brings the flexibility on the plan flow test which can be done in respect to the incoming messages or predefined artificial messages.

The same mechanism is also used to simulate organizational abstraction. In the current version, we support FIPA's Directory Facilitator standard to manage organizational aspects of the multi-agent system. To create a fake Directory Facilitator service, a reusable message structure has been developed. This structure is used to generate FIPA messages that includes DF ontology instance with given concept values. Then this message is inserted into the message set to provide agent organization interaction.

To facilitate the plan implementation, an additional interface is included in the Flow Test Module. This interface monitors the plan events such as execution of a task, generation of an outcome or arrival of a message, in order to debug the plan in a comprehensive way.

During the structural and action test level, the plan is built structurally; primitive tasks are tested and coded. At the structural and action test phases other agents that play defined roles within the scenario are not needed. However, at the flow test phase, the plan is tested at runtime.

For our example plan, the interactions with the hotel role have not been defined yet. So, the "find and book a room" plan has to be isolated from the organization and tested at runtime. In order to accomplish this, message sets

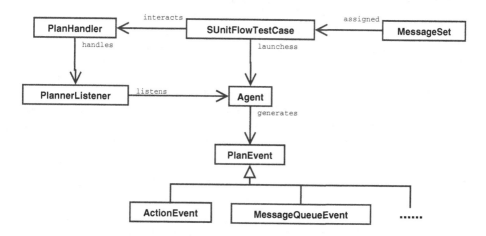

Fig. 9. Class Diagram of the Flow Test Module

```
public class FullIsolatedTest extends SunitFlowTestCase {
    ...
    public MessageSet assignMessageSet() {
        MessageSet mySet= new MessageSet();
        FIPAMsg aMessage = new FIPAMsg();
        ...
        mySet.addMessage(aMessage);
        ...
        return mySet;
    }
    public void testForFirstLevel(){
        ...
        assertActionOutcome(getReservationInformation ,"OK");
        assertActionExecuted (getReservationInformation);
        assertMessageArrived (aMessage);
    }
}
```

Fig. 10. A sample flow test case

are used. To simulate all of the communicating agents in the task execution, a message for each interaction is created to provide external messages and added to message set. Then a test case is written for each message set to validate interactions. An example case is shown in figure 10.

The first assert method named "assertActionOutcome" checks whether the "getReservationInformation" action generates "OK" outcome when the plan is executed with the defined messageSet. If not; asserts false.

The second assert method named "assertActionExecuted" checks whether the "getReservationInformation" action is executed during the plan operation. If not; asserts false.

The third assert method named "assertMessageArrived" checks whether a message identified with "aMessage" is received during the plan execution. If not; asserts false.

Although the developer insures the plan execution against the message sets, the real interactions with other agents are also a crucial issue to implement the scenario. At the following cycles of the AOTDD, each message from the message set is transfered to the real agents that play the corresponding role following again the same cycle. During the implementation of these plans, the AOTTD cycle is followed for the each plan. With the guidance of the test case failure messages, accurate interactions between the agents are accomplished.

5   Evaluation

AOTDD and SUnit framework have been evaluated during the development of an experimental case study implemented by Seagent Research Group by collaborating with an industrial partner. The case is in the tourism domain and industrial partner is one of the well-known hotel information system developers in Turkey. The case study is experimental, since its main goal is to convince the industrial partner to the applicability of MAS technology to their domain.

Two main stories have been implemented so far. These stories were developed using the AOTDD approach. First one deals with room booking based on user preferences defined in a semantic way. Traveler agent initiates this scenario. In this scenario, a proper hotel is found first, then the hotel is queried for an available room, and if a room can be found, that room is booked. Traveler agent interacts with the DF, hotel agent and negotiator agent during the scenario execution. Second scenario is initiated by the hotel agent to find a customer for an empty room. Details of the design of the system can not be added to this paper because of space limitations. Here, we aim to present our group's observations and experiences about the effectiveness of SUnit framework in terms of iterative and incremental MAS development.

When we started to develop SUnit framework, we did not include structural test module in the requirements, since nobody realized its benefits at that moment. But our experiences have showed that it is difficult to develop HTN structures which include more than 20 tasks and lots of levels. Hence, we added structural test module to the SUnit. During the development of this case study, all developers agree on that structural test module was very helpful while constructing HTN structures incrementally.

Best example for the use of structural test module is the plan of traveler agent which books a proper room. This plan is the core of the scenario and has a very complex HTN structure. Developers constructed this plan first including only proper hotel selection and then added new requirements (such as negotiation) in an incremental way. Structural test module directly supported this incremental construction by verifying the correctness of each of the newly added task in terms of the correctness of the plan at hand.

Action test module verified the functionality of the developed plan by verifying each primitive task of the plan. During development, the project group wrote action tests firstly for critical and complex actions and action test module worked effectively to develop robust primitive tasks as in ordinary test driven development. Our experiences showed that developers deeply understood the plan structure when they wrote action tests. So, action tests also helped to improve the quality of plan structure.

All of case study developers agree on the effectiveness of the flow test module. Moreover, they think that implementation of a MAS system is very difficult without such a support. During the development, we observed that flow test module directly supports the iterative development. For example, development group first implemented and verified the traveler agent plans by using the simple mock agents. We observed that creation of real agents is relatively simple since their implementation requirements are defined during the mock agent implementation process. After the development of an agent using the mock agents, new agent(s) can be added to the organization in an iterative and robust way since flow test module secures the previously developed agent plans. Also, new agents can more easily construct since mock agents include necessary protocol implementation for collaboration of the previous developed agents.

6   Conclusion

It is clear that iterative and incremental development is the most critical practice of any kind of software development. So, we think that development of MAS tools and processes that support iterative and incremental MAS development is a very important research topic for agent oriented software engineering community. In this paper, a new approach called as AOTDD and SUnit testing framework that supports this approach have been proposed for developing MASs in an iterative and incremental style. This approach and SUnit framework have been used by our group during the development of an experimental MAS. Our observations and feedbacks from the developers show that, this approach and SUnit framework are very effective in designing the systems iteratively and incrementally. This approach also supports early fault detection in every cycle of development with the support of SUnit and simplifies maintenance of the system. The source code and javadoc files of SUnit framework and the tourism demo developed are accessible on the SUnit project web site: *http://seagent.ege.edu.tr/wiki/index.php/SeaUnit*

References

1. Wooldridge, M., Ciancarini, P.: Agent-oriented software engineering: the state of the art. In: First international workshop, AOSE 2000 on Agent-oriented software engineering, Secaucus, NJ, USA, Springer-Verlag New York, Inc. (2001) 1–28
2. Wooldridge, M., Jennings, N.R., Kinny, D.: The gaia methodology for agent-oriented analysis and design. Autonomous Agents and Multi-Agent Systems **3** (2000) 285–312
3. Zambonelli, F., Jennings, N.R., Wooldridge, M.: Developing multiagent systems: The gaia methodology. ACM Trans. Softw. Eng. Methodol. **12** (2003) 317–370
4. Omicini, A.: Soda: societies and infrastructures in the analysis and design of agent-based systems. In: First international workshop, AOSE 2000 on Agent-oriented software engineering, Secaucus, NJ, USA, Springer-Verlag New York, Inc. (2001) 185–193
5. Padgham, L., Winikoff, M.: Prometheus: a methodology for developing intelligent agents. In: AAMAS '02: Proceedings of the first international joint conference on Autonomous agents and multiagent systems, New York, NY, USA, ACM Press (2002) 37–38
6. Gómez-Sanz, J., Pavón, J.: Agent oriented software engineering with ingenias. In: Proceedings of the 3rd Central and Eastern Europe Conference on Multiagent Systems, Springer Verlag, LNCS (2005) 394–403
7. Bresciani, P., Perini, A., Giorgini, P., Giunchiglia, F., Mylopoulos, J.: Tropos: An agent-oriented software development methodology. Autonomous Agents and Multi-Agent Systems **8** (2004) 203–236
8. Beck, K., Andres, C.: Extreme Programming Explained: Embrace Change (2nd Edition). Addison-Wesley Professional (2004)

9. Cernuzzi, L., Cossentino, M., Zambonell, F.: Process models for agent-based development. Journal of Engineering Applications of Artificial Intelligence **18 (2)** (2005)

10. Zambonelli, F., Omicini, A.: Challenges and research directions in agent-oriented software engineering. Autonomous Agents and Multi-Agent Systems **9** (2004) 253–283

11. Knublauch, H.: Extreme programming of multi-agent systems. In: AAMAS '02: Proceedings of the first international joint conference on Autonomous agents and multiagent systems, New York, NY, USA, ACM Press (2002) 704–711

12. Knublauch, H., Rose, T.: Tool-supported process analysis and design for the development of multi-agent systems. In Giunchiglia, F., Odell, J., Weiß, G., eds.: AOSE. Volume 2585 of Lecture Notes in Computer Science., Springer (2002) 186–197

13. Chella, A., Cossentino, M., Sabatucci, L., Seidita, V.: From passi to agile passi: Tailoring a design process to meet new needs. In: IEEE/WIC/ACM International Joint Conference on Intelligent Agent Technology (IAT-04). (2004)

14. Caire, G., Cossentino, M., Negri, A., Poggi, A., Turci, P.: Multi-agent systems implementation and testing. In: From Agent Theory to Agent Implementation, Fourth International Symposium (AT2AI-4). (2004)

15. Cossentino, M., Seidita, V.: Composition of a new process to meet agile needs using method engineering. In Choren, R., Garcia, A.F., de Lucena, C.J.P., Romanovsky, A.B., eds.: SELMAS. Volume 3390 of Lecture Notes in Computer Science., Springer (2004) 36–51

16. Dikenelli, O., Erdur, R.C., Gumus, O.: Seagent: a platform for developing semantic web based multi agent systems. In: AAMAS '05: Proceedings of the fourth international joint conference on Autonomous agents and multiagent systems, New York, NY, USA, ACM Press (2005) 1271–1272

17. Link, J., Frolich, P.: Unit Testing in Java: How Tests Drive the Code. Morgan Kaufmann Publishers Inc., San Francisco, CA, USA (2003)

18. Fowler, M.: Refactoring - Improving the Design of Existing Code. Addison-Wesley, Reading/Massachusetts (1999)

19. Williamson, M., Decker, K., Sycara, K.: Unified information and control flow in hierarchical task networks. In: Theories of Action, Planning, and Robot Control: Bridging the Gap: Proceedings of the 1996 AAAI Workshop, Menlo Park, California, AAAI Press (1996) 142–150

20. Paolucci, M., Kalp, D., Pannu, A.S., Shehory, O., Sycara, K.: A planning component for retsina agents. In: Lecture Notes in Artificial Intelligence, Intelligent Agents VI. (1999)

21. Graham, J.R., Decker, K.S., Mersic, M.: Decaf - a flexible multi agent system architecture. Autonomous Agents and Multi-Agent Systems **7** (2003) 7–27

Monitoring Group Behavior in Goal-Directed Agents Using Co-efficient Plan Observation

Jan Sudeikat and Wolfgang Renz

Multimedia Systems Lab,
Faculty of Engineering and Computer Science,
Hamburg University of Applied Sciences,
Berliner Tor 7, 20099 Hamburg, Germany
{sudeikat|wr}@informatik.haw-hamburg.de

Abstract. Purposeful, time– and cost–oriented engineering of Multi–Agent Systems (MAS) requires developers to understand the relationships between the numerous behaviors exhibited by individual agents and the resulting global MAS behavior. While development methodologies have drawn attention to verification and debugging of single agents, software producing organizations need to validate that the MAS, as a cooperative system exhibiting group behavior, is behaving as expected. Recent research has proposed techniques to infer mathematical descriptions of macroscopic MAS behavior from microscopic reactive and adaptive agent behaviors. In this paper, we show how similar descriptions can be adjusted to MAS composed of goal–directed agent architectures. We argue that goal-hierarchies found in Requirements Engineering and Belief Desire Intention (BDI) architectures are suitable data structures to facilitate a stochastic modeling approach. To enable monitoring of agent behaviors, we introduce an enhancement to the well-known capability concept for BDI agents. So-called co–efficient capabilities are a novel approach to modularize crosscutting concerns in BDI agent implementations. A case study applies co–efficient plan observation to exemplify and confirm our modeling approach.

1 Introduction

Agents as a basic design metaphor introduce a novel modeling approach to complex systems. Autonomous entities as atomic design artifacts enable an intuitive decomposition of software systems as independent actors, interacting with each other. Their interplay forms the actual application. Due to the autonomous nature of the entities, the inherent complexity of these kinds of systems introduces new levels of uncertainty [1]. Individual agent knowledge and reasoning capabilities may lead to unexpected individual behaviors, inhibiting predictions of the microscopic agent actions and interactions. The sum of these microscopic behaviors cause macroscopic system behavior, enabling self–organized properties and emergent phenomena [2].

To enable purposeful, time– and cost–oriented engineering of Multi–Agent Systems (MAS) it is necessary to ensure the developed system will behave as intended. Up to date, a few facilities to monitor and visualize MAS (e.g. [3,4,5]) as

L. Padgham and F. Zambonelli (Eds.): AOSE 2006, LNCS 4405, pp. 174–189, 2007.

well as individual agents [6] have been reported for this purpose. These allow developers to examine macroscopic and/or microscopic behaviors via simulations. While *testing* is extensively and successfully used to ensure system behavior in traditional (e.g. procedural, object–oriented) development efforts, the lack of a general methodology to infer global from local behavior [7], impairs similar approaches for MAS behaviors. Therefore, this paper discusses how to derive mathematic models of macroscopic system behaviors from MAS implementations under averaged environmental conditions.

The well–known *Belief–Desire–Intention* (BDI) architecture has been established to develop deliberative agents [8,9]. Implementations use the concrete concepts of *beliefs*, *goals* and *plans*, to design and implement individual agents [10,11]. While these abstractions aid development by sophisticated modeling and development methodologies (e.g. [12,13]), the applied reasoning facilities amplify the inherent uncertainty in MAS [1].

Recent research [14,15,16] has developed means to infer mathematical descriptions of the *macroscopic* system behavior from *microscopic* agent behaviors. These can be used to estimate MAS behavior in typical environments, supporting MAS refactoring and redesign while reducing the need for expensive simulation cycles. Inferring stochastic models from these hierarchies requires to map plans and goals to macroscopic observable agent behaviors, resulting in coarse–grained agent models. In this paper we argue that *goal–hierarchies*, found in *Requirements Engineering* (RE) and BDI architectures, can be exploited to guide the identification of suitable mappings and therefore derive similar, phenomenologic models, which postulate an underlying stochastic process. These models can be used to validate the overall system behavior and guide the identification of relevant observables for performance measurement. Being able to quantify the expected macroscopic MAS behavior and therefore to revise the expectations on simulation results has impact on system evaluation and validation. We exemplify this process and present tool support.

Modularization [17] is justified by the *separation of concerns* principle. The functionality of a modular software system can be divided in *core* and *crosscutting concerns* which commonly describe non-functional properties [18]. Aiming towards automated monitoring of the identified observables with minimum intrusion to the original agent code, we introduce a novel modularization approach for BDI agents. Modularization has been introduced to BDI–based AOSE by *capabilities* [19,20]. While these are currently used to capture core concerns, we introduce an enhancement to this concept, which allows to define crosscutting concerns inside BDI agents. Exploiting the event based execution mechanism of a BDI agent platform[1], it is possible to register capabilities for contributive processing on certain BDI reasoning events.

This paper is structured as follows. The next section summarizes current approaches to model macroscopic MAS behaviors, followed by a description of how to derive similar mathematical descriptions from goal hierarchies. Tool support for evaluation of these models is based on the concept of co–efficient capabilities

---

[1] The Jadex system – presented in section 4.1.

which are introduced in section 4. The following section 5 exemplifies our approach by a case study including mathematical analysis and evaluation results. Finally, we conclude and give prospects for future work.

2   Stochastic Models for Global MAS Behavior

A certain method to derive quantitative, macroscopic descriptions for the mean occupation number of the agents states has been introduced for reactive agents by Lerman et al. [14,15,21]. Such descriptions are essentially given by so–called Rate Equations, which are a well established tool for describing average particle numbers in homogeneous systems, e.g. steered tank reactors in chemical reaction systems or population dynamics of biological species and other fields. These equations result from Master Equations describing the underlying Markov processes of these systems [22]. Focusing on reactive agent architectures, namely homogenous robotic applications, these equations have been successfully applied to study numerous examples, e. g. foraging [15] and coalition formation [14].

The rationale for a stochastic description of a MAS is the observation that the sum of the microscopic agent behaviors directly reflects the overall system behavior. When agents have a fixed number of executable behaviors or states (e.g. searching and homing), a state of the system can be described by the fraction of agents executing either of them. In order to quantify these fractions, the reactive agents are modeled as Finite State Automaton and the macroscopic behavior of a MAS can be characterized by the fractions of agents executing in certain microscopic states [15]. The dynamics of the MAS can be described by Rate Equations for these occupation numbers postulating an underlying time–continuous Markov process.

In [15] a structured process to derive these equations automatically from microscopic agent models has been proposed. This process is composed of four steps: (1) identification of discrete actions in the agent behavior, (2) induction of an automaton to describe agent reasoning, (3) translation of the automaton into a set of coupled differential equations and finally, (4) solving the derived equations for appropriate initial conditions and parameter regimes. In relation to [15] we present a process, adjusted to derive stochastic models from BDI–based MAS. We argue that that there is actually no automaton needed, but reactive planing systems can be described in similar ways.

3   Deriving Models from Goal–Hierarchies

Derivation of the above described models, expressing the intended system behavior, demands two major modeling efforts. First, appropriate agent states need to be identified, depending on the intended observations on the overall system. Secondly, the parameters – rates quantifying state transitions – need to be measured to be adjusted, according to implementation details and environmental constraints. The following section shows how goal/plan–hierarchies can guide the first effort. The second effort is exemplified in a case study in section 5 applying tool support which is presented in section 4.

3.1 Goal–Hierarchies

Goal Oriented Requirements Engineering (GORE) uses *goals* to elaborate, structure, specify and analyse requirements for systems under development [23]. Goals in this respect are prescriptive statements of intent, their satisfaction requires (active) components of the system and the environment to cooperate [24]. These range from strategic objectives to fine–grained responsibilities of the individual agents and are typically organized in AND/OR graphs, describing refinement and abstraction of single goals. An AND refinement of a goal requires all subgoals to be satisfied, while OR refinement denotes alternative ways to goal satisfaction.

The usage of goals in the design phase is especially inviting for Agent Oriented Software Engineering (AOSE) methodologies (e.g. [12,13]) aiming towards implementations based on the well–known BDI architecture [9,10]. This model has been successfully applied to the development of cognitive agents, applying *reactive planing*. Bratman [8] developed a theory of human practical reasoning, which describes rational behavior by the notions *Belief, Desire* and *Intention*. Implementations of this model introduced the concrete concepts of *Goals* and *Plans*, leading to a formal theory and an executable model [9].

Beliefs represent the local information of agents about both the environment and its internal state. The structure of the beliefs defines a domain dependent abstraction of the environment. This describes the *view–point* of an agent toward its self and its surrounding. Goals represent agent desires, commonly expressed by certain target states inside agent beliefs (see [25] for a discussion of goals in available BDI systems). Finally, plans are the executable means by which agents satisfy their goals. Single plans are not just a sequence of basic actions, but may also dispatch sub-goals. Therefore goal/plan hierarchies of actual BDI implementations are composed of interleaved sequences of these (cf. figure 1).

While plans can be generated at runtime (e. g. [26]), BDI agents typically choose from a *library* of available plans. Since these are developed at design time, BDI agents apply *reactive planing*. Agent internal reasoning decides which goals to pursue – *goal deliberation* [27] – and which plans to execute in order to achieve the selected goals – *meta-level reasoning* (problems of this are discussed in [20]), leading to both pro–active and reactive behaviors. To enable reasoning, goals and plans are annotated with conditions that constrain their instantiation (creation condition) and execution context (context condition). While these conditions are typically defined in terms of belief values, describing agent and environment (sensor input) states.

3.2 Deriving Agent States from Subtrees

Figure 1 gives an impression of the goal hierarchies identified in RE and AOSE methodologies. Following a notation introduced by the Tropos methodology [12], it displays a goal dependency inside an agent. To accomplish a top–level goal (Goal 1). The agent can either pursue Goal 2 or Goal 3 (OR decomposition), leading to different courses of action, *observable* on a macroscopic level. The distinct behaviors are described by the resulting subtrees, which have the decomposed goals as root nodes. Therefore, a GPS can be divided into underlying subtrees (cf. figure 1) when goals/plans are found to be OR decomposition, forcing agents to decide which course of actions to take. In the following, we will examine the interplay of the distinct behavioral pattern that are expressed by these *goal/plan subtrees* (GPS). In figure 1, these trees are surrounded by cubes.

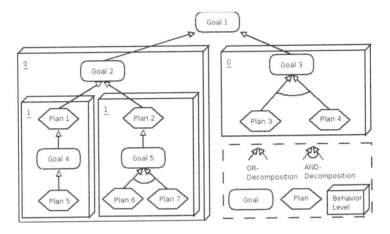

Fig. 1. Goal hierarchy inside a deliberative agent

The decomposition into distinct GPS is necessary but not sufficient to identify *observable* agent behaviors. While different courses of actions will allow to be distinguished by their GPSs, human intervention is necessary to identify appropriate, macroscopic *observable* agent states based on the application domain and the intended level of granularity. BDI implementations provide different types of goals (summarized in [25]), but these do not influence the structure of the GPSs, since they are used to abstract from the detailed conditions that lead to plan execution.

Due to the applied reactive planing mechanism (cf. section 3.1), the interplay with the environment causes agent actions. Thus in many cases, a Markov assumption will be justified. In this respect our abstraction approach aligns with research in [28], where the relation between *Markov Decision Processes* (MDP) and BDI architectures is examined. The obtained results stress that BDI agents can be understood as reactive systems and vice versa. The fractions of agents executing in the distinct GPSs are candidates for states in a corresponding Markov Model. So the microscopic behaviors can be abstracted to be described as macroscopic agent states by phenomenological, macroscopic Rate Equations. This is exemplified in section 5. Identification of the GPSs in an available BDI-implementation is guiding the search for the macroscopic observables of interest. After the possible states of execution for the types of agent have been identified at the intended level of granularity, a stochastic model, composed of couples Rate Equations, can be assumed [14,15].

In order to compare these models to actual MAS implementations in an actual environment the transition rates between the states need to be measured to be compared to expected values. The next section introduces tool support for this purpose.

4   Monitoring Agent Execution

The distributed and concurrent nature of MAS complicates the comprehension of MAS behavior, which is crucial for systematic development processes. Therefore, analysis and visualization tools have been developed [3,5,6,29]. These mainly rely on two mechanisms. First, messages between agents can be tapped by a third party, e .g. observing agents, and secondly logging messages generated inside agent source code can be analysed.

Once the relevant observables have been identified (section 3.2), we want to measure in which goal/plan subtrees the agents are actually executing, depending on environmental conditions. In general, the macroscopic observable behavior of individual agents or their exchanged messages do not allow to infer directly which plans are executed. The annotation of plans with logging information requires additional effort from developers. This section describes a mechanism — inspired by the notion of *crosscutting concerns* in modular software structures [18,30] — to enable automatic observation of plan execution with minimum intrusion to the original agent code.

4.1   Co–efficient Capabilities

In [20] *capabilities* have been proposed to modularize BDI agents in functional clusters. These capabilities comprise beliefs, goals, plans and a set of visibility rules of these elements to the surrounding agent, referenceable under a specific namespace. They allow recursive inclusions of capabilities an are used to define specific functionalities which can be imported by different agent types. In [20] the usage of capabilities is exemplified by *client* and *bidder* capabilities which encapsulate the functionality for initialization and participation of a negotiation.

In [19], a general and coherent *export/import* mechanisms for the comprised elements has been proposed. In addition, the *creation semantics* of capability elements and the *parametrization* of imported capabilities have been enabled by the adoption of *initial mental states* which provide a set of default configurations.

Aiming towards minimal–intrusive measurement of GPS transitions, we propose an enhancement to this modularization concept, which allows to define *crosscutting concerns* in agent implementations. Modularization [17] is a key aspect in software engineering. The functionality of a software system can be decomposed into *core concerns*, which are to be separated into different components or modules and so–called *Aspects* [30], which crosscut them. Crosscutting prime examples are inter alia failure recovery, monitoring and logging. While conventional development paradigms (e.g. procedural, object–oriented) capture these aspects as non–functional requirements, aspect–oriented programming explicitly express these as software artifacts to be *weaved* into the static structure of a software system. According to the aspectual terminology, *pointcuts* define of a set of *join points*. These are well–defined points in a program's execution, e.g. the call of specific methods. When a pointcut evaluates to true, it triggers the execution of *advices*. These hold the executable code of an aspect and define when it is executed. This terminology will be revisited in 4.1.

In this respect capabilities [19,20,31] intend to define and modularize core concerns in BDI agents. Figure 2 (left) shows modularization by capabilities between agents. Two agent types share functionality by inclusion of the same capability. Similar to conventional development efforts — without the notion of aspects — non–functional concerns can be captured in modules, resp. capabilities and executed by explicit references [19] to elements inside these modules.

The right hand side in figure 2 shows a *co–efficient capability* (CC), which automates this referencing, by exploitation of the local reasoning mechanisms. Being registered at an agent allows BDI reasoning events, like the instantiation of plans or belief changes, to trigger processing in the CC (arcs towards the capability) without code change in the executed agent. Reasoning inside the CC may cause BDI specific events inside the surrounding agent, e. g. the adoption of goals or the change of belief values (arc from the capability). We name these capabilities *co–efficient*, because they register for contributive processing on certain BDI reasoning events. This allows crosscutting functionalities, like logging, failure recovery etc., to be automatically triggered, without explicit references in goals or plans.

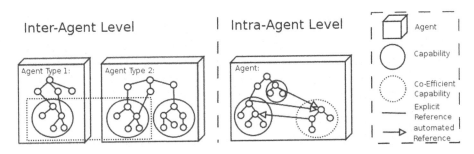

Fig. 2. Modularization of concerns in MAS – left: capabilities are shared by different agents; right: co–efficient capabilities

Implementation Issues. The described mechanism has been implemented using the *Jadex* system[2]. A suite of tools facilitate development, deployment and debugging of Jadex–based MAS. The single agents consist of two parts. First, they are described by *Agent Definition Files* (ADF), which denote the

---

[2] http://vsis-ww.informatik.uni-hamburg.de/projects/jadex

structures of beliefs and goals among further implementation dependent details in XML[3] syntax. The ADF describe agents as well as capabilities. Agents include capabilities by referencing the corresponding XML file in their ADF. Secondly, the activities agents can perform are coded in plans, these are ordinary Java[4] classes.

The Jadex platform allows implementations of a certain interface (jadex. runtime.ISystemEventListener), to be registered at individual agents. The *Jadex Introspector* and *Tracer* development tools [32], accompanying the Jadex distribution, use this mechanism to observe agent reasoning. A CC comprises an implementation of this interface in order to register for a set of events of interest. Being automatically notified by occurences of these events for a specific agent allows to respond, e.g. by dispatching novel BDI events in the capability itself or the surrounding agent.

The available reasoning events comprise *structural changes, processing events* and *communication*. Structural changes may be the addition and removal of beliefs, goals, plans and capabilities. Processing events denote the activities performed by agents, like reading/writing access to beliefs as well as so–called *internal events*, e.g. timeouts. Communicative events denote reception and sending of messages. Since the implementation of CCs relies on an available capability implementation [19], the recursive inclusion of these is possible. Several CCs can be present in one agent and these can respond to overlapping sets of events.

Usage of Crosscutting Concerns. The notion of crosscutting concerns, namely aspect-oriented programming [30], has found minor attention in development efforts for MAS. While aspects have been utilized in object–oriented implementations of agent models and agent infrastructures (e. g. [33,34,35]), only recently have aspects been proposed to structure agent models [36,37]. While in [36] an agent oriented modeling language has been extended with aspects, proposes [37] a modeling framework and meta-model for aspects in MAS. In this paper we transfer the notion of crosscutting concerns to the BDI architecture with respec to the pro–active reasoning cycle of these agents, utilizing an established modularization concept for their encapsulation.

We adopt vocabulary from aspect–oriented programming to express similar modularization in BDI agents. All Jadex reasoning events are possible join points. They define points in the agent reasoning which possibly trigger processing inside a CC. Pointcuts are expressed by different implementations of the listener object, allowing several pointcuts and therefore several distinct concerns in one co–efficient capability. These pointcuts are responsible to initiate reasoning inside the co–efficient capability or modify the agent, according to triggering events.

In aspect–oriented programming advices may execute *before*, *after* or *around* join points [30]. To date, the BDI advices can only be executed after the join point has been processed. While aspect–oriented programming is concerned with

---

[3] http://www.w3.org/XML/

[4] http://java.sun.com/

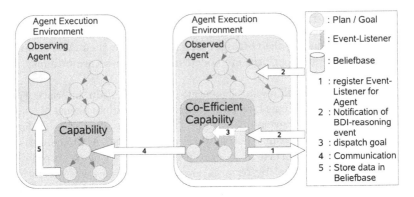

Fig. 3. Implemented monitoring architecture. Description see text.

the sequence of execution, a classification of advices in BDI agents has to take the influence of events into account. In the previous section it has been shown that the available join points can be grouped in structural, processing and communicative events. The influence of these needs to be distinguished between *introducing* and *removing* events, which change the structure of the agent. Examples are the addition or deletion of new beliefs or goals. The Processing Events comprise *affecting* and *informing* events. While the former ones affect the agent state, e. g. writing belief values, the latter ones describe the processing inside agents, like reading beliefs.

Aiming towards comprehensive software systems based on BDI technology, modularization and reusability of BDI agent code is a topic of growing concern. The capability concept [19,20] has been introduced to BDI agent architectures in order to allow decomposition of agents. Developers can structure agent code according to the primary functionalities and have to ensure that crosscutting concerns are addressed whenever appropriate. The presented mechanism allows developers to separately express crosscutting concerns in BDI agents to be automatically unified into working systems.

However, the mechanism should be applied with care. Performance of the agent will be reduced by exhaustive processing inside pointcuts. These should be implemented as instantaneous actions. In addition, the crosscutting behavior of the CC reduces the *traceability* of the agent actions.

4.2   Monitoring Architecture

The described mechanism has been used to enable monitoring of GPS transitions. Goals, responsible for message transfer to an observing agent, are dispatched according to the introduction and removal of plans. This logging mechanism is encapsulated in a CC. Figure 3 describes how a CC has been used to monitor agent execution. The implementation is separated in two capabilites that encapsulate the *observing* (left) and the *observed* (right) functionalities. The observing agent mainly handles incoming messages that inform about state transitions in the observed agents and stores the transmitted informations. This functionality can be straightforward clustered according to [20,19]. In the observed agent(s) the CC mechanism is utilized to allow an automated recording of state transitions. On agent startup the CC registers itself for a set of events at the surrounding agent (1). Therefore it is notified when one of these events occures (2), examines the kind of event and dispatches an according event in the capability. If a state transitions has been registered, an according message is send to the observing agent (resp. capability), which stores the obtained information in its beliefbase for further processing (5).

5   Case Study

To confirm the above described modeling and analysis approach, we examine an example MAS from the Jadex–Project. This example scenario has been inspired by a case study in [38], where hierarchical structures of static, predefined roles are examined. In order to allow for cooperative behavior, the system has been generalized as follows. The objective for a group of robots (agents) in the so-called *Marsworld*, is to mine ore on a far distant planet. The mining process is composed of (1) locating the ore, (2) mining it on the planets surface and (3) transporting the mined ore to the home base. Therefore, a collection of three distinct types of agents are released from a home base to a bounded environment. All of them have a sensor range to detect occurrences of ore in the soil an start immediately a searching behavior. In order to search for occurrences of ore randomly selected locations are visited. Sensed occurrences of ore are reported to the so-called *sentry* agent. This robot is equipped with a wider sensor range and can verify, whether a suspicious spot actually accommodates ore (constant time delay). When ore is found, the location is forwarded to a randomly selected *production* agent, equipped with a dedicated mining device. After mining is finished (constant time delay) a group of *carry* agents is ordered to transport ore to the home base (constant number of round trips). When the ordered actions have been performed agents continue searching.

5.1   Rate Equations

In the outlined scenario agents change between two distinct behaviors. They either search for ore or perform a dedicated action, i.e. sense ore, mine ore or transport ore. As discussed in section 3.2, these behaviors will be reflected by distinct goal/plan subtrees in BDI–based implementations. The goal–hierarchy of each agent type is OR–decomposed in 2 GPSs. Therefore all agent types can be represented with two distinct states, where one is responsible for the searching behavior (free state) and the other one for the agent specific action (bound state). Since both behaviors include movement and further actions, implemented by goal/plan structures, more fine grained views on the MAS are possible and can be treated similar to the following exemplification. Furthermore, it can get important to include states of the environment into the dynamic description, as for our case study. These are the states of the targets, which attract the different agents.

Since detections of ore generate sensing actions by the sentry agents, leading to orders for the remaining agent types, the MAS can be described similar to a chemical reaction chain as shown in figure 4. The generation of orders is reflected by inclusion of *targets* (T). These resemble occurrences of ore which attract the different agent types (sentries, producers, carriers resp. M_s, M_p, M_c).

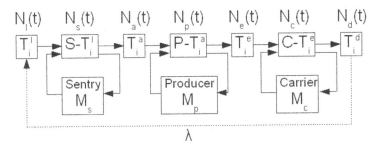

Fig. 4. Reaction chain inside the marsworld case study with free and bound states. Explanation of the parameters in see text.

The Rate Equations are derived from an underlying stochastic model defined by Master Equations for the assumed Markovian process. State changes then occur at certain rates, i.e. certain transition probabilities per time unit. Therefore, agent states are described by time–dependent space–averaged continuous occupation numbers. This is correct, if the occupation numbers are determined as an average over an ensemble of simulations run with the same initial conditions and identical environment. Identification of these states is a major modeling effort, guided by the GPSs (cf. section 3.2). Once the agent states have been identified the rates can be described by examination of the events that trigger state transition. After these preliminaries, we write down the macroscopic rate equations for our MAS (cf. [15]), assuming that state changes occur at certain rates, i.e. certain transition probabilities per time unit and explain the meaning of the variables and terms in the following:

$$\dot{N}_L(t) = -\alpha_{Ls} (M_s - N_s) N_L - \alpha_{Lp} (M_p - N_p) N_L - \alpha_{Lc} (M_c - N_c) N_L$$
$$\dot{N}_s(t) = \alpha_{Ls} (M_s - N_s) N_L + \alpha_{Lp} (M_p - N_p) N_L + \alpha_{Lc} (M_c - N_c) N_L - \mu_s N_s$$
$$\dot{N}_a(t) = -\alpha_{ap} (M_p - N_p) N_a + \mu_s N_s$$
$$\dot{N}_p(t) = \alpha_{ap} (M_p - N_p) N_a - \mu_p N_p$$
$$\dot{N}_e(t) = -\alpha_{ec} (M_c - N_c) N_e + \mu_p N_p$$
$$\dot{N}_c(t) = \alpha_{ec} (M_c - N_c) N_e - \mu_c N_c$$
$$\dot{N}_d(t) = \mu_c N_c$$

In both figure 4 and the above Rate Equations, $N_k, k \in \{L, a, e, d\}$ denote the number of targets *loaded*, *activated*, *exhausted* or *dead* respectively. The $N_j, j \in \{s, p, c\}$ denote the number of agents (sentries, producers or carriers resp.) being bound to a target, namely sentry bound to loaded target for examination, producer bound to an activated target for exploration and career bound to an exhausted target for transporting the material to the home-base. The non–linear terms describe that in order to reach these bound states, a free agent has to meet an appropriate target with rate coefficients $\alpha_{kj} > 0$ denoting the overall binding rates. Since the number of agents of each type is a fixed number $M_j > 0$, the number of free agents in the walking state is $M_j - N_j \geq 0$. The linear terms describe the finite life–time of these bound states due to the agents finishing their work with the bound target. The corresponding release rates $\mu_j > 0$ are mean inverse working times per target for each agent of type $j \in \{s, p, c\}$. Each binding starts when the agent either encounters an appropriate target or receives a message containing an appropriate targets position. In the latter case, the binding time includes the time for moving to the targets location and for processing the target.

The general solution of the system of differential equations may not be necessary because some approximations can be made. Since some of the variables are fast, i.e. assume quasistationary values without delay, such variables can be eliminated by setting their derivative to zero. In this way N_a and N_e can be eliminated since the sentries and producers will send messages when they finish their work with the target, leading to an instantaneous binding of the target to the next agent to get involved. By this approximation the system is simplified but exhibits still interesting non–linear behavior. On the other hand, effects due to spatial inhomogeneities are not included.

5.2   Simulation Results

Simulations were performed for up to ten agents, up to ten targets and up to several hundred runs to ensure good statistics comparable to the Rate Equations. The average occupation number of the bound states for the three agent types are displayed in figure 5 as a function of time. As expected, the sentries start to work followed by the producers and finally the carriers with some time delay. Since the sentries are mainly in the search state and finish their work with the targets fast, the corresponding amplitude is small. Most of the work has to be done by the carriers since they need to shuttle between the target and the homebase several times according to their limited transport capacity.

In our simulations targets are given random but, for all runs, identically fixed locations (frozen-in disorder). This is a realistic szenario for simulating the MAS behavior in a given environment. As a consequence, additional delay times occur according to the minimum path length necessary for an agent starting at the home base to get bound. These initial delay times are due to the initial spatial inhomogeniety of the system and thus not included into the rate equations given above but need to be introduced for describing our set-up. We have initial delay times of 2, 6 and 16 seconds for the sentries, producers and carriers, respectivly. Apart from the latter effects of spatial propagation and frozen-in disorder, the rate equations describe very well the time evolution of the BDI–based MAS measured through the occupation numbers of the GPSs representing the bound states.

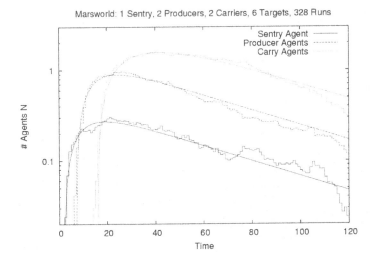

Fig. 5. The average occupation number of the bound states, i. e. the GPSs for the three agent types as a function of time, simulation data and theory (parameters cf. figure 5)

The analytical solutions of the rate equations fit the data very well, justifying that the derived equations resemble the actual system dynamics which are implementation dependent. The long–time behavior, for all agent types, is dominated by the slow, approximately exponential decay of the loaded target number according to the agents limited search efficiency $\mu_L := \alpha_{Ls}M_s + \alpha_{Lc}M_c + \alpha_{Lp}M_p$ which is $\mu_L = 0.019s^{-1}$ corresponding to a mean decay time of 53 seconds in figure 5. The onset is dominated by two effects, the mean time to reach the target after receiving the message and the mean working time. Both effects are combined in the release rates $\mu_j, j \in \{s, p, c\}$. The onset of the sentries is fitted well with $\mu_s = 0.13s^{-1}$. Producers are faster ($\mu_p < \mu_s$) and follow the sentries with the same rate (obvious from the differential equations). Only the carriers are slower with $\mu_c = 0.07^{-1}$.

The system is interesting also for it exhibits non–linear and cooperative behavior. At the low agent numbers we explore, the discreteness of the occupation numbers plays an important role. So all carry agents are booked up when a target gets exhausted leading to a saturation effect, which is contained in the rate equations. Furthermore search efficiency depends on the activities of all agents. In the beginning, all three agent types search for targets. Then the effective search success diminishes since a large amount of producers and carriers gets bound and cannot search anymore. Thus the number of activated targets will decrease leading to a reduction of work for producers and carriers and search efficiency will increase again. This system instability according to the agents cooperativity is certainly not wanted. But again the rate equations for the GPSs occupation numbers give clear evidence of such unexpected and unwanted behavior including estimations of corresponding parameter ranges.

6   Conclusions

In this paper, we showed how macroscopic models of MAS behavior can be derived from goal/plan hierarchies in BDI implementations of reactive planing agents. These models describe the MAS in typical environment settings, enabling to *estimate* and *redesign* [39] the macroscopic system behavior with minor simulation effort. In order to measure transition rates between different courses of actions an extension to the capability concept, allowing modularization of BDI agents, has been outlined. Inspired by the notion of crosscutting concerns in modular software structures, this extension allowed the automated observation of BDI agent behavior with minimum intrusion to agent source code. The simulation results have been compared to analytical results obtained from Rate Equations.

Future work will examine benefits and limitations of this explicit representation of crosscutting concerns in BDI implementations. Programming of BDI–oriented aspects, demands an automated weaving process and aspect visualization to support traceability for developers[5]. An adoption if this notion in current BDI based development efforts may lead towards a more comprehensive examination how of aspect–oriented concepts, e. g. as defined in the meta–model described in [37], fit in this particular agent architecture. In addition to a novel modularization concept, the described mechanism enables adaptive, e.g. self modifying, behaviors in BDI agents and assertion–like invariant checking in BDI–reasoning [40].

The derived macroscopic model described the intended MAS behavior. We compared this model to the actual MAS implementation by simulation and intend to automate this process, allowing invariants of global MAS properties to be checked in controlled simulation settings. By adoption of automatically weaved co–efficient capabilities and a generic simulation environment it is foreseeable to test BDI–based MAS with minor cost.

The applied modeling approach and mathematical techniques relate microscopic agent actions to global system behavior. We expect further examination of these relations (e. g. in [7]) aided by the presented tool–set to have impact on system design and optimization for cooperative and self–organizing MAS [41]. In addition, the presented abstraction technique may aid the construction of MDPs from BDI agent declarations and vice versa. This has been questioned in [28], as a mean to reuse the domain knowledge, implicitly represented in BDI agent implementation, for the creation of purely reactive agents.

Acknowledgments

One of us (J.S.) would like to thank the *Distributed Systems and Information Systems* (VSIS) group at Hamburg University, particularly Winfried Lamersdorf, Lars Braubach and Alexander Pokahr for inspiring discussion and encouragement.

---

[5] The AJDT-Project exemplifies this – http://www.eclipse.org/ajdt/

References

1. Jennings, N.R.: Building complex, distributed systems: the case for an agent-based approach. Comms. of the ACM **44** (**4**) (2001) 35–41
2. Wolf, T.D., Holvoet, T.: Emergence and self-organisation: a statement of similarities and differences. In: Proc. of ESOA'04. (2004) 96–110
3. Guerin, S.: Peeking into the black-box: Some art and science to visualizing agent-based models. In: Proceedings of the 2004 Winter Simulation Conference. (2004)
4. Ndumu, D.T., Nwana, H.S., Lee, L.C., Collis, J.C.: Visualising and debugging distributed multi-agent systems. In: Proc. of AGENTS '99. (1999) 326–333
5. Szekely, P., Rogers, C.M., Frank, M.: Interfaces for understanding multi-agent behavior. In: Proc. of the 6th int. conf. on Intel. user interfaces. (2001) 161–166
6. Lam, D.N., Barber, K.S.: Comprehending agent software. In: Proc. of the 4th int. joint conf. on autonomous agents and multiagent systems (AAMAS '05). (2005)
7. Yamins, D.: Towards a theory of "local to global" in distributed multi-agent systems (i). In: Proc. of AAMAS '05, ACM Press (2005) 183–190
8. Bratman, M.: Intentions, Plans, and Practical Reason. Harvard Univ. Press. (1987)
9. Rao, A.S., Georgeff, M.P.: BDI-agents: from theory to practice. In: Proceedings of the First Int. Conference on Multiagent Systems. (1995)
10. Georgeff, M.P., Lansky, A.L.: Reactive reasoning and planning: an experiment with a mobile robot. In: Proc. of AAAI 87, Seattle, Washington (1987) 677–682
11. Pokahr, A., Braubach, L., Lamersdorf, W.: A flexible BDI architecture supporting extensibility. In: The 2005 IEEE/WIC/ACM Int. Conf. on IAT-2005. (2005)
12. Bresciani, P., Giorgini, P., Giunchiglia, F., Mylopoulos, J., Perini, A.: Tropos: An agent-oriented software development methodology. Journal of Autonomous Agents and Multi-Agent Systems (2004) Kluwer Academic Publishers.
13. Padgham, L., Winikoff, M.: Developing Intelligent Agent Systems: A Practical Guide. Number ISBN 0-470-86120-7. John Wiley and Sons (2004)
14. Lerman, K., Galstyan, A.: A general methodology for mathematical analysis of multiagent systems. USC Inf. Sciences Tech.l Report ISI-TR-529 (2001)
15. Lerman, K., Galstyan, A.: Automatically modeling group behavior of simple agents. In: Agent Modeling Workshop, AAMAS-04, New York, NY (2004)
16. Lerman, K., Jones, C.V., Galstyan, A., Mataric, M.J.: Analysis of dynamic task allocation in multi-robot systems. Int. J. of Robotics Research **25** (2006) 225–241
17. Parnas, D.L.: On the criteria to be used in decomposing systems into modules. Commun. ACM **15** (1972) 1053–1058
18. Elrad, T., Filman, R.E., Bader, A.: Aspect-oriented programming: Introduction. Commun. ACM **44** (2001) 29–32
19. Braubach, L., Pokahr, A., Lamersdorf, W.: Extending the capability concept for flexible BDI agent modularization. In: Proc. of PROMAS-2005. (2005)
20. Busetta, P., Howden, N., Rönnquist, R., Hodgson, A.: Structuring BDI agents in functional clusters. In: ATAL '99, Springer-Verlag (2000) 277–289
21. Lerman, K., Martinoli, A., Galstyan, A.: A review of probabilistic macroscopic models for swarm robotic systems. In: ISAB-04. Volume 3342 of LNCS. (2004)
22. Van Kampen, N.G.: Stochastic Processes in Physics and Chemistry. Elsevier (2001)
23. van Lamsweerde, A.: Goal-oriented requirements engineering: A guided tour. In Proc. RE01 - Int. Joint Conference on Requirements Engineering (2001)
24. Van Lamsweerde, A.: Goal-oriented requirements engineering: A roundtrip from research to practice. In: Proc. of RE'04. (2004) 4–8 (Invited Keynote Paper)

25. Braubach, L., Pokahr, A., Lamersdorf, W., Moldt, D.: Goal representation for BDI agent systems. In: Proc. of PROMAS'04. (2004)
26. Walczak, A., Braubach, L., Pokahr, A., Lamersdorf, W.: Augmenting bdi agents with deliberative planning techniques. In: The 5th International Workshop on Programming Multiagent Systems (PROMAS-2006). (2006)
27. Pokahr, A., Braubach, L., Lamersdorf, W.: A bdi architecture for goal deliberation. In: Proc. of AAMAS '05. (2005) 1295–1296
28. Simari, G., Parsons, S.: On the relationship between mdps and the bdi architecture. In: Proc. of the Fifth International Joint Conference on Autonomous Agents and Multiagent Systems. (2006)
29. Padgham, L., Winikoff, M., Poutakidis, D.: Adding debugging support to the prometheus methodology. Engin. Applications of Art. Intel. **18** (2005) 173–190
30. Kiczales, G., Lamping, J., Menhdhekar, A., Maeda, C., Lopes, C., Loingtier, J.M., Irwin, J.: Aspect-oriented programming. In: Proc. of ECOOP. Springer (1997)
31. Padgham, L., Lambrix, P.: Agent capabilities: Extending bdi theory. In: Proceedings of the Seventeenth National Conference on Artificial Intelligence and Twelfth Conference on Innovative Applications of Artificial Intelligence. (2000) 68–73
32. Pokahr, A., Braubach, L., Leppin, R., Walczak, A.: Jadex Tool Guide - Release 0.93. Distributed Systems Group, University of Hamburg, Germany. (2005)
33. Garcia, A., Silva, V., Chavez, C., Lucena, C.: Engineering multi-agent systems with aspects and patterns. Journal of the Brazilian Computer Society **8** (2002) 57–72
34. Robbes, R., Bouraqadi, N., Stinckwich, S.: An aspect-based multi-agent system. In: Research Track of the ESUG 2004 Smalltalk Conference, Köthen (Anhalt), Germany (2004)
35. Garcia, A., Kulesza, U., SantAnna, C., Chavez, C., Lucena, C.: Aspects in agent-oriented software engineering: Lessons learned. In: Proceedings of the 6th Workshop on Agent-Oriented on Software Engineering, in conjunction with the AAMAS05 Conference, Utrecht, The Netherlands (2005)
36. Garcia, A., Chavez, C., Choren, R.: Enhancing agent–oriented models with aspects. In: AAMAS '06: Proceedings of the fifth international joint conference on Autonomous agents and multiagent systems, ACM Press (2006)
37. Garcia, A., Chavez, C., Choren, R.: An aspect–oriented modeling framework for designing multi–agent systems. In: Proc. of the 7th Inernational Workshop on Agent Oriented Software Engineering (AOSE'06). (2006)
38. Ferber, J.: Multi-Agent Systems. Addison Wesley (1999)
39. Sudeikat, J., Renz, W.: On the redesign of self–organizing multi–agent systems. International Transactions on Systems Science and Applications **2** (2006) 81–89 Special Issue on SOAS'06.
40. Sudeikat, J., Braubach, L., Pokahr, A., Lamersdorf, W., Renz, W.: Validation of bdi agents. In: Proc. of the Fourth International Workshop on Programming Multi-Agent Systems (ProMAS'06). (2006)
41. Renz, W., Sudeikat, J.: Mesoscopic modeling of emergent behavior - a self-organizing deliberative minority game. In: Engineering Self-Organising Systems. (2005) 167–181

Evaluating a Model Driven Development Toolkit for Domain Experts to Modify Agent Based Systems[*]

Gaya Buddhinath Jayatilleke, Lin Padgham, and Michael Winikoff

School of Computer Science and Information Technology,
RMIT University,
GPO Box 2476V, Melbourne, VIC 3001, Australia
{gjayatil, linpa, winikoff}@cs.rmit.edu.au

Abstract. An agent oriented approach is well suited for complex application domains, and often when such applications are used by domain experts they identify modifications to be made to these applications. However, domain experts are usually limited in agent programming knowledge, and are not able to make these changes themselves. The aim of this work is to provide support so that domain experts are able to make modifications to agent systems. In this paper we report on an evaluation of our Component Agent Framework for domain Experts (CAFnE) framework and toolkit, giving a detailed account of a usability study we conducted with a group of experienced meteorologists.

1 Introduction

The agent oriented paradigm is becoming increasingly popular for building systems which are relatively complex, and which operate in dynamic domains. One advantage of agent based architectures is that it is relatively easy to extend and expand an application as new conditions are discovered or prioritised. Often there are many nuances in the application domain which are understood by domain experts, but may not be fully captured initially in a requirements analysis. Our aim in the work reported here has been to empower domain experts who take delivery of an agent based software application, to be able to modify and evolve it without the assistance of agent programmers.

To facilitate this we have developed a detailed model of agent based systems that facilitates modelling of the system at a level of detail sufficient to produce code for real applications. Our vision is that a software developer would use this approach and the associated toolkit to develop agent applications. Domain experts who are not programmers (and certainly not programmers of agent applications) would then be able to modify and evolve the application to deal with both growing requirements, and developing understanding of nuances of desired behaviour.

In order to evaluate our approach we have taken a simplified version of an actual agent application developed in collaboration with an industry partner, and implemented it in our system. We have then identified some changes that the actual application had

---

[*] This work was supported by the Australian Research Council (Linkage Grants LP0347025 and LP0453486) in collaboration with the Australian Bureau of Meteorology and Agent Oriented Software Pty. Ltd.

L. Padgham and F. Zambonelli (Eds.): AOSE 2006, LNCS 4405, pp. 190–207, 2007.

undergone, and have asked domain experts (meteorologists) to attempt to make these changes using our system. We have observed and recorded these attempts and analysed the extent to which our approach and toolkit appear to be successful.

In this paper we first (section 2) provide a brief overview of the experimental application, which was a meteorological alerting system developed as part of a collaborative grant with the Victorian branch of the Australian Bureau of Meteorology, and Agent Oriented Software Group. We then briefly describe our approach and toolkit (section 3). Additional publications [1,2] provide greater detail on both the toolkit and the application. The major part of the paper, and its main contribution, is a description of the evaluation of our system based on sessions with five meteorologists (sections 4 and 5). Section 4 presents the evaluation methodology, and in section 5 we analyse the success of our approach at four different conceptual levels. We conclude that while the user interface could be improved, the approach appears to be quite successful. The fact that the study is based on a real system, and that the changes parallel actual changes made to the initial system, lends credibility to the study.

2 Overview of the Sample Application

The application on which this study was based is an alerting system which has been developed between 2002 and 2005, as part of a collaboration between the Australian Bureau of Meteorology, RMIT, and Agent-Oriented Software Group. This system, and some of the success in using the agent paradigm has been reported previously [1]. The purpose of the system is to monitor a wide range of meteorological data, alerting personnel to anomalous situations, interactions between data from different sources that may not otherwise be noticed, extreme or escalating situations, and so on. The initial prototype version of the system (see Figure 1) monitored for discrepancies between data from forecasts for airport areas (Terminal Area Forecasts: TAFs) and data from automated weather stations (AWSs) on the ground at airports. Significant discrepancies resulted in an alert to a relevant human operator.

This system was designed and implemented as a multiagent system because it had a number of characteristics that were a good match with the agent paradigm, including the environment being highly dynamic, and there being a need for the system to be able to exhibit both reactive behaviour (responding rapidly to changes in the weather) and proactive behaviour (e.g. initiating monitoring of certain conditions such as tracking a storm). Finally, the system consists of a number of entities that may join and leave the system dynamically, and this is important for the system's reliability and extensibility [1]. However, it should be noted that the scope of the system used for this evaluation did not include some of these aspects, for instance the system did not incorporate proactive behaviour.

We re-implemented a simplified version of the system using our toolkit, where data (TAFs and AWSs) were generated by a simulator, and alerts were simply pop-up windows on the machine running the system. The initial system consisted of five agents: one for receiving TAF data, one for receiving AWS data, one for doing discrepancy

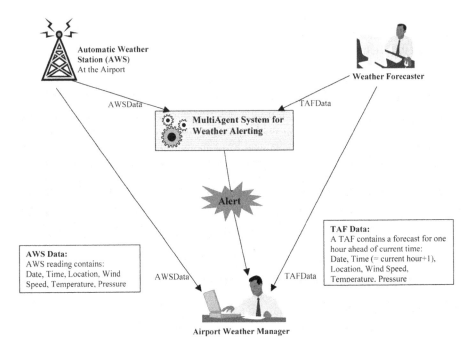

Fig. 1. The Weather Alerting Application

calculations, and two for providing alerts to end users (one for Melbourne, one for Sydney). The system overview diagram, depicting the high level system architecture, can be seen in Figure 5. Note that two of the agent instances, those providing alerts to end users, are of the same agent type (GuiAgent), thus there are five agent instances, but only four agent types.

Figure 2 shows an agent overview diagram for the AlertAgent. This shows how the agent's internals are structured in terms of plans, messages which trigger these plans, and data. Although both the system and agent overview diagrams show the *static* structure of the system, i.e. what parts are connected to what other parts, it is often possible to fairly easily understand the dynamics of an agent from its overview diagram. For example, from Figure 2 we can see that an AWSDataEv message triggers the HandleAwsDataPlan which in turn triggers checking for discrepancies in temperature and pressure. The plans that check for discrepancies can trigger a warning (SendWarningToSubscribed).

After re-implementing the system in our framework, we then identified some early changes (or types of changes) that had been made to the actual system, on the request of meteorologists (i.e. domain experts) involved in the project. These included adding an agent for receiving alerts at a new location, alerting on more of the available data, adding the ability to process completely new meteorological data (volcanic ash readings), and adding a more flexible alerting threshold. This then provided the basis for our evaluation activity with meteorologists.

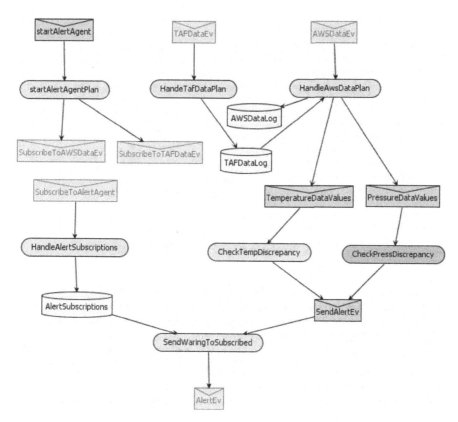

Fig. 2. Agent Overview Diagram for the AlertAgent. Envelopes depict messages, the "pill" shapes are plans, and cylinders are data.

3   CAFnE Framework and Toolkit

The CAFnE[1] toolkit supports the generation of complete executable code from a structured model of the application. It is envisaged that an application is developed, by an application developer, using the toolkit to define the relevant conceptual components. It is hoped that due to the intuitive nature of the agent model a domain expert will be able to readily understand the application design, and will in fact be able to modify and further develop it. Because fully executable code is generated based on the model, the domain expert is thus able to modify and extend the application.

3.1   Conceptual Structure

Starting with the modelling of agents done in SMART [3], and reviewing this against application needs based on our experiences, we developed a simple agent model shown in Figure 3. This model identifies a list of basic component types required for

---

[1] CAFnE stands for Component Agent Framework for domain Experts.

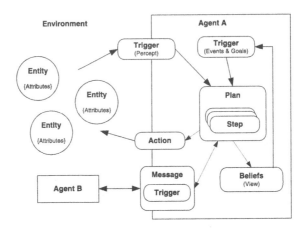

Fig. 3. Simple agent model used in CAFnE

modelling an agent application, namely: *attribute, entity, environment, goal, event, trigger, plan, step, belief* and *agent*. Further details of these, along with a discussion of the relationship between the CAFnE and the SMART concepts, can be found in [4].

In order to generate executable code from these basic components we adopted a Model Driven Development approach as used in the Model Driven Architecture (MDA) [5] of the Object Management Group (OMG). We use three (M0, M1 and M2) of the four levels used in MDA for application modelling. Figure 4-(a) shows these modelling levels and examples of entities in each layer from the meteorology application.

Each level in the model hierarchy is an instance of the level above. At the meta-meta level (M2 equivalent) we define the domain and platform independent generic component types listed earlier. These generic types are then used in the meta level (M1 equivalent) to define domain dependent component types. This specifies the types of entities required for the particular application domain. The M0 level defines the runtime components of the system which are bound to the domain and also to a runtime platform. In other words, M0 represents the runtime system in a given agent programming language.

We use XML Schema for representing M2, XML for M1 and JACK [6] agent language as M0, the runtime platform. The transformation from M1 (XML) to M0 (JACK code) is done using a set of transformation rules written in XSLT[2].

Figure 4-(b) gives an overview of the main modules of the toolkit. The Component Definition Generation (CDG) Module is responsible for generating the appropriate XML specifications for the components defined by the user via the UI Module. The output of the CDG Module is a set of XML files that comply with the XML Schema definitions of the component types.

The Transformation Module transforms the platform independent XML specifications to executable code in an agent language. This is achieved by applying a set of XML-Transformations (XSLT) to the XML component specifications generated by the

---

[2] http://www.w3.org/TR/xslt

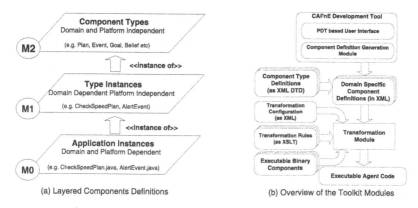

Fig. 4. An overview of CAFnE concepts

CDG Module. Specifics of the Transformation modules including the rules and how it operates are described in [4]. Currently the Transformation Module generates JACK agent language code. However, if one wishes to run a CAFnE application in a different agent platform (such as Jadex) it is only required to change the XSLT rules. Thus a technical advantage of the CAFnE platform is that it allows an application to be transformed and run in different runtime platforms without changing the high level application model.

3.2 Relationship to the Prometheus Methodology for Software Design

Many of the domain independent concepts exist in a range of agent design and development methodologies, which can therefore be adapted for building the application using the CAFnE toolkit. We build on the Prometheus methodology [7] and the support tool available for development using this methodology called PDT[3] [8].

Prometheus supports development of the level M1 entities for *goal, event, trigger, plan, belief* and *agent*. In addition, the developer using CAFnE must define the *environment* and its *attributes* as well as the plan *steps*. Steps are executable units used in plans, making it easier to formulate plans. CAFnE constrains (and guides) the developer in modelling the application with these components, thus making it easier for domain experts to understand and make modifications. However CAFnE also provides additional flexibility, by allowing plan steps to have arbitrary target platform code (currently JACK/Java). This provides a mechanism for greater flexibility where needed.

3.3 Usage for Modifications

Once an application is developed, what the domain expert is provided with is a set of graphical and textual models that present the information from level M1. One of the most important graphical models for an overview of the system is the Prometheus system overview diagram. Figure 5 shows this, (upper right frame) within the toolkit, for the experimental meteorology application.

---

[3] Prometheus Design Tool. (http://www.cs.rmit.edu.au/agents/pdt)

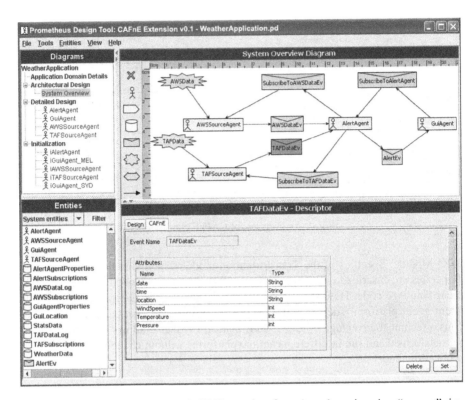

Fig. 5. The Prometheus Design Tool (PDT) user interface. A starburst icon is a "percept", i.e. information from the environment. A box with a stick figure is an agent, and an envelope shape denotes a message.

Clicking on a particular agent type opens up an "agent overview diagram" in this frame which shows the domain dependent types of plans, events, triggers and goals within an agent type. The details of plan steps, attributes and beliefs are available in the CAFnE text based frame at the bottom right of figure 5, called the "Descriptor pane".

The specific agent instances, and their corresponding initial beliefs are accessible from the "Initialization" option in the "Diagrams" pane in the upper left frame (figure 5). When expanded these can be viewed graphically in the upper right frame. CAFnE allows the user to specify what agent instances will exist at runtime, including their names, and what agent types they instantiate. Additionally, it is possible to specify, for each agent instance, what initial beliefs the agent will have. This allows different agent instances to be given different beliefs, for example, an agent instance that is responsible for displaying alerts for the city of Melbourne would begin with a belief that it is covering the region of Melbourne, whereas another agent instance of the same type that was responsible for, say, Sydney, would begin its life with the belief that it is covering the region of Sydney.

The domain expert who wishes to modify an application does this by interacting with the model available via the CAFnE toolkit. For example to add a new type of agent, this can be introduced graphically into the system overview diagram. Expanding it then allows introduction of relevant plans and events which the agent can handle. The tool also supports copying existing entities (together with their included components) and then modifying. This is a particularly useful way for non-programmers to envisage and realise system additions. To add a new instance of an existing type requires addition into the initialization model. Further detail on using the CAFnE tool is available in [4].

4   Evaluation Methodology

4.1   Participants

In order to evaluate our toolkit and approach, we identified, through our relationship with the Bureau of Meteorology, five experienced forecasters who were willing to spend a couple of hours in an individual interview, using the toolkit. None of the forecasters had been previously involved with our project with the Bureau of Meteorology.

All five participants had at least fifteen years of experience in weather forecasting. Three participants had varying levels of experience in programming (shown in table 1) with only two of them currently being involved in programming activities (shown in the "Comments" column). None of the participants had designed or implemented agent based systems prior to the study.

Table 1. Domain Expert Profiles: Programming Experience

Participant	Familiarity	Experience	Comments
A	C, Python	10yrs	Current work involves programming
B	Java	10yrs	Current work involves programming
C	-	0yrs	No Programming Experience
D	C, C++	-	Past programming experience
E	-	0yrs	No Programming Experience

4.2   Materials

Participants were emailed a description of the evaluation process along with three documents that provided an overview of the toolkit and the sample application, one week prior to the evaluation session. The documents included a Brief User Guide to the CAFnE Toolkit, a document describing the functions available as plan steps for the sample application and a design overview of the Sample Weather Alerting System. Participants were also given a web link[4] for downloading and experimenting with the toolkit prior to the exercise.

As none of the participants had actually been able to find time to read the documentation or experiment with the toolkit prior to the evaluation interview, the first 30-45

---

[4] http://www.cs.rmit.edu.au/~gjayatil/cafneEval

minutes of the interview was spent going through these materials. The participants were then presented with the descriptions of the requested changes along with a description of the observable outcome once each change was successfully made.

4.3 Modifications Specified

We developed descriptions of four[5] different modifications to be made to the system, which paralleled enhancements or modifications that had been made by programmers to the actual system. The changes were:

1. Show alerts for Darwin - a new city;
2. Add ability to alert on wind data - a new weather data type;
3. Add ability to show volcanic ash alerts - a new type of alert and data source; and
4. Change the threshold for alerting from a fixed to a variable value.

Of these the third change is the most difficult, and the first is the most straightforward. Table 2 shows these changes, with the right column indicating the entities which require modification in order to realise the change. This information was not given to participants, what was given to participants was a detailed description of the requirements for each change, along with an indication of what would be seen once the change was successfully made (see Table 3 for an example description of change number 2, as it was provided to the forecasters).

4.4 Data Collection

There were three types of data collected: recording of all verbal comments and interaction; noting of timing information; and a questionnaire (see appendix A) which was filled in at the end of each session asking a set of questions regarding how easy they found the tool and the concepts with respect to understanding and realizing the changes. This questionnaire also included a set of questions on the background of the participants regarding their experience in the weather domain, programming in general and agent programming.

While making the changes, participants were asked to think out loud and ask questions as they worked on understanding and making the changes. The interviewer (who was the first author) was limited to observing, capturing data and providing assistance on clarifying agent concepts and toolkit functions. The interviewer was not involved in helping the user in any way with deriving design solutions for the changes given. Questions answered by the interviewer included ones such as "How do I copy a plan?", "Do I have to fill all these description boxes?", and "How do I change this link from Plan A to Plan B?". Questions not answered by the interviewer included ones such as "Am I supposed to create a Plan here?", "Ah! I need an agent instance here, don't I?", and "Do I need to send this data to Agent B?".

Timing information was recorded for each change, starting when a subject began reading the description of the required change and ending when the subject declared it as complete.

---

[5] We actually had five changes, but as no-one had time to look at the fifth change we have excluded it from the study.

Table 2. Changes List

No	Change title	Description	Related Concepts
1	Make the system show alerts for the City of Darwin	The initial system only showed alerts for the cities of Sydney and Melbourne. The change is intended to make the system show alerts for Darwin.	Agent Type, Agent Instance
2	Add the ability to alert on Wind Data	The initial system only alerted on discrepancies based on Temperature and Pressure data. Modifications are to be made to process Wind data and generate alerts on any Wind speed based discrepancies.	Plan, Event
3	Add the ability to show Volcanic Ash Alerts	This change required users to add a new reading (Volcanic Ash levels in atmosphere) by using a new agent type (Volcanic Ash Agent) and generate alerts if the ash levels were above a certain limit.	Agent, Type, Events, Plan, Step
4	Implement a variable threshold for alerting	The original version of the system used a fixed discrepancy threshold for all regions. For any region, if the discrepancy between the actual reading and the forecast is over this value, an alert was generated. With this modification, the system is to have variable thresholds based on the region (i.e. Sydney, Melbourne and Darwin)	Plan, Belief

5 Analysis

Within the available time most participants were able to complete (or attempt) three changes. Table 4 shows the time (in minutes) taken by each subject, and whether the change was successfully accomplished. A ✓ next to the time indicates a successful implementation and ✧ indicates a partial completion.

One interesting observation here is the consistency in the times taken by each user. The amount of time taken to make a change is quite consistent between users. The time taken also confirms our assessment of the first change as being the easiest, but does not clearly indicate the third change as being harder than changes 2 or 4.

These results clearly indicate that a domain expert with only a short introduction (of around 40 minutes) to the concepts and the toolkit, is able to make moderately complex modifications to an existing agent system, without the help of an expert agent developer. However some difficulties were also experienced and not all attempts were successful within the time available. We analysed our data to determine where improvements may be needed in order to facilitate greater ease of use and success.

In analysing and evaluating the data collected from our interviews, we refer to the cognitive model of program understanding developed by Letovsky et al. [9,10]. In [9] Letovsky identifies three components in the cognitive model of program understanding. A *knowledge base* that includes programming expertise and problem-domain knowledge; a *mental model* that specifies the understanding of the existing program and an

Table 3. Change Description

CHANGE 2: Add the ability to alert on WindData
Background: The current system only supports generating alerts based on the temperature (data type TEMP) and pressure (data type PRESS) data discrepancies between AWS and TAF. However the AWS and TAF also contain details about Wind (data type WIND) such as wind speed. This data is not used to generate alerts.
Required Change: You are to make the necessary changes to the system in order to generate alerts on wind forecasts. The tolerance level for issuing an alert for a discrepancy between TAF and AWS reading for wind should be 10 units.
Expected Outcome: Alerts on Wind will be displayed

Table 4. Times taken (in minutes)by each subject (Note: dna = did not attempt; ✓ = complete implementation; ✧ = partial implementation)

Participant	Change 1	Change 2	Change 3	Change 4
A	15 ✓	30 ✓	25 ✧	dna
B	15 ✓	30 ✓	dna	dna
C	20 ✓	30 ✓	30 ✧	dna
D	15 ✓	35 ✓	30 ✓	30 ✓
E	20 ✓	25 ✓	dna	35 ✧

assimilation process used to construct the mental model using the knowledge base and stimulus material (such as program code, design documents etc.). The *assimilation process* used by programmers in software maintenance is further evaluated in [10] where a Systematic Strategy of understanding a program is claimed to be superior to an As-Needed Strategy in maintenance tasks. The Systematic Strategy refers to a programmer understanding the global view of the application before attempting a modification whereas the As-Needed Strategy refers to limiting this knowledge to the part or parts of the system affected by the change.

In the following we evaluate to what extent the participants were able to develop an adequate knowledge base, in terms of the required agent concepts. We then explore to what extent they have succeeded in obtaining a mental model of the application program, with a focus on a global understanding (facilitating the Systematic Strategy) rather than understanding only of relevant parts (for an As-Needed Strategy). We then look at the participants' ability to make the changes at two levels: the design level covering what changes need to be made, in what components, and the implementation level covering actually realising these changes through the CAFnE toolkit user interface.

5.1   Agent Concept Knowledge

The Knowledge Base as identified in the Letovsky model is the understanding of the programming environment and the problem domain. As we are working with domain experts, we assume understanding of the problem domain. Therefore in our case the Knowledge Base evaluation concerns understanding of the agent concepts used in the CAFnE framework.

None of the participants had prior experience in building or modifying agent systems. Subjects spent an average of 40 minutes in browsing the CAFnE user guide and the sample application to acquire this knowledge. Subjects thought out loud while going through the application and seeing the concepts in use appeared to solidify their understanding. When asked if they understood the functions of the basic components (e.g. plan, event, belief) and the agent model (figure3-(a)), they commented that the concepts are easy to grasp and intuitive.

However, while the users understood the simple agent model, some of the users faced difficulties and had to clarify their understanding while attempting the changes. The majority of the difficulties could be categorised as conceptual problems and interface problems. A common conceptual problem was the difference between the design diagrams (at the M1 level) and the instance diagram (at the M0 level). Subjects such as C and E, who were new to programming, needed further explanations in how these two levels differ. Another example is the use of Attributes. Subjects needed help in understanding the use of Attributes in Steps and Events, and how they hold values at runtime. While part of this may be attributable to the newness of the ideas, the representation of the concepts in the tool was sometimes confusing and led to interface based problems. For example the Trigger in a plan descriptor form is represented with a drop down list of all incoming triggers. This confused the users as a plan by definition can only have one trigger. In these situations the subjects asked questions to clarify the view they had in mind. These are areas we plan to improve on, especially to narrow the gap between the agent model and the representation in the toolkit.

5.2 Program Knowledge

Program Knowledge is the mental model of Letovsky [9]. It refers to the understanding of the existing design of the application. In particular we are interested in whether the participants were able to develop a holistic overall understanding suitable for a Systematic Strategy of modification.

In the case of the evaluation, the participants were totally new to the application design, but they were familiar with the data and the domain requirements. For example, the participants were familiar with the AWS and TAF data formats and contents, and the process of alerting based on discrepancies. This allowed the participants to easily understand the high level view (i.e. the inter-agent level) of the application. They were all able to easily explain how the data flowed through the system. CAFnE helps this process by visualising the application at the inter-agent (System Overview Diagram) and intra-agent (Agent Overview Diagram) levels. All the participants first got a broader view of the application using the System Overview Diagram, and then drilled down for further details using the Agent Overview Diagrams. By following the data flow in these diagrams, subjects were able to develop an understanding of the causal relationships between components in the system at different levels, such as between agents, between plans and between events. As indicated in [10], the ability to understand the causal relationships between application components forms *strong* mental models that lead to correct modifications. However, developing this understanding did require the participants to manually follow through processes based on data flow. One improvement could be to provide some inbuilt mechanism for visualizing the data flow.

However, although participants were able to develop a good understanding of the application's design, there were a number of areas where they struggled somewhat, and where ways of providing additional support should be investigated.

One area where participants struggled was in understanding some details of the application design that were less related to the domain. For example, the use of a subscription mechanism between the agents. When it was explained, participants were able to readily understand this architecture and later use it correctly in making the new regional agent instance (i.e. change 1) receive alerts from the AlerterAgent.

Another area where users struggled was in understanding what each plan does within an agent. They often referred to plan steps or followed the flow of information in and out of the plan to understand its use. Again, some mechanism that allows visualisation of the dynamic process where plans are used is likely to assist in this area.

Finally, another aspect which caused some difficulties was some of the details around runtime initialization of agents, including the use of start up plans[6] in agents, and the use of beliefsets to hold configuration details. It is expected that better design documentation would address many of these issues.

It should be noted that the participants were operating in time-limited conditions, gaining their understanding of the application's design, as well as the CAFnE concepts, within 40 minutes or so. Nearly all the users commented that they needed more time with the application, to, in their words "play around", to understand it better. However, they did feel that it was sufficiently clear and intuitive that, given more time, they would develop a strong understanding.

5.3   Conceptual Design of Change

Conceptual Design of Change is the derivation of a solution to the problem given in the change description at the conceptual level without actually implementing it using the tool. It is a product of the agent concept knowledge, domain knowledge, program knowledge and the users' capacity to use these in formulating a design change.

In all the changes attempted by users, they were able to come up with a design change relatively easily and rapidly. This was indicated by the thinking out loud practice they adhered to through out the session. Following are some statements made by participants in this stage:

"I need an agent instance for Darwin, don't I?"
  — attempting change 1

"I need to make a copy of this plan [pointing to CheckTemperatureDiscrepancy] and this event [pointing to TemperatureData]"
  — attempting change 2

"I have to make an agent type similar to AWSSourceAgent and rename it."
  — attempting change 3

---

[6] Plans that are run automatically when the agent is created.

The basic agent model used in CAFnE and the Prometheus based graphical notation used to represent the concepts appeared to be successful in providing the understanding necessary to conceptualise the changes required. This is further highlighted by the fact that the partially completed changes shown in table 4 (with a ✧), were all solutions which were correct at the conceptual level, though the users were unable to implement them within the time frame.

As expected, users looked for patterns similar or close to the one they needed in the change. By examining these available patterns users derived partial or complete solutions to the changes. A good example of this is change 2, where users recognised the similarity between Wind data and Temperature data and developed their solution for handling Wind data by looking at how the Temperature data was handled.

While users understood what needed to be done conceptually, realisation of this via the tool interface was somewhat more problematic.

5.4 Implementation

Implementation refers to the encoding of the desired modifications or additions using the CAFnE toolkit interface. During this phase users were given assistance when specific questions were asked about carrying out a certain operation, such as "how do I copy a plan?", or "how do I change this link from plan A to plan B?". The assumption here was that more time to find the information in the manual, or greater familiarity, would allow the users to resolve these questions without assistance. However in the context of limited evaluation time, it made sense to directly provide this information. On the other hand, no assistance was given in deciding *what* to do - only in the details of *how* to accomplish it via the tool interface.

Most users indicated that they found the diagrams and the graphical notation easy to understand. They commented that these diagrams reflected how they pictured an agent system, especially the system overview diagram. This was consistent with feedback from a preliminary evaluation with students where the tool did not provide overview diagrams. This lack was a significant issue in gaining an understanding of how individual entities (plans, events, etc.) fitted together and what role they played in the system.

Users heavily utilized the copy and paste functions in replicating patterns similar to the one they needed to implement. Examples include copying and renaming an agent instance in change 1, and copying plans and events in changes 2 and 3. Another useful feature was the ability, at the click of a button, to transform the application model to executable code and run it, in order to see the outcome of a change. Two of the users realized after making change 2 that alerts for wind were not being displayed at runtime. With further investigation they were able to find the problem[7] and correct it. Users also found the warnings and errors shown at the transformation level useful. This allowed them to eliminate model based errors such as missing inputs in Steps, and plans without triggers.

The main complaint from the users while using the prototype tool was the lack of features in the user interface which are normally found in other Windows applications.

---

[7] They had copied and pasted from the Temperature handling parts of the system, but hadn't changed all references to Temperature to be references to Wind.

These included features such as an Edit menu with Undo, Copy, Cut and Paste, right click popup menu for diagram components and drag & drop functions where applicable.

Users like A and B with a programming background had comments on things such as "use of Java standards for GUIs" and "more textual access to steps than with GUI widgets". Others highlighted the need for using less computer science terms such as "Initialization", and "Instance" and more training to overcome some of the usability issues. However these do not impact our fundamental concerns regarding the adequacy of the framework and of the tool functionality.

Most users commented that working at the more abstract diagram and form level seemed much easier than directly working with textual code. For example, when shown the Java code generated, participant E with no programming experience commented:

"Wow! It's lot easier than typing all that [Java code]. "

"that's neat stuff [code generation], I mean in the end you could have domain experts, people that just know their job but hopeless at coding do just this [clicking diagrams] and do that [filling forms] and run"
— participant C

6   Conclusion and Future Work

This paper described an evaluation of a conceptual framework of domain independent component types and the associated toolkit which enables applications to be built and modified in a structured manner, using these component types. The evaluation of the toolkit and approach was done by five meteorologists, using a simplification of an actual agent-based system, making changes that the real system had undergone.

We have provided a detailed analysis of related work in [4] and found the only similar work in the agent setting to be [11]. Most existing agent toolkits are made for experienced programmers and do not provide the same level of support for domain experts.

Our approach is consistent with Model Driven Development (MDD), since fully functional executable code is derived from the models. One area for future work is to compare our (agent-based) approach with more mainstream approaches to MDD such as the OMG's Model Driven Architecture[8] (MDA). Our belief is that the MDA is not well suited for domain experts since it relies on the UML, which is not likely to be known by domain experts, and which is considerably more complex than our models. However, clearly an experimental evaluation of this opinion would be valuable, although it is beyond the scope of this work.

Overall, the findings of our work can be summarised as:

1. Domain experts with varying programming experience, and with no experience with agent design or programming were able to rapidly (35-40 minutes) become familiar with the CAFnE concepts and begin comprehending an agent system design.
2. Users were able to go through the system and understand the functionality from the various diagrams provided.

---

[8] http://www.omg.org/mda

3. Participating domain experts could make moderately complex changes and run the system, without any prior knowledge of the agent approach or (in some cases) of programming.
4. Users found it easier to work at the higher level of abstraction given by the tool, and the overview diagrams provided were seen as useful.
5. Additional support for understanding the flow of processes within the system would probably be helpful.
6. Realizing the changes was hampered by various issues in the GUI, such as non-adherence to user interface standards, due to its prototype nature. In future work we plan to improve the user interface and to provide some mechanism for more readily understanding the role of a component and visualizing the data flow in a particular process.

In conclusion, we were able to demonstrate clearly that domain experts who are not expert programmers, and in some cases had *no* programming experience, were able to make modifications to an agent system using CAFnE. Furthermore, the domain experts were able to learn the concepts of CAFnE, become familiar with the design of the system, and make a number of changes, all within two hours. That the system in question is based on a real system, and that the changes parallel actual changes made to the real system, lends strength to this conclusion.

References

1. Mathieson, I., Dance, S., Padgham, L., Gorman, M., Winikoff, M.: An open meteorological alerting system: Issues and solutions. In: Proceedings of the 27th Australasian Computer Science Conference, Dunedin, New Zealand (2004) 351–358
2. Jayatilleke, G.B., Padgham, L., Winikoff, M.: A model driven component-based development framework for agents. International Journal of Computer Systems Science and Engineering **20/4** (2005)
3. Luck, M., d'Inverno, M.: A conceptual framework for agent definition and development. In: Proceedings of the fourth International Workshop on Agent Theories, Architectures, and Languages (ATAL). (1998) 155–176
4. Jayatilleke, G., Padgham, L., Winikoff, M.: Component agent framework for non-experts (CAFnE) toolkit. In Unland, R., Calisti, M., Klusch, M., eds.: Software Agent-Based Applications and Prototypes, Birkhaeuser Publishing Company (2005) 169–196
5. Kleppe, A., Warmer, J., Bast, W.: MDA Explained, The Model Driven Architecture: Practice and Promise. Addison-Wesley Publishing Company, ISBN: 0-321-19442-X (2003)
6. Busetta, P., Rönnquist, R., Hodgson, A., Lucas, A.: JACK Intelligent Agents - Components for Intelligent Agents in Java. Technical Report 1, Agent Oriented Software Pty. Ltd, Melbourne, Australia (1999) Available from http://www.agent-software.com.
7. Padgham, L., Winikoff, M.: Developing Intelligent Agent Systems: A Practical Guide. John Wiley and Sons, ISBN 0-470-86120-7 (2004)
8. Padgham, L., Thangarajah, J., Winikoff, M.: Tool support for agent development using the Prometheus methodology. In: First international workshop on Integration of Software Engineering and Agent Technology (ISEAT). (2005) 383–388

9. Letovsky, S.: Cognitive processes in program comprehension. In: Papers presented at the first workshop on Empirical studies of programmers, Norwood, NJ, USA (1986) 58–79

10. Littman, D.C., Pinto, J., Letovsky, S., Soloway, E.: Mental models and software maintenance. In: Papers presented at the first workshop on Empirical studies of programmers, Norwood, NJ, USA (1986) 80–98

11. Goradia, H.J., Vidal, J.M.: Building blocks for agent design. In: Fourth International Workshop on Agent Oriented Software Engineering. (2003) 17–30

A   Questionnaire

Domain Expert's Name: Date/Time:

1. Understanding BDI concepts and process   [/10]
Understanding of Data-Event-Plan (theoretically BDI) based agents.

1.1 Have you heard about BDI agent concepts before?   **YES   NO**
If yes, give details.

1.2 Did you find the description about the agent model provided in the Toolkit Help easy to
understand?   **YES   NO**
If not,
      1.2.1 What parts did you find difficult to understand? (most to least)

1.3 Can you briefly explain how a Trigger-Plan based agent (used in CAFnE) works?

2- Understanding sample application idea   [/10]
Understanding the design of the application.

2.1 Did you understand the purpose of the sample application? (explain)

2.2 Did you find the details given in the design document sufficient to understand how the
application works?
(if yes)
      2.2.1 Can you provide a brief description of what each agent does?

(if no)
      2.2.1 What aspects did you find hard to understand?
      2.2.2 What can you suggest to improve the understanding?

3- Understanding changes and how they are realized
This is the clear understanding of what is required of a particular change, what changes are
needed in the design and using the tool to do it.
[*Note: these questions were asked for each change*]

Change 1: Show Alerts for Darwin   [/10]
3.1.1. Do you understand what the change is about? (explain)

3.1.2. Do you understand what modifications are required in the design (explain)

3.1.3 What aspects of using the tool did you find difficult in making this change?
      3.1.3.1 How do you think it can be improved?

3.1.4 If the change was not correctly done, find and note the reasons for the cause. Might
include reasons such as wrong understanding of the model, design etc.

3.1.5 If the change was correctly done, but deviated significantly from the anticipated design
change, find and note the reasons for the design decisions.

Building the Core Architecture of a NASA Multiagent System Product Line*

Joaquin Peña[1], Michael G. Hinchey[2], Antonio Ruiz-Cortés[1], and Pablo Trinidad[1]

[1] University of Seville, Spain
{joaquinp, aruiz}@us.es, trinidad@lsi.us.es
[2] NASA Goddard Space Flight Center, USA
Michael.G.Hinchey@nasa.gov

Abstract. The field of Software Product Lines (SPL) emphasizes building a family of software products from which concrete products can be derived rapidly. This helps to reduce time-to-market, costs, etc., and can result in improved software quality and safety. Current Agent-Oriented Software Engineering (AOSE) methodologies are concerned with developing a single Multiagent System. The main contribution of this paper is a proposal to developing the core architecture of a Multiagent Systems Product Line (MAS-PL), exemplifying our approach with reference to a concept NASA mission based on multiagent technology.

1 Introduction

Many organizations, and software companies in particular, develop a range of products over periods of time that exhibit many of the same properties and features. The multiagent systems community exhibits similar trends. However, the community has not as yet developed the infrastructure to develop a core multiagent system (hereafter, MAS) from which concrete (substantially similar) products can be derived.

The software product line paradigm (hereafter, SPL) augurs the potential of developing a set of core assets for a family of products from which customized products can be rapidly generated, reducing time-to-market, costs, etc. [1], while simultaneously improving quality, by making greater effort in design, implementation and test more financially viable, as this effort can be amortized over several products. The feasibility of building MASs product lines is presented in [2], but no specific methodology is proposed. In this paper, we propose an approach for performing the first stages in the lifecycle of building a multiagent system product line (MAS-PL).

* The work reported in this article was supported by the Spanish Ministry of Science and Technology under grants TIC2003-02737-C02-01 and TIN2006-00472 and by the NASA Software Engineering Laboratory, NASA Goddard Space Flight Center, Greenbelt, MD, USA.

L. Padgham and F. Zambonelli (Eds.): AOSE 2006, LNCS 4405, pp. 208–224, 2007.

For enabling a product line, one of the important activities to be performed is to identify a core architecture for the family of software products. Unfortunately, there is no AOSE methodology that demonstrates how to do this for MAS-PLs. Our approach is based on the Methodology for analysing Complex Multiagent Systems (MaCMAS) [3], an AOSE methodology focused on dealing with complexity, which uses UML as a modeling language and builds on our current research and development experience in the field of SPLs.

Roughly, our approach consists of using goal-oriented requirement documents, role models, and traceability diagrams in order to build a first model of the system, and later use information on variability and commonalities throughout the products to propose a transformation of the former models that represent the core architecture of the family.

The main contributions of this paper are: (i) we introduce feature models in the agent field in order to document variabilities and commonalities across products; (ii) we provide an automatic algorithm and a prototype for performing commonality analysis (that is to say, to automatically analyze the probability that a feature appears in a product); (iii) we propose an operation to compose the models corresponding to a feature that allows us to build the core architecture which includes those features whose probability of appearing is above a given threshold.

2   Motivating MAS-PL with a NASA Case Study

There has been significant NASA research on the subject of agent technology, with a view to greater exploitation of such technologies in future missions.

The ANTS (Autonomous Nano Technology Swarm) concept mission,[1] for example, will be based on a grouping of agents that work jointly and autonomously to achieve mission goals, analogous to a swarm in nature.

Lander Amorphous Rover Antenna (LARA) is a sub-mission, envisaged for the 2015-2020 timeframe, that will use a highly reconfigurable-in-form rover artifact. Tens of these rovers, behaving as a swarm, will be used to explore the Lunar and Martian surfaces. Each of these "vehicles" or rovers will have the ability to change its form from a snake-like form, to a cylinder, or to an antenna, which will provide them with a wide range of functional possibilities. They are envisaged as possible building materials for future human lunar bases.

Prospecting Asteroid Mission (PAM) is a concept sub-mission based on the ANTS concepts that will be dedicated to exploring the asteroid belt. A thousand pico-spacecraft (less than 1kg each) may be launched from a point in space forming sub-swarms, and deployed to study asteroids of interest in the asteroid belt. Saturn Autonomous Ring Array (SARA) is also a concept sub-mission similar to PAM but whose goal is analysis of the Rings of Saturn.

Although based on mainly the same concepts, these sub-missions differ. For example, in PAM, spacecraft should be able to protect themselves from solar storms, while in SARA this is not of concern, but as a higher gravitational force

---

[1] http://ants.gsfc.nasa.gov/

exists, the spacecraft should be capable of avoiding gravitational "pull" and collisions with particles of the rings, as well as with other spacecraft. Another example is the mechanism used for motion in these missions. Some of them require ground-based motion, i.e. LARA, while other missions involve flying spacecraft employing gas propulsion and solar sails for power.

Thus, ANTS represents a number of sub-missions, each with common features, but with a wide range of applicability, and hence several products.

Being able to build a MAS-PL for these sets of sub-missions, with a set of reusable assets at all the levels (software artifacts, software processes, engineering knowledge, best practices, etc.), can drastically reduce temporal and monetary costs in the development of such missions.

In [2], a number of challenges are presented in the context of MAS-PL. In this paper we cover some of these challenges, which has motivated this research to address the following issues:

SPL for distributed systems. Distributed systems have not been a hot topic in the SPL field. We will explore a case study based on the ANTS concept mission presented above, which is a highly complex distributed system. Thus, this represents a first step towards addressing this challenge.

AOSE deficiencies. AOSE does not cover many of the activities of SPL. These are mainly concentrated on commonality analysis, and its implications for the entire SPL approach. This motivates us to cover this issue, validating our approach with the case study presented.

3   Background Information

As a result of combining two different fields, we have to contextualize our work in both research areas. In this section, we provide an overview of SPL and AOSE illustrating the points of synergy between them.

3.1   Software Product Lines

The field of software product lines covers the entire software lifecycle needed to develop a family of products where the derivation of concrete products is achieved systematically or even automatically when possible.

Its software process is usually divided into two main stages: *Domain Engineering* and *Application Engineering*. The former is responsible for providing the reusable core assets that are exploited during application engineering when assembling or customizing individual applications [4]. Although there are other activities, such as product management, in this section we do not try to be exhaustive, but only discuss those activities directly related to this paper and relevant to our approach. Thus, following the nomenclature used in [4], the activities, usually performed iteratively and in parallel, of domain engineering that correlate with our approach are:

The *Domain Requirements Engineering* activity describes the requirements of the complete family of products, highlighting both the common and variable features across the family. In this activity, commonality analysis is of great importance for aiding in determining which are the common features and which of them are present only in some products. The models used in this activity for specifying features show when a feature is optional, mandatory or alternative in the family. One of the most accepted models here is *feature models* [5]. A feature is a characteristic of the system that is observable by the end user [6]. Features represent a concept quite similar to system goals (used in AOSE) and the models used to represent them present a correlation with hierarchical system goal requirement documents [2]. Our approach is based on this correlation.

In Figure 1, we show a subset of the feature model from our case study. As can be seen, in this kind of model the features for all products are shown along with information on whether they are mandatory, optional, or alternative. For example, the feature *flight and orbit* is mandatory, while the feature *walk* is optional. In addition, the features *snake*, *amoeba*, and *rolling* must be present only if their parent is present, and, as they are related by an or-relation, when a product possesses the feature *walk* it must also possess at least one of the former features.

The *Domain Design* activity produces architecture-independent models that define the features of the family and the domain of application. Many approaches have been discussed in the literature to perform this modeling. Some of these approaches use role models to represent the interfaces and interactions needed to cover certain functionality independently (a feature or a set of features). The most representative are [7,8], but similar approaches have appeared in the OO field, for example [9,10]. We build on this correlation using agent-based role models at the acquaintance organization to represent features independently.

Then, in the *Domain Realization* activity, a detailed architecture of the family is produced adding mechanisms such as components that can be customized, or frameworks for these components, in order to enable the rapid derivation of products. In SPL, there exist some approaches where collaboration-based models (role models) are composed to produce the core architecture, e.g. [7,8]. In these approaches, component-based models are used where each component is assigned a set of interfaces and a set of connectors to specify interactions among them. Again, this is similar approach to the approach of some AOSE methodologies in building the architecture of the system, called the *structural organization*, e.g. [11].

3.2   Overview of MaCMAS/UML

The organizational metaphor has been proven to be one of the most appropriate tools for engineering a MAS, and has been successfully applied, e.g., [12,13,11]. It shows that a MAS organization can be observed from two viewpoints [11]:

Acquaintance point of view: shows the organization as the set of interaction relationships between the roles played by agents.

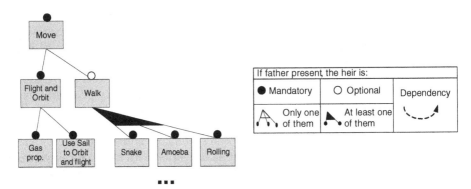

Fig. 1. Sub-set of the feature model of our case study

Structural point of view: shows agents as artifacts that belong to sub-organizations, groups, teams. In this view agents are also structured into hierarchical structures showing the social structure of the system.

Both views are intimately related, but they show the organization from
radically different viewpoints. Since any structural organization must include
interactions between agents in order to function, it is safe to say that the acquaintance organization is always contained in the structural organization. Therefore,
a natural map is formed between the acquaintance organization and the corresponding structural organization. This is the process of assigning roles to agents
[11]. Then, we can conclude that any acquaintance organization can be modeled
orthogonally to its structural organization [14].

MaCMAS is the AOSE methodology that we use for our approach and is based
on previously developed concepts [3]² It is specially tailored to model complex
acquaintance organizations [15].

We have adopted this approach because it presents several common features
with SPL approaches, that eases the integration of both fields. Going into details,
the main reasons are: First, after applying it we obtain a hierarchical diagram,
the traceability diagram, that is quite close to a feature model. Second, it matches
well with product lines, since it also produces a set of role models that represent
the materialization of each system goal at the analysis level. Third, it provides
UML-based models which are the de-facto standard in modeling, and which
will decrease the learning-curve for engineers. Fourth, it provides techniques
for composing acquaintance models, which is needed for building the structural
organization of the system, allowing us to group together those features that
are common to all of the products in the product line and thus, build the core
architecture.

For the purposes of this paper we only need to know a few features of MaC-
MAS, mainly the models it uses. Although a process for building these models
is also needed, we do not address this in this paper, and refer the interested

---

² See http://james.eii.us.es/MaCMAS/ for details and case studies of this methodology.

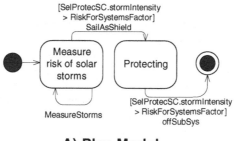

A) Plan Model

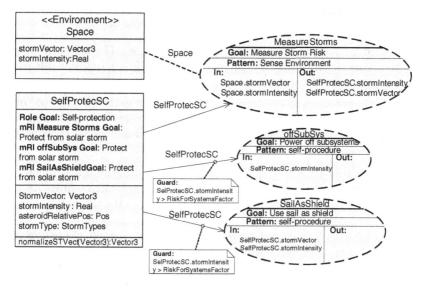

B) Role Model

Fig. 2. "Self-protection from solar storms" autonomic property model

reader to the literature on this methodology. From the models it provides, we are interested in the following:

a) **Static Acquaintance Organization View:** This shows the static interaction relationships between roles in the system and the knowledge processed by them. In this category, we can find models for representing the ontology managed by agents, models for representing their dependencies, and role models. For the purposes of this paper we only need to detail role models:

  Role Models: show an acquaintance sub-organization as a set of roles collaborating by means of several *multi-Role Interactions* (mRI) [16]. mRIs are used to abstract the acquaintance relationships amongst roles in the system. As mRIs allow abstract representation of interactions, we can use these models at whatever level of abstraction we desire.

In Figure 2.B), we show the role model corresponding to an autonomic feature of our case study that models how to materialize protection from a solar storm at the domain design level. Roles are represented as UML-interface-like shapes, and mRIs are shown as UML-collaboration-like shapes. Both notations are extended with some information required for modeling agents, such as goals, or collaboration patterns. One example of role a is *SelfProtectSC*; it shows its goals, the knowledge that should be managed to fulfill these goals, and the services it provides to be able to achieve its goals. One example of an mRI is *Measure Storms*: it is linked to its participant roles, and it shows the goal it fulfills, the pattern of collaboration between its participating roles, and the knowledge it both needs and produces in order to fulfill the goal.

b) **Behavior of Acquaintance Organization View:** The behavioral aspect of an organization shows the sequencing of mRIs in a particular role model. It is represented by two equivalent models:

Plan of a role: separately represents the plan of each role in a role model showing how the mRIs of the role sequence. It is represented using UML 2.0 ProtocolStateMachines [17]. It is used to focus on a certain role, while ignoring others.

Plan of a role model: represents the order of mRIs in a role model with a centralized description. It is represented using UML 2.0 StateMachines [17]. It is used to facilitate the understanding of the whole behavior of a sub-organization.

In Figure 2.A), we show the plan of the role model. As can be seen, each transition in the state machine represents an mRI execution. In this model, we can show that we have to execute the mRI *measure storms* until the risk of solar storms is higher than a constant, shown with a guard. Thus, when the guard holds, we have to execute the mRI *sailAsShield*.

c) **Traceability view:** This model shows how models in different abstraction layers relate. It shows how mRIs are abstracted, composed or decomposed by means of *classification, aggregation, generalization* or *redefinition*. Notice that we usually show only the relations between interactions because they are the focus of modeling, but all the elements that compose an mRI can also be related. Finally, since an mRI presents a direct correlation with system goals, traceability models clearly show how a certain requirement system goal is refined and materialized. Notice that we do not show this model since, adding commonalities and variabilities, it is equivalent to the feature model that we show later.

4   Overview of Our Approach for Building the Core Architecture

From all the activities that have to be performed for setting up a product line, we show here a subset concerning the development of the core architecture from

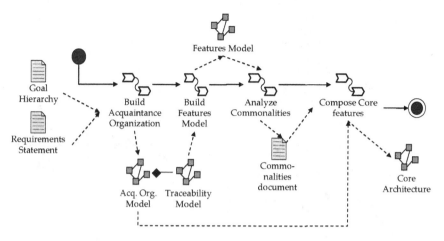

Fig. 3. Overview of our approach

the modeling point of view. Thus, we do not cover activities such as product management since it falls out of the scope of this paper.

In Figure 3, we show the Software Process Engineering Metamodel (SPEM) definition of the software process of our approach. The first stage to be performed consist of developing a set of models in different layers of abstraction where we obtain a MaCMAS traceability model and a set of role models showing how each goal is materialized. This is achieved by applying the MaCMAS software process. The second activity shown is responsible for adding commonalities and variabilities to the traceability model. Later, we perform a commonality analysis to find out which features, called core features, are more used across products. Finally, we compose the role models corresponding to these features to obtain the core architecture. The following sections describe these activities.

5   Building the Acquaintance Organization and the Feature Model

After applying MaCMAS, as we were building a MAS that covers the functionality of all products in the family, we obtain a model of the acquaintance organization of the system: role models, plan models and a traceability model. Once we have built the acquaintance organization, we have to modify the traceability diagram to add information on variability and commonalities, as shown in Figure 5, to obtain a feature model of the family. We do not detail this process since it relies on taking each node of the traceability diagram and determining if it is mandatory, optional, alternative, or-exclusive, or if it depends on other(s), as shown in the figure.

MaCMAS guides this entire process using hierarchical goal-oriented requirement documents from which all of the models are produced. Thus, there is a direct traceability between system goals and role models. This traceability is

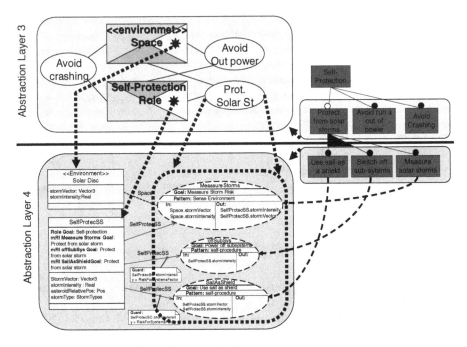

Fig. 4. Role model/features relationship

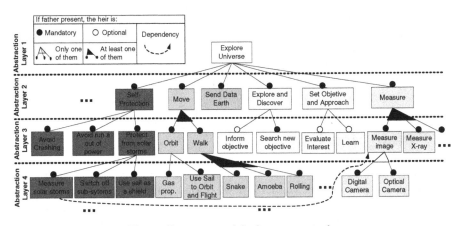

Fig. 5. Features model of our case study

feasible since when a system goal is complex enough to require more than one agent in order to be fulfilled, a group of agents are required to work together. Hence, a role model shows a set of agents, represented by the role they play, that join to achieve a certain system goal (whether by contention or cooperation). MaCMAS uses mRIs to represent all of the joint processes that are required and are carried out amongst roles in order to fulfill the system goal of the role model. These also pursue system sub-goals as shown in Figure 4, where we can see the correlation between these elements and the feature model obtained from the traceability diagram. Note that the role model of this figure can be also seen in Figure 2.

6   Commonality Analysis

To build the core architecture of the system we must include those features that appear in all the products and those whose probability of appearing in a product is high. In [18,19] the authors define the commonality of a feature as the percentage of products defined within a feature model that contains the feature. A calculation method for this and many other operations related to feature models analysis is proposed using Constraint Satisfaction Problems (CSP). The definition of commonality is the following:

Definition 1 (Commonality). *Let M be a feature model and F the feature within M whose commonality we want to calculate. Let P be the set of products defined by M and P_F the subset of products P containing F. commonality(F) is defined as follows:*

$$commonality(M, F) = \frac{|P_F| \cdot 100}{|P|}$$

Considering the previous definition, for any full-mandatory feature (this means a feature that appears in all the products in the family) $P_F = P$, its commonality will be 100%. For any other non-full-mandatory feature, $P_F \subset P$ and therefore its commonality will be less than 100%.

Calculating the commonality of every feature, we can easily determine which are the full-mandatory features and consequently the role models that must be used to build the core architecture. For those features whose commonality is less that 100%, we have to consider which of them will be part of the core and which will not. We propose to use a threshold, that must be calculated empirically for each domain, to make this decision. Consequently those features whose commonality is above the threshold will be also used to build the core architecture.

In addition, tools that help engineers with automated analysis of features models are of high value [18]. We have extended the prototype[3] presented in [18] to automatically calculate the commonality of all the features of our case study. The results obtained with the prototype are shown in Figure 6. As shown in this figure, these features are ordered by their commonality. The figure also show the threshold that we have selected, set up at the 60%, for considering a feature to be core or not.

We use the following fictitious scenario to document our example: We have realized that the commonality for the features *self-protection from a solar storm* and *orbiting* is 100%. Thus we have to add them to the core architecture, since they appear in all the possible products.

---

[3] This prototype along with this and other case studies is available at http://www.tdg-seville.info/topics/spl

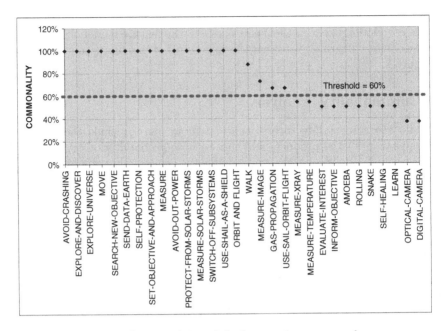

Fig. 6. Commonalities of the features in our example

As these features are related, since if a spacecraft is orbiting and measuring and it determines that there exists a risk of a solar storm, the spacecraft must first escape the orbit and later power down subsystems or use its sail as a shield to avoid crashing, we are forced to compose them to model their dependencies and provide agents with all the roles needed to safely protect from solar storms in any situation. Notice that we have limited our example to two role models to simplify the example, but in the real world we must also take into account the rest of the related features.

Once we have determined the set of features, and thus, the set of role models to be taken into account for the core architecture, we must compose them as described in the following section.

7 Composition of the Core Features

We have to take into account that when composing several role models, we can find: *emergent roles* and *mRIs*, artifacts that appear in the composition yet they do not belong to any of the initial role models; *composed roles*, the roles in the resultant models that represent several initial roles as a single element; and, *unchanged roles* and *mRIs*, those that are left unchanged and imported directly from the initial role models.

Once those role models to be used for the core architecture have been determined, we must complete the core architecture by composing role models.

Importing an mRI or a role requires only adding it to the composite role model. The following shows how to compose roles and plans.

7.1 Composing Roles

When several roles are merged in a composite role model, their elements must be also merged as follows:

Goal of the role: The new goal of the role abstracts all the goals of the role to be composed. This information can be found in requirements hierarchical goal

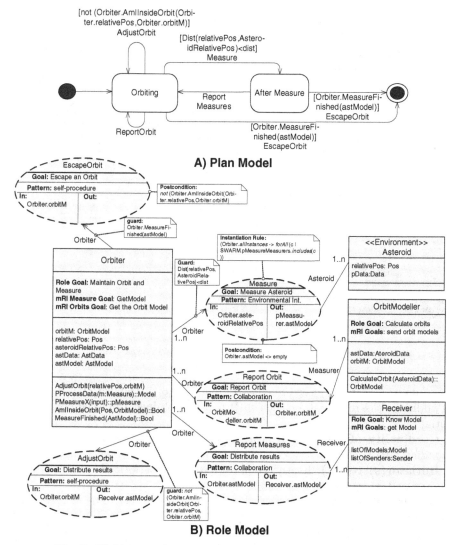

Fig. 7. "Orbiting and measuring an asteroid" autonomous property

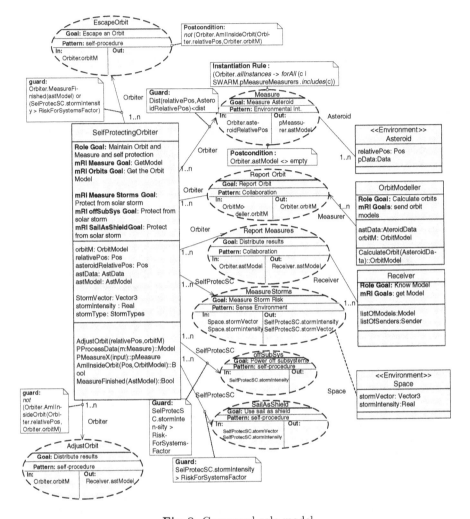

Fig. 8. Composed role model

diagrams or we can add it as the *and* (conjunction) of the goals to be composed. In addition, the role goal for each mRI can be obtained from the goal of the initial roles for that mRI.

Cardinality of the role: It is the same as in the initial role for the corresponding mRI.

Initiator(s) role(s): If mRI composition is not performed, as in our case study, this feature does not change.

Interface of a role: All elements in the interfaces of roles to be merged must be added to the composite interface. Note that there may be common services and knowledge in these interfaces. When this happens, they must be included only once in the composite interface, or renamed, depending on the composition of their ontologies.

Guard of a role/mRI: The new guards are the *and* (conjunction) of the corresponding guards in initial role models if roles composed participate in the same mRI. Otherwise, guards remain unchanged.

In our case study, we have to compose the role models corresponding to the features *self-protection from a solar storm* and *orbiting*. The model for the former feature was shown in Figure 2, and the role model of the later is shown in Figure 7.

After applying the approach described above, the composed role model obtained is shown in Figure 8. As we can see, the roles *Orbiter* and *SelfProtectSC* have been composed into a single role called *SelfProtectingOrbiter*. These roles has been composed because the agent that plays one of the roles also has to play the other as they are dependent (mRIs *escape orbit*, *power off sub-systems*, and *use sail as a shield* have to be sequenced in a certain way).

Since the rest of the roles are orthogonal, that is to say they do not interact with each other, they have been left unchanged and all mRIs have been also added without changes.

7.2 Composing Plans

The composition of plans consists of setting the order of execution of mRIs in the composite model, using the role model plan or role plans. We provide several algorithms to assist in this task: extraction of a role plan from the role model

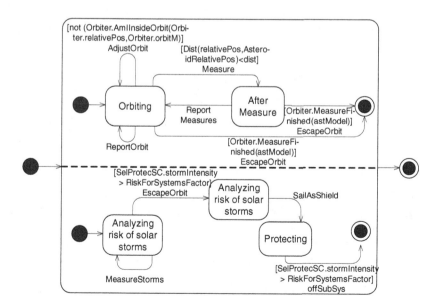

Fig. 9. Composed plan model

plan and vice versa, and aggregation of several role plans; see [20] for further details of these algorithms.

Thanks to these algorithms, we can keep both plan views consistent automatically. Depending on the number of roles that have to be merged we can base the composition of the plan of the composite role model on the plan of roles or on the plan of the role model. Several types of plan composition can be used for role plans and for role model plans:

Sequential: The plan is executed atomically in sequence with others. The final state of each state machine is superimposed with the initial state of the state machine that represents the plan that must be executed, except the initial plan that maintains the initial state unchanged and the final plan that maintains the final state unchanged.

Parallel: The plan of each model is executed in parallel. It can be documented by using concurrent orthogonal regions of state machines (cf. [17]).

Interleaving: To interleave several plans, we must build a new state machine where all mRIs in all plans are taken into account. Notice that we must usually preserve the order of execution of each plan to be composed. We can use algorithms to check behavior inheritance to ensure that this constraint is preserved, since to ensure this property the composed plan must inherit from all the initial plans [21].

The composition of role model plans has to be performed following one of the plan composition techniques described previously. Later, we are interested in the plan of one of the composed roles, as it is needed to assign the new plan to the composed roles; we can extract it using the algorithms mentioned previously.

We can also perform a composition of role plans following one of the techniques to compose plans described previously. Later, if we are interested in the plan of the composite role model, for example for testing, we can obtain it using the algorithms mentioned previously.

Regarding our example, as the self-protection must be taken into account during the whole process of orbiting and measuring, and not in a concrete state, we must perform a parallel composition of their plans, with a minor interleaving of the mRI *escape orbit* in the self protection plan, as is shown in Figure 9.

8   Conclusions

The field of software product lines offers many advantages to organizations producing a range of similar software systems. Reported benefits of the approach include reduced time-to-market, reduced costs, and reduced complexity. Simultaneously, the ability to spread development costs over a range of products has enabled adopters to invest more significantly in software quality.

Multiagent systems have a wide field of applicability, across a whole plethora of domains. However, many key features, including communication, planning, replication, security mechanisms, to name but a few, are likely to be very similar across all MAS, particularly in a given domain.

Key to the development of MAS-PLs is the identification of the core MAS from which a family of concrete products may be derived. We have described an initial approach to building this part of the infrastructure needed to enable a product line approach in MAS.

The approach matches well with existing AOSE methodologies and promises to open a field of research and development that may make MAS and MAS-based systems more practical in an industrial context.

We are continuing to investigate the use of such an approach in current and future NASA missions. For example, we have applied MAS-PL to manage evolutionary systems that benefits from the results of this paper [22]. Initial results are promising and over time we envisage significant benefits from employing a product line approach to such missions.

References

1. Clements, P., Northrop, L.: Software Product Lines: Practices and Patterns. SEI Series in Software Engineering. Addison–Wesley (2001)
2. Peña, J., Hinchey, M.G., Ruíz-Cortes, A.: Multiagent system product lines: Challenges and benefits. Communications of the ACM (2006)
3. Pena, J.: On Improving The Modelling Of Complex Acquaintance Organisations Of Agents. A Method Fragment For The Analysis Phase. PhD thesis, University of Seville (2005)
4. Pohl, K., Böckle, G., van der Linden, F.: Software Product Line Engineering : Foundations, Principles and Techniques. Springer (2005)
5. Czarnecki, K., Eisenecker, U.: Generative Programming: Methods, Tools, and Applications. Addison–Wesley (2000)
6. Kang, K., Cohen, S., Hess, J., Novak, W., Peterson., A.: Feature-oriented domain analysis (foda) feasibility study. Technical Report CMU/SEI-90-TR-021, Software Engineering Institute, Carnegie-Mellon University (1990)
7. Jansen, A., Smedinga, R., Gurp, J., Bosch, J.: First class feature abstractions for product derivation. IEE Proceedings - Software **151** (2004) 187–198
8. Smaragdakis, Y., Batory, D.: Mixin layers: an object–oriented implementation technique for refinements and collaboration-based designs. ACM Trans. Softw. Eng. Methodol. **11** (2002) 215–255
9. D'Souza, D., Wills, A.: Objects, Components, and Frameworks with UML: The Catalysis Approach. Addison–Wesley, Reading, Mass. (1999)
10. Reenskaug, T.: Working with Objects: The OOram Software Engineering Method. Manning Publications (1996)
11. Zambonelli, F., Jennings, N., Wooldridge, M.: Developing multiagent systems: the GAIA methodology. ACM Transactions on Software Engineering and Methodology **12** (2003)
12. Odell, J., Parunak, H., Fleischer, M.: The role of roles in designing effective agent organisations. In Garcia, A., Castro, C.L.F.Z.A.O.J., eds.: Software Engineering for Large-Scale Multi-Agent Systems. Number 2603 in LNCS, Berlin, Springer–Verlag (2003) 27–28
13. Parunak, H.V.D., Odell, J.: Representing social structures in UML. In Müller, J.P., Andre, E., Sen, S., Frasson, C., eds.: Proceedings of the Fifth International Conference on Autonomous Agents, Montreal, Canada, ACM Press (2001) 100–101

14. Kendall, E.A.: Role modeling for agent system analysis, design, and implementation. IEEE Concurrency **8** (2000) 34–41

15. Peña, J., Levy, R., Corchuelo, R.: Towards clarifying the importance of interactions in agent-oriented software engineering. International Iberoamerican Journal of AI **9** (2005) 19–28

16. Peña, J., Corchuelo, R., Arjona, J.L.: A top down approach for mas protocol descriptions. In: ACM Symposium on Applied Computing SAC'03, Melbourne, Florida, USA, ACM Press (2003) 45–49

17. (OMG), O.M.G.: Unified modeling language: Superstructure. version 2.0. Final adopted specification ptc/03–08–02, OMG (2003) www.omg.org.

18. Benavides, D., Ruiz-Cortés, A., Trinidad, P.: Automated reasoning on feature models. LNCS, Advanced Information Systems Engineering: 17th International Conference, CAiSE 2005 **3520** (2005) 491–503

19. Benavides, D., Ruiz-Cortés, A., Trinidad, P., Segura, S.: A survey on the automated analyses of feature models. XV Jornadas de Ingeniería del Software y Bases de Datos,JISBD 2006 (2006)

20. Peña, J., Corchuelo, R., Arjona, J.L.: Towards Interaction Protocol Operations for Large Multi-agent Systems. In: Proceedings of FAABS'02. Volume 2699 of LNAI., MD, USA, Springer–Verlag (2002) 79–91

21. Liskov, B., Wing, J.M.: Specifications and their use in defining subtypes. In: Proceedings of the eighth annual conference on Object-oriented programming systems, languages, and applications, ACM Press (1993) 16–28

22. Peña, J., Hinchey, M.G., Resinas, M., Sterritt, R., Rash, J.L.: Managing the evolution of an enterprise architecture using a mas-product-line approach. In: 5th International Workshop on System/Software Architectures (IWSSA'06), Nevada, USA, CSREA Press (2006) to be published

Author Index

Lecture Notes in Computer Science

For information about Vols. 1–4289

please contact your bookseller or Springer